NSW Targeting Maths

Year 6

Gloria Harris

PASCAL
PRESS

Contents

Term 1

Term 2

Term 3

Term 4

New Edition

Targeting Maths Australia's Favourite Maths Program

Australian Curriculum/ NSW Alignment

This NEW Edition fully aligns each student page with both the new NSW Syllabus (2024) and the new Australian Curriculum: Mathematics F-10 version 9.0. The NSW Syllabus outcome codes and content groups appear with the Australian Curriculum strand and code on each student page.

iPad Apps

With an app for each year, from Foundation/Kindergarten to Year 6, the Targeting Maths Apps include all the essential maths content that children need to know in an amazing app that makes learning maths fun, motivating and full of rewards. Look for it in Apple's App Store today! Made especially for the iPad and aligned to each student page in this book.

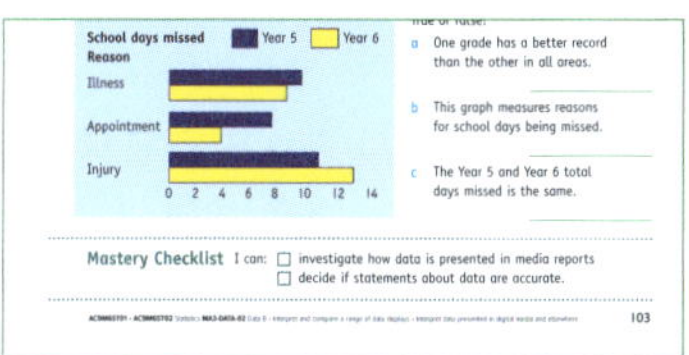

Mastery Checklists

Each unit has a Mastery Checklist. These checklists engage students in visible learning as they recognise and reflect on the specific maths skills learnt in each unit.

Integrated Problem-solving Program

Includes an integrated problem-solving program that actively builds students' problem solving capabilities.

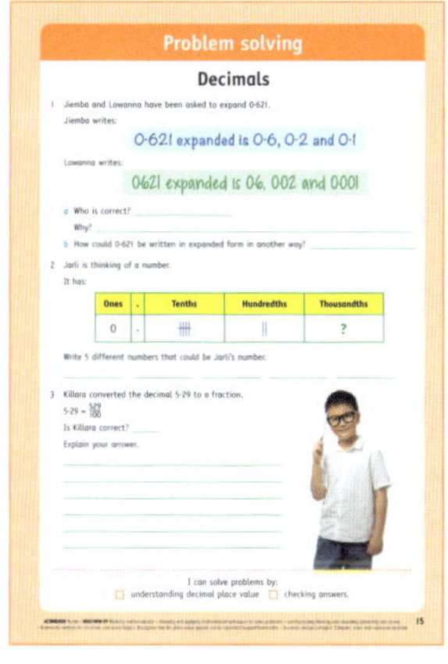

In-stage Topic Alignment for Composite Classes

Great for composite classes too, the contents of each book in one stage, eg Year 5 and Year 6, match topic by topic.

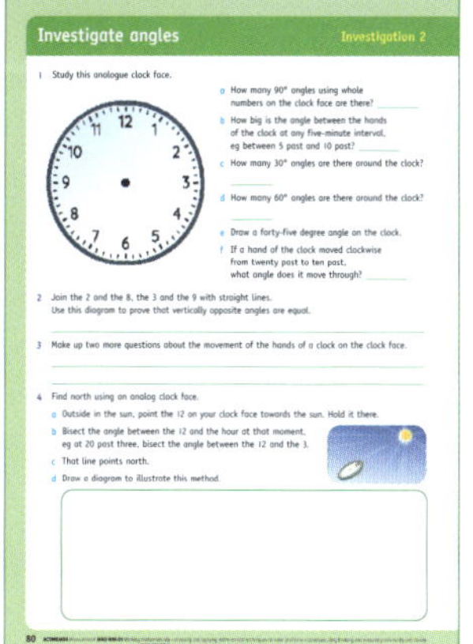

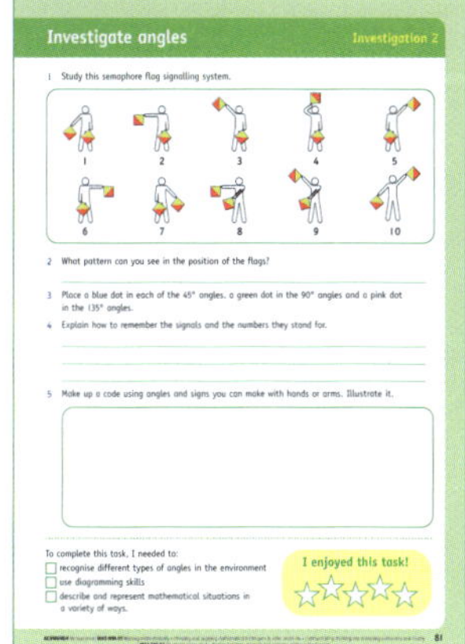

Term Investigations

Each term includes an investigation that will get students planning and working through an extended problem.

Regular Revision

Revision pages appear both at mid term and at the end of each term to revise key concepts.

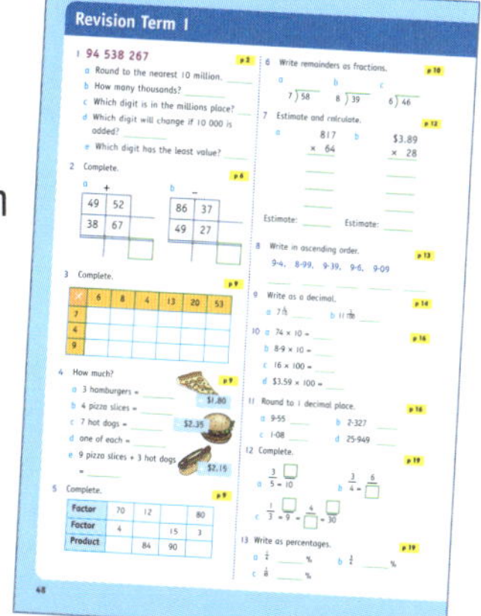

Hands-on Activities

Various hands-on activities are included in each term, asking students to measure and make, count and compare, using objects from around the classroom or home.

Year 6 Outcomes

NSW Syllabus Outcomes	Student pages
Working Mathematically	
MA1-WM-01 develops understanding and fluency in mathematics through exploring and connecting mathematical concepts	2–184
MA1-WM-01 develops understanding and fluency in mathematics through choosing and applying mathematical techniques to solve problems	7, 11, 15, 20, 24, 25, 30, 61, 75, 80, 81, 90, 92, 99, 109, 120, 128, 130, 131, 147, 168, 182, 183
MA1-WM-01 evelops understanding and fluency in mathematics through communicating their thinking and reasoning coherently and clearly	15, 20, 24, 25, 61, 75, 80, 81, 90, 109, 120, 128, 130, 131, 147, 168, 182, 183
Number and Algebra	
Representing whole numbers	
MA3-RN-01 applies an understanding of place value and the role of zero to represent the properties of numbers	2, 3, 4, 60, 61
MA3-RN-02 compares and orders decimals up to 3 decimal places	13, 14, 15, 16, 69, 115, 116, 117, 120
MA3-RN-03 determines percentages of quantities, and finds equivalent fractions and decimals for benchmark percentage values	19, 20, 21, 75, 76, 77, 78, 79, 108, 121, 122, 123, 124, 125
Additive relations	
MA3-AR-01 selects and applies appropriate strategies to solve addition and subtraction problems	5, 6, 7, 17, 28, 29, 30, 60, 106, 107, 116, 118, 120, 126, 127, 131, 139, 155, 161
Multiplicative relations	
MA3-MR-01 selects and applies appropriate strategies to solve multiplication and division problems	8, 9, 10, 11, 12, 16, 19, 28, 29, 30, 58, 59, 65, 66, 67, 68, 109, 110, 111, 112, 113, 114, 126, 154, 155, 157, 158, 159, 160, 178, 179, 180, 181
MA3-MR-02 constructs and completes number sentences involving multiplicative relations, applying the order of operations to calculations	62, 63, 64, 127, 154, 155, 156, 157, 158
Fractions	
MA3-RQF-01 compares and orders fractions with denominators of 2, 3, 4, 5, 6, 8 and 10	18, 19, 69, 70, 71, 146, 162, 163, 165, 166, 168
MA3-RQF-02 determines $\frac{1}{2}$, $\frac{1}{4}$, $\frac{1}{5}$ and $\frac{1}{10}$ of measures and quantities	72, 73, 74, 167
Measurement and Space	
Geometric measure	
MA3-GM-01 locates and describes points on a coordinate plan	31, 32, 96, 98, 99, 100, 101, 128, 129
MA3-GM-02 selects and uses the appropriate unit and device to measure lengths and distances including perimeters	33, 34, 86, 87, 97, 99, 111, 112, 115, 169, 170, 171, 172
MA3-GM-03 measures and constructs angles, and identifies the relationships between angles on a straight line and angles at a point	35, 36, 37, 38, 39, 41, 42, 80, 81, 144, 145, 146
Two-dimensional (2D) spatial structure	
MA3-2DS-01 investigates and classifies two-dimensional shapes, including triangles and quadrilaterals based on their properties	40, 41, 42, 140, 141, 142, 143, 146, 147
MA3-2DS-02 selects and uses the appropriate unit to calculate areas, including areas of rectangles	34, 84, 85, 86, 87, 171, 172, 173, 182, 183
MA3-2DS-03 combines, splits and rearranges shapes to determine the area of parallelograms and triangles	134, 135
Three-dimensional (3D) spatial structure	
MA3-3DS-01 visualises, sketches and constructs three-dimensional objects, including prisms and pyramids, making connections to two-dimensional representations	24, 25, 186, 187, 188, 189, 190
MA3-3DS-02 selects and uses the appropriate unit to estimate, measure and calculate volumes and capacities	88, 89, 90, 91, 92
Non-spatial measure	
MA3-NSM-01 selects and uses the appropriate unit and device to measure the masses of objects	90, 115, 136, 137, 138, 139, 175, 176, 177
MA3-NSM-02 measures and compares duration, using 12- and 24-hour time and am and pm notation	93, 174
Statistics and Probability	
Data and Chance	
MA3-DATA-01 constructs graphs using many-to-one scales	47, 192, 194
MA3-DATA-02 interprets data displays, including timelines and line graphs	22, 43, 44, 45, 46, 94, 95, 102, 103, 148, 149, 150, 151, 191, 192, 193
MA3-CHAN-01 conducts chance experiments and quantifies the probability	22, 23, 195, 196, 197

Australian Curriculum Content Descriptions *Students learn to:*	Student pages
Number and Algebra	
Number	
AC9M6N01 recognise situations, including financial contexts, that use integers; locate and represent integers on a number line and as coordinates on the Cartesian plane	31, 32, 60, 61, 96, 98, 99, 100, 101, 106
AC9M6N02 identify and describe the properties of prime, composite and square numbers and use these properties to solve problems and simplify calculations	58, 59, 110, 126
AC9M6N03 apply knowledge of equivalence to compare, order and represent common fractions including halves, thirds and quarters on the same number line and justify their order	18, 19, 20, 69, 71, 110, 122, 162, 163, 164, 165, 166
AC9M6N04 apply knowledge of place value to add and subtract decimals, using digital tools where appropriate; use estimation and rounding to check the reasonableness of answers	13, 14, 15, 17, 106, 107, 109, 116, 118, 127
AC9M6N05 solve problems involving addition and subtraction of fractions using knowledge of equivalent fractions	18, 19, 20, 70, 71, 74, 165, 166, 167, 168
AC9M6N06 multiply and divide decimals by multiples of powers of 10 without a calculator, applying knowledge of place value and proficiency with multiplication facts; using estimation and rounding to check the reasonableness of answers	10, 16, 111, 112, 113, 114, 119
AC9M6N07 solve problems that require finding a familiar fraction, decimal or percentage of a quantity, including percentage discounts, choosing efficient calculation strategies and using digital tools where appropriate	21, 69, 72, 73, 74, 75, 76, 77, 78, 79, 108, 121, 122, 123, 124, 125, 157, 167
AC9M6N08 approximate numerical solutions to problems involving rational numbers and percentages, including financial contexts, using appropriate estimation strategies	12, 108, 156
AC9M6N09 use mathematical modelling to solve practical problems, involving rational numbers and percentages, including in financial contexts; formulate the problems, choosing operations and efficient calculation strategies, and using digital tools where appropriate; interpret and communicate solutions in terms of the situation, justifying the choices made	5, 6, 7, 8, 9, 11, 12, 17, 21, 29, 30, 33, 60, 61, 65, 66, 67, 68, 77, 78, 79, 92, 99, 107, 109, 112, 117, 120, 121, 123, 125, 139, 154, 155, 158, 159, 160, 161
Algebra	
AC9M6A01 recognise and use rules that generate visually growing patterns and number patterns involving rational numbers	30
AC9M6A02 find unknown values in numerical equations involving brackets and combinations of arithmetic operations, using the properties of numbers and operations	29, 62, 63, 64, 126, 127, 154, 155, 156, 157, 158, 161
AC9M6A03 create and use algorithms involving a sequence of steps and decisions that use rules to generate sets of numbers; identify, interpret and explain emerging patterns	28, 130, 131
Measurement and Geometry	
Measurement	
AC9M6M01 convert between common metric units of length, mass and capacity; choose and use decimal representations of metric measurements relevant to the context of a problem	33, 34, 88, 89, 90, 91, 115, 120, 136, 137, 138, 139, 169, 170, 182, 183
AC9M6M02 establish the formula for the area of a rectangle and use it to solve practical problems	34, 84, 85, 86, 87, 92, 111, 134, 135, 171, 172, 173
AC9M6M03 interpret and use timetables and itineraries to plan activities and determine the duration of events and journeys	93, 174, 175
AC9M6M04 identify the relationships between angles on a straight line, angles at a point and vertically opposite angles; use these to determine unknown angles, communicating reasoning	35, 36, 37, 38, 39, 40, 41, 42, 80, 81, 144, 145, 146, 147
Space	
AC9M6SP01 compare the parallel cross-sections of objects and recognise their relationships to right prisms	24, 25, 189, 190
AC9M6SP02 locate points in the 4 quadrants of a Cartesian plane; describe changes to the coordinates when a point is moved to a different position in the plane	31, 32, 96, 98, 99, 100, 101, 128, 129
AC9M6SP03 recognise and use combinations of transformations to create tessellations and other geometric patterns, using dynamic geometric software where appropriate	140, 141, 142, 143
Statistics and Probability	
Statistics	
AC9M6ST01 interpret and compare data sets for ordinal and nominal categorical, discrete and continuous numerical variables using comparative displays or visualisations and digital tools; compare distributions in terms of mode, range and shape	22, 43, 44, 47, 103, 148, 149, 150, 191, 192, 194, 195
AC9M6ST02 identify statistically informed arguments presented in traditional and digital media; discuss and critique methods, data representations and conclusions	45, 46, 102, 103, 150, 151, 192
AC9M6ST03 plan and conduct statistical investigations by posing and refining questions or identifying a problem and collecting relevant data; analyse and interpret the data and communicate findings within the context of the investigation	193, 194
Probability	
AC9M6P01 recognise that probabilities lie on numerical scales of 0 – 1 or 0% – 100% and use estimation to assign probabilities that events occur in a given context, using common fractions, percentages and decimals	23, 148, 196, 197
AC9M6P02 conduct repeated chance experiments and run simulations with an increasing number of trials using digital tools; compare observations with expected results and discuss the effect on variation of increasing the number of trials	22, 195, 196

How to Solve a Problem

Read • Plan • Work • Check

Read the problem carefully. Read it again. Underline important words.

Plan what you are going to do — add, subtract, multiply or divide.

Work Write the steps you take to work out the answer. Write your answer in full.

Check your answer! Make sure that your answer makes sense and that you answered the question.

Draw a diagram

Draw a simple picture.
Use symbols if you can.

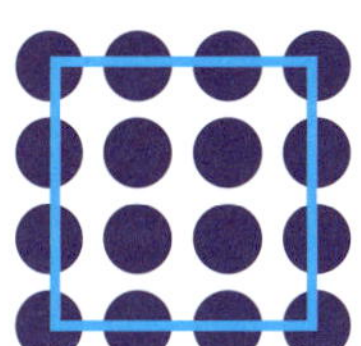

16 *is* a square number.

Trial and Error

Make a guess and write it down. Check if it is right. If not, work out if your guess should be higher or lower. Make another guess and write it down. Check if it's right. Keep going until you have the correct answer.

Look for patterns

Study the numbers in the problem.
Write them down in a list.
Can you see a pattern?
What comes next in the pattern?
Write it as your answer.

Cindy cycles 3 km, then 6 km, then 9 km on 3 days. How far should she cycle on the 4th day to keep to her pattern?

3, 6, 9, ?   *3, 6, 9, 12*

Cindy should cycle 12 km.

Use a table

Put the information from the problem in columns. Can you see the pattern? The information is clearer in a table.

Use this to work out the answer.

Answer: 14 people = 14 cars

Work backwards

Read the problem all the way through. Find one piece of information. Write it down. Find another piece of information that relates and put them together. Write it down. Keep working backwards until you solve all the pieces of the problem.

Kell has $2 more than Matt, who has $3 less than Jan. Jan has $10. How much do they each have?

Jan = $10

Matt = $10 – $3 = $7

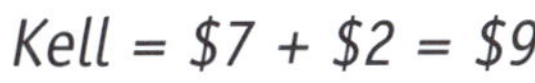

Kell = $7 + $2 = $9

Dictionary

angle

The amount of turning between two straight lines that meet at a point.

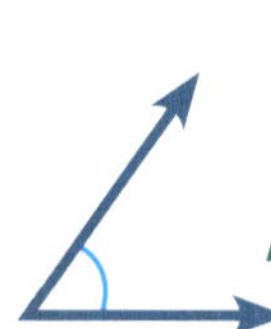

Acute angles are less than 90°.

Straight angles are 180°.

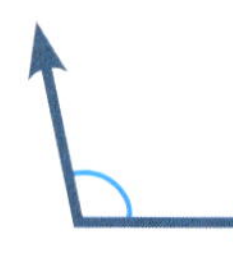

Obtuse angles are larger than 90° but less than 180°.

Reflex angles are larger than 180° but less than 360°.

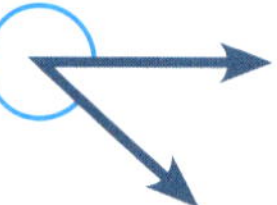

Revolutions are 360°.

A protractor is used to measure angles.

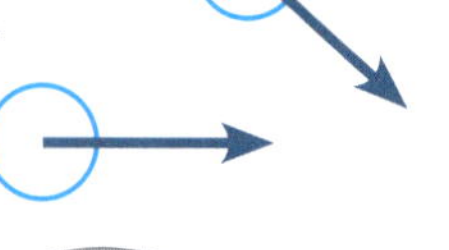

area

Area is the size of the surface.
It is measured in square units.
square centimetres (cm^2)
square metres (m^2)
hectares (ha) (1 ha = 10 000 m^2)
square kilometres (km^2)

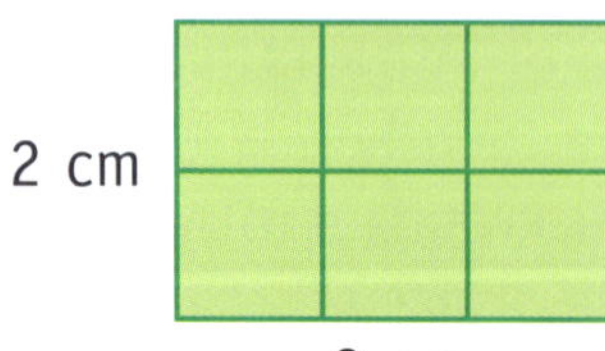

Area = 2 cm × 3 cm
= 6 cm^2

average

Average = sum of scores ÷ number of scores

average of 7, 9, 12, 16 = $\frac{7 + 9 + 12 + 16}{4}$
= 11

capacity

The amount a container can hold.

The capacity of this bottle is 1 litre.

Cartesian plane

The Cartesian plane is sometimes referred to as the number plane. The coordinates of a point refer to an ordered pair *(x, y)* describing the horizontal position *x* first, followed by the vertical position *y*.

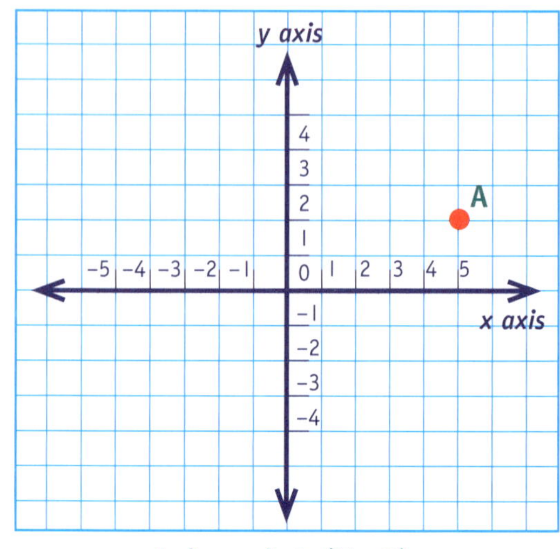

A is point (5, 2).

cross-section

The surface that is seen when a solid shape is cut through.

edge/face/vertex

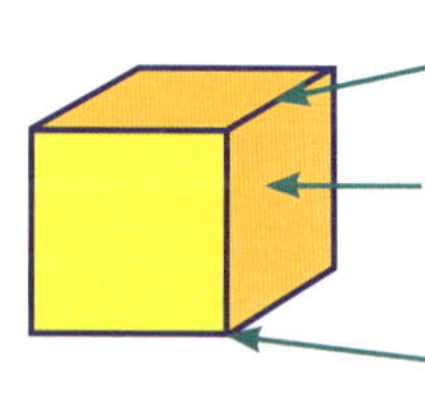

An edge is where two flat surfaces meet.
A face is the flat surface of a solid shape.
A vertex is where the edges meet to make a corner.

factor

A whole number that can be divided exactly into another number.

6 is a factor of 42.

Dictionary

fraction

Any part of a group or whole.

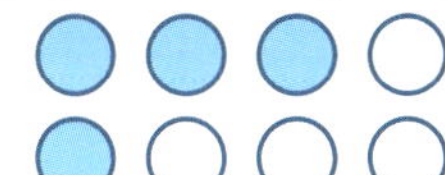

$\frac{4}{8}$ ← numerator ← denominator

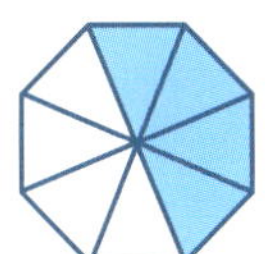

$\frac{4}{8} = \frac{1}{2}$

Equivalent fractions are fractions that have the same value, eg $\frac{4}{8} = \frac{1}{2}$.

Decimal fractions are ones written using a decimal point to show the tenths, hundredths etc. eg 3·63.

Mixed numbers have a whole number and a fraction, eg $4\frac{1}{2}$

graphs

A diagram that shows a collection of data.

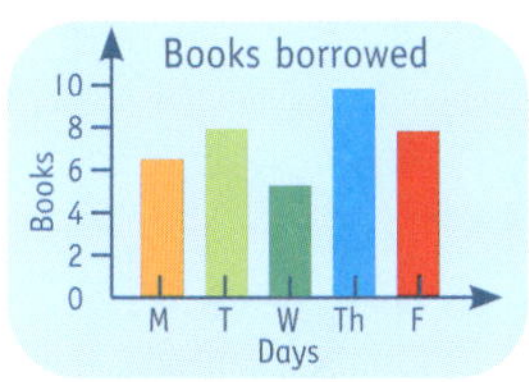

column graph

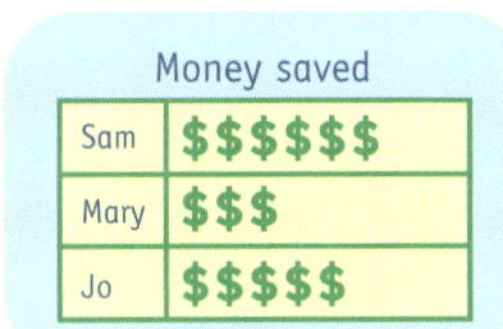

picture graph

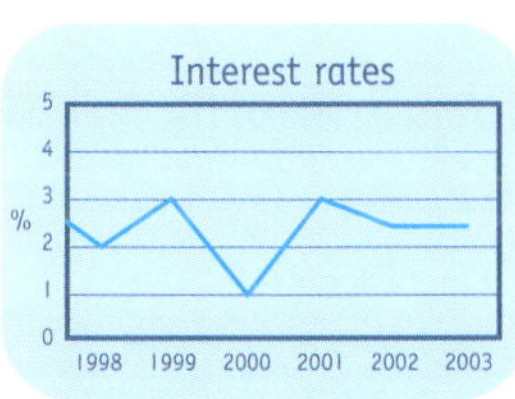

line graph

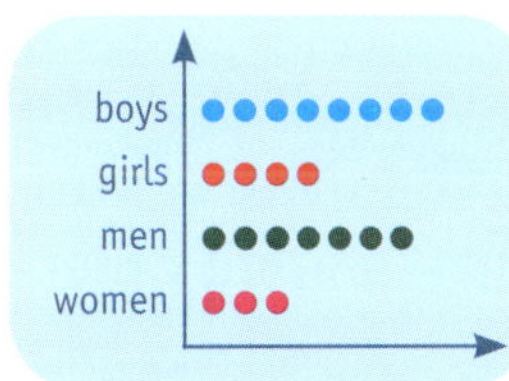

dot plot

highest common factor

The HCF is the highest number which is a factor of two or more numbers, eg the HCF of 9 and 15 is 3.

length

The distance from one end to another. Length is measured in millimetres (mm), centimetres (cm), metres (m) and kilometres (km).

10 mm = 1 cm   100 cm = 1 m
1000 m = 1 km

lines

Parallel lines never meet.

Perpendicular lines are at right angles.

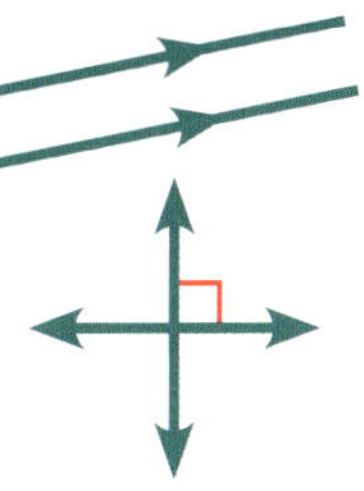

lowest common multiple

The LCM is the lowest number which is a multiple of two or more numbers, eg LCM of 4 and 3 is 12.

mass

Mass is measured in grams (g), kilograms (kg) and tonnes (t).

1000 g = 1 kg   1000 kg = 1 t

mean

Mean is the average of a set of scores.

Scores: 4, 6, 2, 4, 5, 3, 5
Mean: $29 \div 7 = 4\frac{1}{7}$

multiple

The product of two or more factors.

$3 \times 2 \times 4 = 24$

24 is a multiple of 2, 3 and 4.

outcome

A result of an experiment or trial eg rolling a die has 6 outcomes:

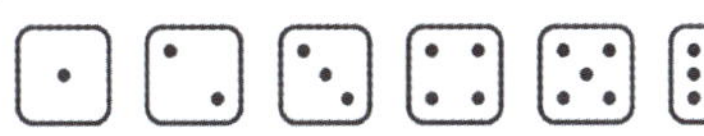

percent

An amount out of one hundred (%).

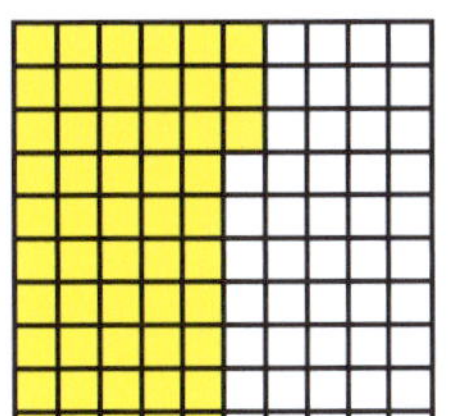

$\frac{53}{100}$ fraction

0·53 decimal

53% percentage

perimeter

The length of the outside boundary of a shape.

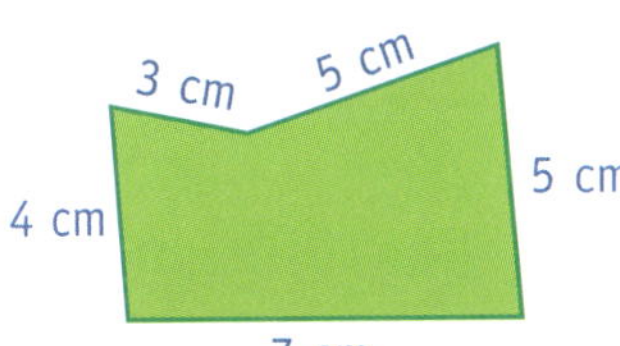

P = 4 cm + 3 cm + 5 cm + 5 cm + 7 cm
P = 24 cm

Dictionary

prime number
A number which has only two factors – itself and one.

2 has factors 2 and 1.
19 has factors 19 and 1.
2 and 19 are prime numbers.

Numbers with more than two factors are composite numbers.

probability
The chance of something happening. Probability can be described in:

words: certain, impossible, likely, unlikely.

decimals from 0 to 1: 0·5, 0·75

percentages: 10% chance, 50% chance

spreadsheet
A table used to organise data into rows and columns

	A	B	C	D	E
1	5	6	11		
2	6	7	13		
3	7	8	15		
4	8	9	17		

A1 + B1 = C1

surface
The flat or curved outside layer of a solid shape.

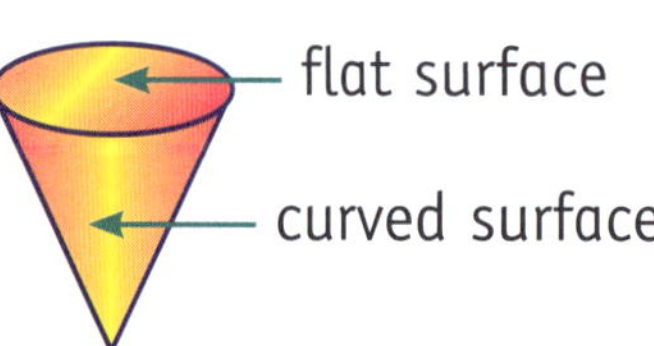

symmetry
A shape has **line symmetry** if both halves match exactly when it is folded on the axis of symmetry.

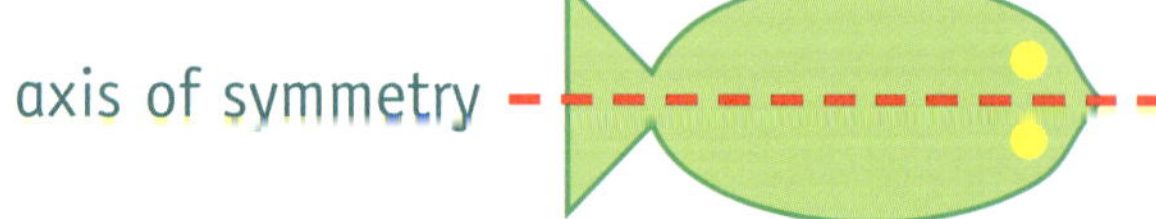

A shape has **rotational symmetry** when a tracing of the shape matches the original as it rotates around its centre.

tally
A mark made to represent an item when counting. Four vertical marks are made and crossed horizontally with the fifth to keep them in bundles of fives.

卌 卌 ||| = 13

tessellation
A pattern made by identical shapes fitting together without gaps or overlaps.

three-dimensional (3D) objects
A 3D object has length, width and height. They include:

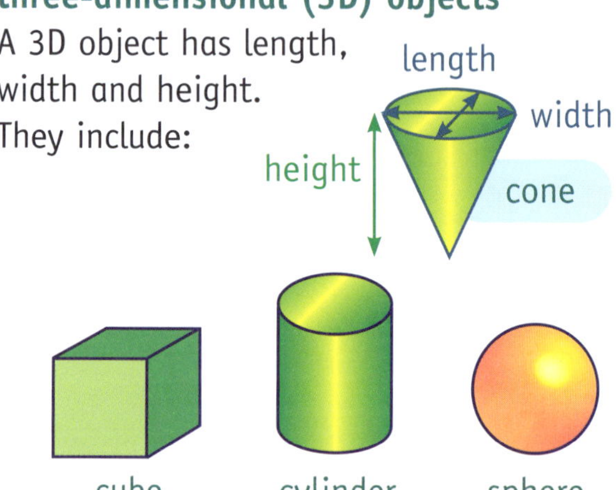

prisms – objects which have a uniform cross-section, two end faces which give a prism its name and all other faces are rectangles.

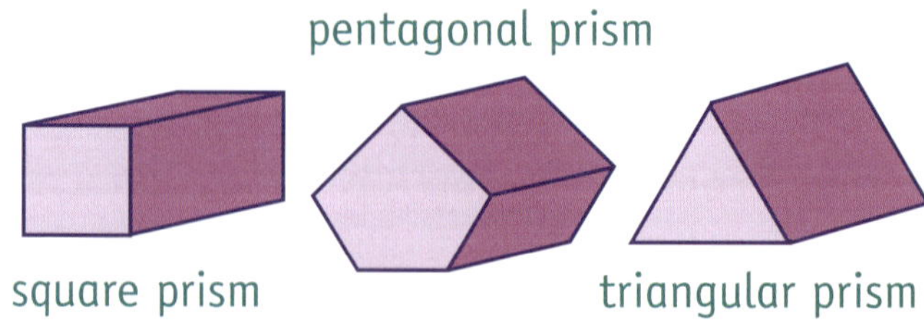

pyramids – objects which have polygons as a base and all other sides are triangles.

Dictionary

time

Time can be displayed in 12-hour or 24-hour form.

analogue

digital

1 hour = 60 minutes
1 minute = 60 seconds

transformations

The three types of transformations are:

Translation: slide a 2D shape without changing it in any way

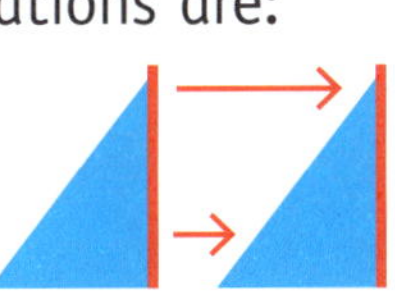

Reflection: flip a shape over to make a mirror image

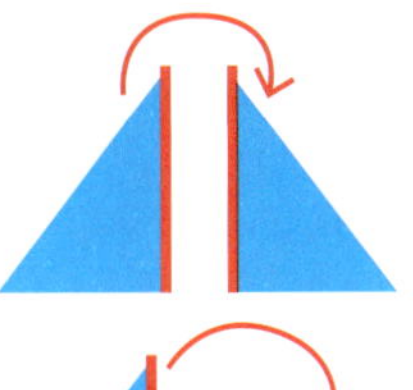

Rotation: turn a shape around a fixed point.

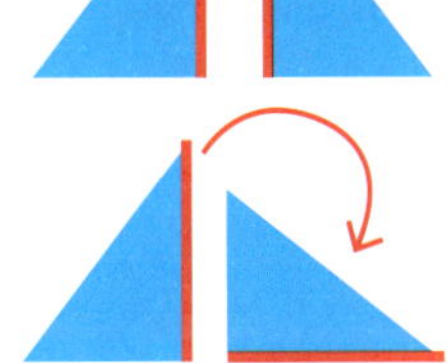

triangle

A polygon with three angles and three sides. There are 4 types of triangles.

equilateral — All sides are equal. All angles are equal.

isosceles — Two sides are equal. Two angles are equal.

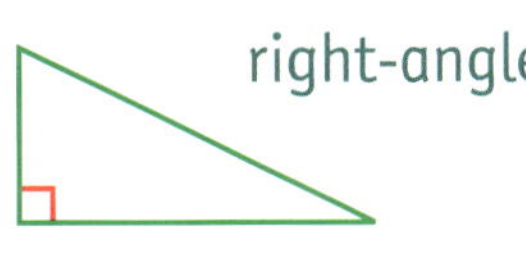

right-angled — One angle is a right angle (90°).

scalene — Each side is a different length.

two-dimensional (2D) shapes

Shapes that have only two dimensions – length and width. They include:

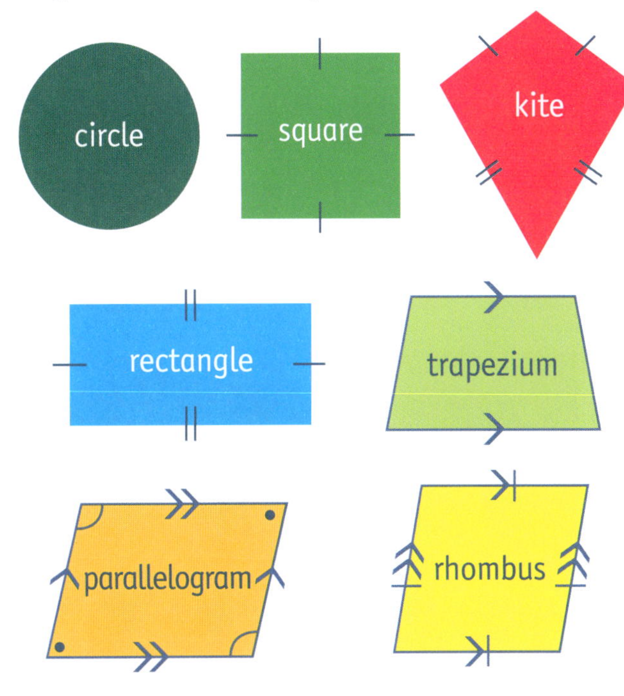

polygons: 5 sides – pentagon
6 sides – hexagon
7 sides – heptagon
8 sides – octagon
9 sides – nonagon
10 sides – decagon

regular polygons – All sides are equal and all angles are equal.

volume

The amount of space a solid object takes up.

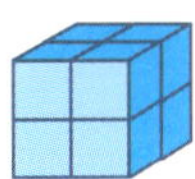

Volume = 2 × 2 × 2
= 8 cubic units

Units of volume:
cubic centimetres (cm^3)
cubic metres (m^3)

Unit 1 Numbers over one million

Country	Population *	Area km²	City	Population *
Australia	26 473 055	7 692 024	Sydney Melbourne	5 121 000 5 235 000
Indonesia	277 534 122	1 919 931	Jakarta	11 249 000
Thailand	71 801 279	513 120	Bangkok	11 070 000
Malaysia	34 308 525	330 803	Kuala Lumpur	8 622 000

* 2023 Estimates

1 Order the countries by population in ascending order. Round the numbers to millions.

Australia 26 million

2 Order the cities in descending order of size.

3 Look at Australia's and Indonesia's populations and areas. Comment.

Unit 1 Large numbers

Expanded notation
1 760 415 = 1 000 000 + 700 000 + 60 000 + 400 + 10 + 5

1 Write these in expanded notation.

a 513 120 ______

b 330 803 ______

c 11 070 000 ______

d 8 622 000 ______

e 71 801 279 ______

2 Study page 2 again and practise expressing the numbers in different ways using rounding, eg Bangkok's population is about 11 million or eleven million, seventy thousand.

Which city has a population of about:

a 5 million? ______
b 8·6 million? ______
c $5\frac{1}{4}$ million? ______
d 11 000 000 + 250 000? ______

3 Which two countries' populations total about 60 000 000? ______

4 Place the populations of A Australia, B Malaysia and C Thailand on this number line.

0 ... 100 000 000

5 Write the areas of the following countries in words. They are rounded to ten thousand km².

a Thailand 510 000 km² ______

b Indonesia 1 920 000 km² ______

6 Complete these number series.

a 98 500 000 ______ ______ ______ 98 900 000
b 468 947 ______ ______ ______ 472 947
c 2 056 982 ______ ______ ______ 2 456 982

Unit 1 Place value

1 Write the following numerals vertically, placing them correctly according to place value.

	HM	TM	M	HTh	TTh	Th	H	T	O
a forty-three million, eighty thousand and twenty									
b five million, three hundred and seventeen thousand and six									
c eighty-eight thousand, four hundred and ninety-nine									

2 Here is a population counter of Saraban, a growing country.

72 567 345

a When the population increases by one million, which digit will change? ______

b If you change the 6 to a 7, how many more people will there be? ______

c How many times greater is the 7 on the left than the 7 on the right? ______

d How many times greater is the 5 on the left than the 5 on the right? ______

e The population of this country is about seventy-two million, six hundred thousand people. True or false? ______

3 What might the numbers be of men, women, boys and girls in Saraban?

______ + ______ + ______ + ______

4 Write the three countries from page 2 and their population, which are less than Saraban.

______ ______ ______

5 Match the expressions on the right with their numerical value on the left.

a	16 490 000	over five million
b	2 500 250	less than one million
c	58 000 014	roughly sixteen million
d	5 500 000	a little more than two and a half million
e	875 900	slightly less than sixty million

Mastery Checklist I can:
- ☐ use place value to hundred millions
- ☐ understand real-world large numbers
- ☐ write large numbers in different ways
- ☐ use expanded notation.

Unit 2 Addition and subtraction

The State of Xanda is planning a huge advertising campaign to boost tourism. The Tourist Bureau is publishing brochures to advertise the joys of travel by road. Help them to present their material clearly by using tables.

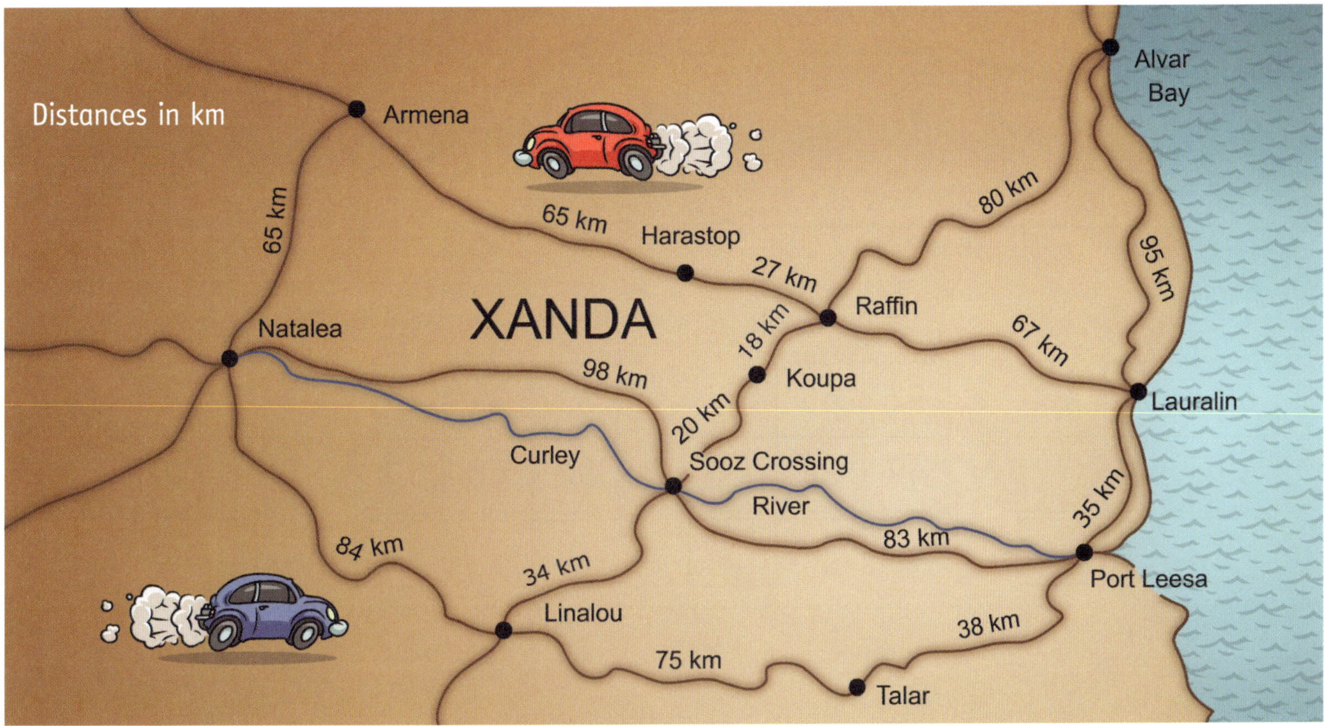

1 Complete the distance chart of shortest distances.

	Talar	Sooz Crossing
Alvar Bay		
Natalea		
Linalou		
Sooz Crossing		
Talar		

2 Help tourists decide which way to go to reach their destinations. Tick the shortest route.

From	To	Via	Distance
a Lauralin	Linalou	Raffin	
b Lauralin	Linalou	Talar	
c		**Difference**	
d Armena	Alvar Bay	Raffin	
e Armena	Alvar Bay	Lauralin	
f		**Difference**	

3 I travelled 262 km, leaving from Port Leesa and passing through three towns. What was my destination? __________

Unit 2 Mental strategies

1 a 50 + 70 = ____ b 40 + 60 = ____ c 80 + 90 = ____ d 50 + 90 = ____ e 30 + 80 = ____

2 Which towns are exactly 100 km apart? [ ]

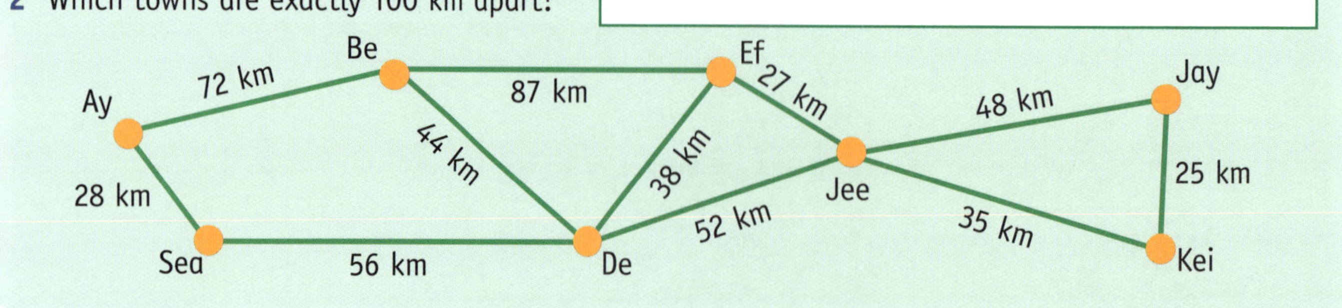

3 a +

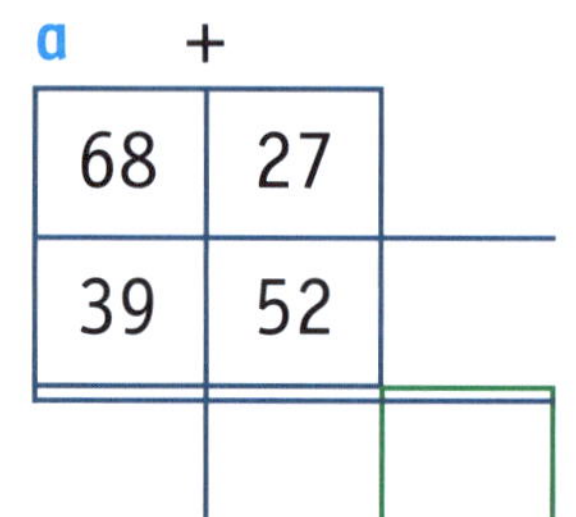

68	27
39	52

b +

52	66
49	29

c +

83	79
92	68

d +

75	28
38	43

4 a 320 + 150 = ____ b 530 + 270 = ____ c 250 + 480 = ____ d 340 + 730 = ____

5 Total each salesperson's distance travelled for the day.

a Tina	b Brett	c Sol	d Jo	e Chen
264 km	256 km	59 km	89 km	397 km
89 km	193 km	326 km	112 km	86 km
164 km	93 km	37 km	76 km	
____	____	____	____	____

SUBTRACTION IS THE REVERSE OF ADDITION 180 – 130 = 50 **Check!** 50 + 130 = 180

6 a 270 – 160 = ____ b 430 – 270 = ____ c 540 – 360 = ____ d 670 – 80 = ____

7 Complete the table of distances for holiday makers. Use count on as your strategy.

Distance	500	1000	400	200	420	300	550	250
Already travelled	305	485	140	85	295	175	321	129
Km to go	a	b	c	d	e	f	g	h

8 Continue these number patterns.

a 300, 272, 244, ____, ____, ____

b 500, 465, 430, ____, ____, ____

c 600, 510, 420, ____, ____, ____

d 800, 755, ____, 665, ____, ____

Mastery Checklist I can: ☐ add to compare distances
☐ use different mental strategies to add.

Problem solving

Using mental strategies

1 a 400 + 300 = ______ b 200 + 900 = ______ c 300 + 800 = ______

2 Total the mass in the shopping baskets. Look for easy combinations!

3 Write the total distance travelled on these journeys.

Road distances in kilometres

	Canberra	Bathurst	Dubbo	Orange
Bathurst	271			
Dubbo	414	209		
Orange	309	53	156	
Sydney	320	219	428	262

a Bathurst → Canberra → Sydney = 271 + 320 = ______

b Dubbo → Orange → Canberra ______

c Sydney → Canberra → Orange ______

4 Count backwards by 28 from 500 until you reach 304.

500 → ______ → ______ → ______ → ______ → ______ → ______ → 304

5 As Harry reaches each town, he calls his wife to tell her how much further he has to go to get home. What distance from home is he at each hotel stop? Count back each time.

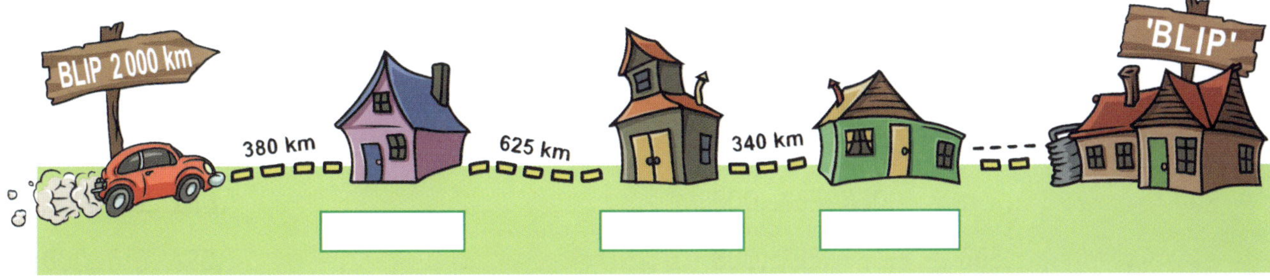

I can solve problems by:

☐ using addition ☐ writing algorithms.

Unit 3 Multiplication and division

SHOP WELL

We serve

Lisa		
Biscuits	5 pks	$11.00
Sim Sauce	3 jars	$9.90
Paper towel	2 rolls	$4.70
Tuna	7 tins	$6.30
Kiwi fruit	12	$6.00
Total		**$37.90**

Best prices!

1 Study the supermarket displays and count the articles in each display. Complete the missing information from the labels. Use multiplication to work out the total.

a Sim Sauce: 12 boxes of ________ jars = ________ jars

b Sim Sauce: 16 boxes of ________ jars = ________ jars

c Paper towel: 12 packs of ________ rolls = ________ rolls

d Paper towel: 8 packs of ________ rolls = ________ rolls

e Biscuits: 5 packs of ________ biscuits = ________ biscuits

f Biscuits: 10 packs of ________ biscuits = ________ biscuits

2 Study the checkout docket.

Write the number sentence. Calculate the cost per item, using division. Check using multiplication.

a Biscuits ________________________________ = ____________ per packet

b Sim Sauce ________________________________ = ____________

c Tuna ________________________________ = ____________

d Paper towel ________________________________ = ____________

e Kiwi fruit ________________________________ = ____________

Unit 3 Multiplication

Factor × Factor = Product

1 Complete.

a

×	2	8	12	15	30	7	9	11
10								
6								
5								

b

×	0	20	9	3	6	7	15	25
4								
11								
8								

2

Factor	7	8	9	11	6	10	5	6	3	12	0	15
Factor	30	40	90	50	70	15	60	50	90	40	11	20
Product												

3

Factor	5		9	7	8			9		8	7	
Factor		40		70		6	3		10	50		7
Product	35	240	360		720	420	270	99	120		140	630

4 Calculate the costs of:

a rolls.
1 doz @ 15c ea.

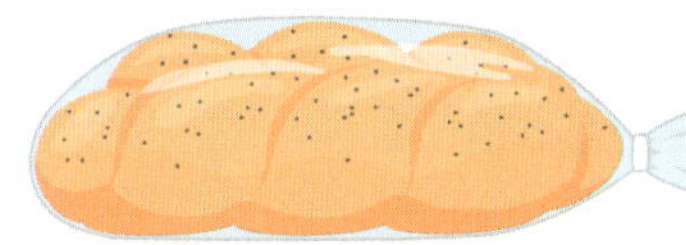

b bread.
4 loaves @ $1.60 ea.

c cake.
10 @ 55c ea.

5

Item	Mass each	Pack of 6	Bag of 10
Choc bar	480 g		
Muffin	1200 g		
Cake	115 g		

Challenge! Circle two factors and a product.

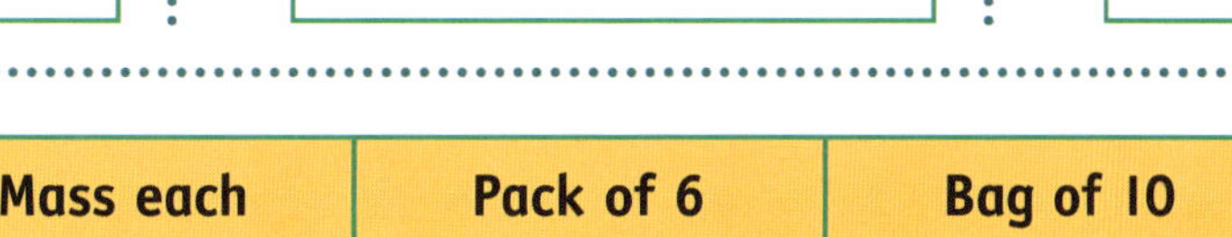

6 240 3 30 90 630 7 40 80 5 0 60 8 48 180 3 60 270 90 4 320
7 40 280 20 60 9 520 8 56 30 6 60 360 9 90 81 7 420 3 80 240

Unit 3 Division

Dividend ÷ Divisor = Quotient + Remainder

1 a 180 ÷ 6 = ____ b 280 ÷ 4 = ____ c 360 ÷ 9 = ____ d 630 ÷ 9 = ____ e 450 ÷ 5 = ____

f 320 ÷ 8 = ____ g 350 ÷ 7 = ____ h 240 ÷ 8 = ____ i 300 ÷ 6 = ____ j 420 ÷ 7 = ____

2 Circle the errors.

a 150 ÷ 3 = 5 b 180 ÷ 9 = 30 c 240 ÷ 6 = 40 d 330 ÷ 11 = 30 e 120 ÷ 5 = 80

f 270 ÷ 4 = 60 g 360 ÷ 3 = 120 h 400 ÷ 8 = 40 i 720 ÷ 90 = 8 j 560 ÷ 70 = 8

3 Complete the tables: Q = Quotient R = Remainder

	Q	R
17 ÷ 3	5	2
a 28 ÷ 5		
b 63 ÷ 8		
c 58 ÷ 7		
d 47 ÷ 6		
e 53 ÷ 9		

	Q	R
23 ÷ 4	5	2
f ÷ 6	3	1
g ÷ 5	7	1
h ÷ 8	1	6
i ÷ 10	5	8
j ÷ 9	6	7

	Q	R
38 ÷ 6	6	2
k 41 ÷		5
l 62 ÷		8
m 14 ÷		3
n 22 ÷		4
o 75 ÷		3

$7\overline{)59}$ = 8 r3 $7\overline{)59}$ = $8\frac{3}{7}$ *Write remainders as fractions.*

4 a $9\overline{)87}$ b $7\overline{)53}$ c $6\overline{)53}$ d $4\overline{)26}$

e $5\overline{)49}$ f $8\overline{)69}$ g $3\overline{)19}$ h $7\overline{)66}$

i $6\overline{)46}$ j $9\overline{)78}$ k $8\overline{)95}$ l $6\overline{)82}$

5 Use multiplication to solve division.

a ▲ ÷ 6 ■ ÷ 3

b ▲ ÷ 6 ■ ÷ 7

c ▲ ÷ 3 ■ ÷ 6

Problem solving

Holiday budget

Make a budget for the Floogles, a family of 2 adults and 2 children.
Plan lots of activities and fun for them for a 5 night/4 day stay.

1 What will it cost them? All food is free.

Accommodation	Car Hire	Entertainment

2 Which item will cost the most on the holiday? ______________________

I can solve problems by:

☐ using different operations ☐ choosing the correct strategy.

AC9M6N09 Number **MAO-WM-01** Working mathematically • choosing and applying mathematical techniques to solve problems • communicating thinking and reasoning coherently and clearly • **MA3-MR-01** • Multiplicative relations B • Select and apply strategies to solve problems involving multiplication and division with whole numbers

Unit 3 Multiplication by 2-digit numbers

1 Estimate the following multiples before working.

a 315 × 40 est. ______

b 184 × 60 est. ______

c 562 × 40 est. ______

475 × 80
Estimate → 500 × 8 tens
4000 tens = 40 000
Actual → 475 × 80 =
38 000 Close!

2 Estimate first.

278
× 27
1946 (278 × 7)
5560 (278 × 20)
7506 (total)

a 268 × 27 est. ______

b 714 × 35 est. ______

c 952 × 49 est. ______

3 Rewrite the ingredients for the extra people.

MAGIC MUESLI MUNCH	MAGIC MUESLI MUNCH	MAGIC MUESLI MUNCH
Ingredients for 2	**Ingredients for 8**	**Ingredients for 12**
60 g puffed wheat		
70 g rolled oats		
50 g pecan nuts		
40 g flaked coconut		
15 g sunflower seeds		
45 g dried apples		
100 g dried apricots		
50 mL maple syrup		

Challenge! Find a recipe and copy it. Rewrite it for:
a 3 people. b 8 people.

Mastery Checklist I can:
- ☐ multiply to find supermarket totals
- ☐ multiply to check division answers
- ☐ multiply prices and masses
- ☐ recognise factors and products
- ☐ complete divisions with remainders
- ☐ use algorithms to multiply by 2 digits.

AC9M6N08 • AC9M6N09 Number MA3-MR-01 • Multiplicative relations A • Select and apply mental and written strategies to multiply 2- and 3-digit numbers by 2-digit numbers • Multiplicative relations B • Select and apply strategies to solve problems involving multiplication and division with whole numbers

Unit 4 Reading and writing decimals

9.755
9.56
9.4
9.459
9.565
9.45
9.6
9.5
9.8
9.75

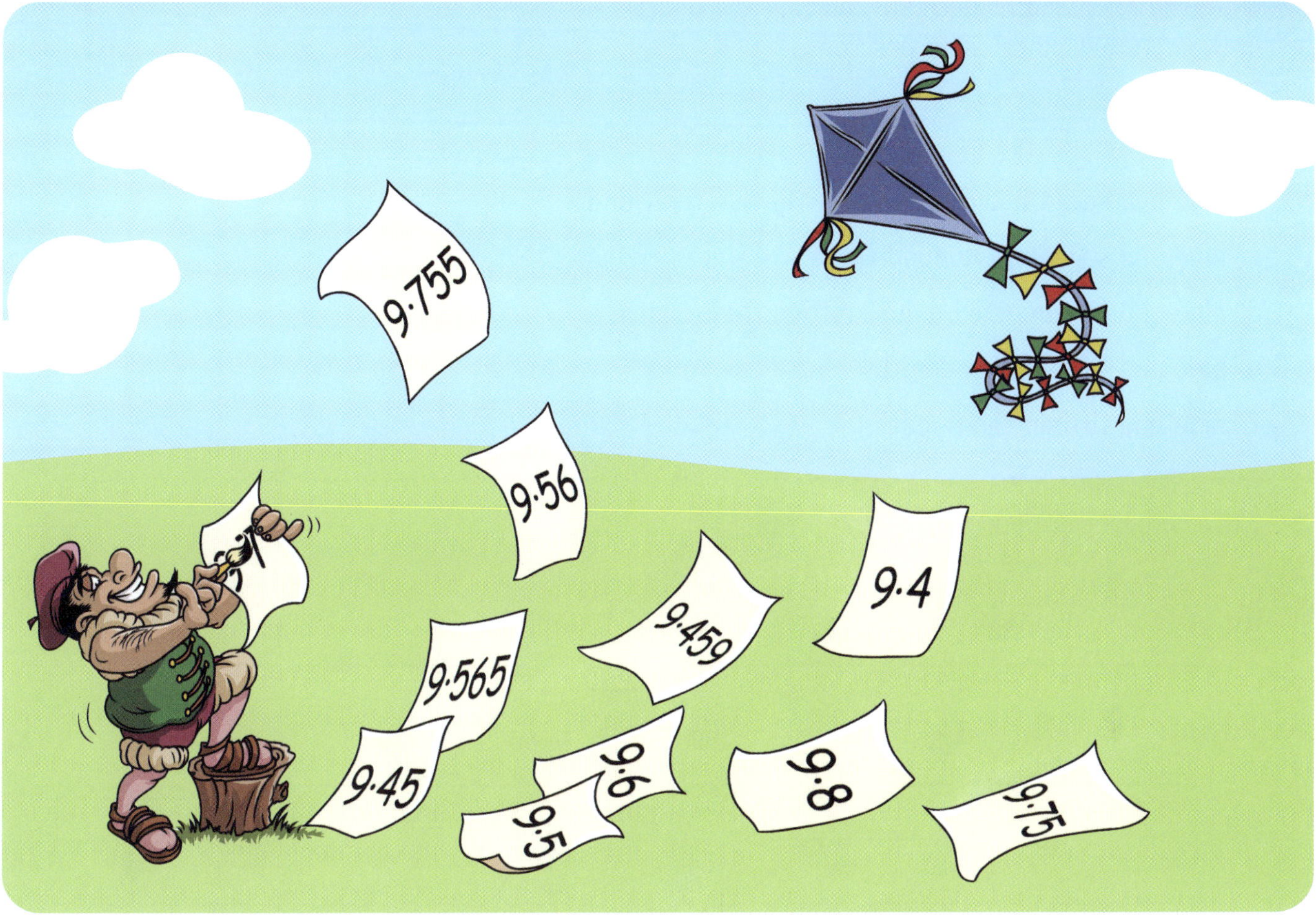

1 Help Mr Eagleye by putting his Best Kite Flier point-score sheets into ascending order.

a	b	c	d	e	f	g	h	i	j

2 What is the difference between:

a the smallest score and the largest score? _______

b h and b _______ c i and c _______ d i and d _______

3 Round each of Mr Eagleye's Best Kite Flier scores to one decimal place.

_________ _________ _________ _________ _________

_________ _________ _________ _________ _________

4 What is the advantage of rounding when making estimates? ______________________________

____

Unit 4 Decimals to three places

Decimal revision

1 Write the following as decimals, placing the digits in their correct place value positions.

ones		tenths	hundredths	thousandths
1	·	$\frac{1}{10}$	$\frac{1}{100}$	$\frac{1}{1000}$

a nine and eight tenths ____________________

b nine and seven hundred and seventy-five thousandths ____________________

c nine and seventy-five hundredths ____________________

d nine and five hundred and sixty-five thousandths ____________________

e nine and fifty-six hundredths ____________________

f nine and fifteen thousandths ____________________

2 Write the decimal indicated by the arrow.

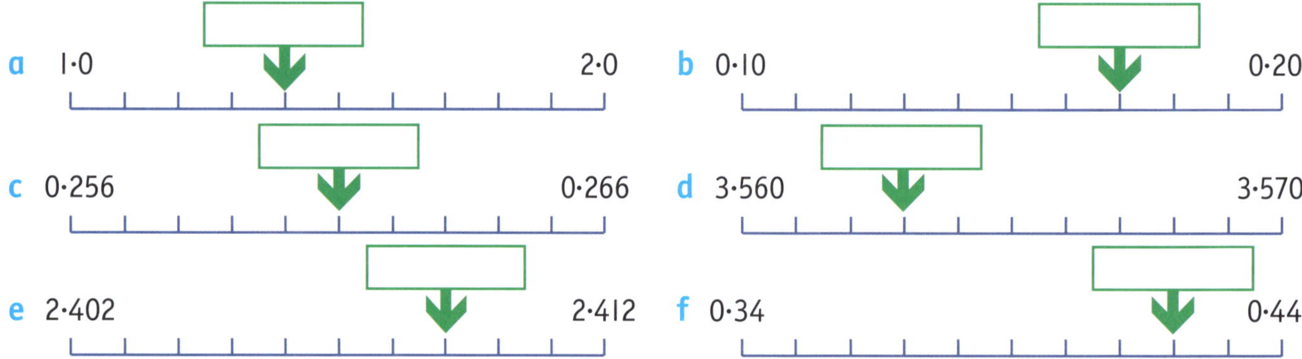

3 Arrange each set of digits to make a decimal number less than one.
eg 7, 4, 3, 0 = 0·734, 0·743, 0·347, 0·374, 0·437, 0·473

a 6, 0, 5, 3 ____________

b 9, 0, 1, 7 ____________

c 5, 1, 0 ____________

d 8, 0, 3 ____________

4 What is the value of the:

a 3 in 5·35? ________ b 7 in 2·697? ________ c 1 in 1·095? ________

d 6 in 7·06? ________ e 2 in 0·328? ________ f 4 in 0·854? ________

5 Place the following in descending order on the ladders.

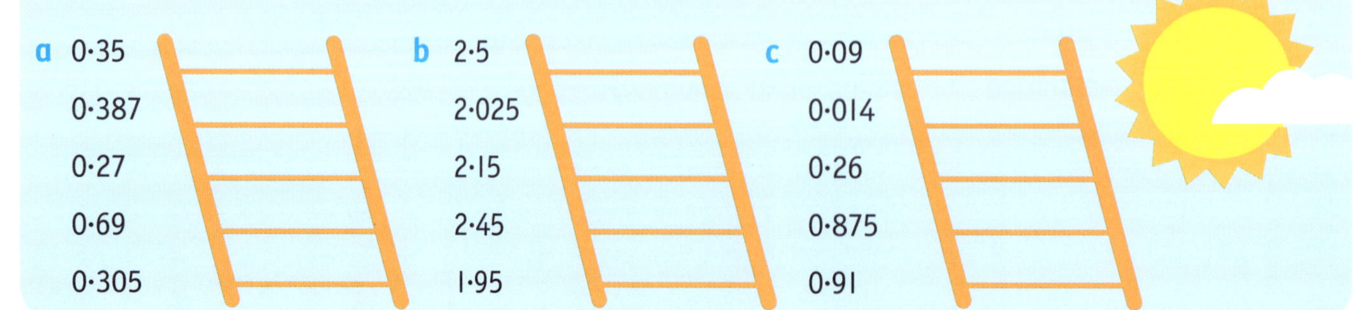

Problem solving

Decimals

1 Jiemba and Lowanna have been asked to expand 0·621.

Jiemba writes:

0·621 expanded is 0·6, 0·2 and 0·1

Lowanna writes:

0·621 expanded is 0·6, 0·02 and 0·001

a Who is correct? ____________

Why? ____________

b How could 0·621 be written in expanded form in another way? ____________

2 Jarli is thinking of a number.

It has:

Ones	.	Tenths	Hundredths	Thousandths
0	.	𝍸 (5 tally marks)	‖ (2 tally marks)	?

Write 5 different numbers that could be Jarli's number.

________ ________ ________ ________ ________

3 Killara converted the decimal 5·29 to a fraction.

$5{\cdot}29 = \frac{529}{100}$

Is Killara correct? ______

Explain your answer.

____

____

____

____

____

____

I can solve problems by:

☐ understanding decimal place value ☐ checking answers.

Unit 4 Multiply decimals by 10 and 100

Multiply by 10
Move decimal point one place to right.
Multiply by 100
Move decimal place two places to right.
eg 7·31 × 10 = 73·1
8·52 × 100 = 852

1 Write the money amount for a calculator reading, eg 6·7 = $6.70.

a 3·2 ______ b 15·4 ______ c 264·35 ______
d 0·28 ______ e 792·07 ______ f 1·78 ______

2 Multiply by 10.

a $4.35 ______ b $5.65 ______ c $2.70 ______
d $1.65 ______ e $0.85 ______ f $54.25 ______
g $0.58 ______ h $13.30 ______

3 Increase these amounts tenfold.

a $22.50 ______ b $10.10 ______ c $24.75 ______
d $15.25 ______ e $0.45 ______ f $543.20 ______

4 Multiply these numbers by 100.

a 7·894 ______ b 13·605 ______ c 3·0 ______ d 72·94 ______
e 14·003 ______ f 135·32 ______ g 78·5 ______ h 1·6 ______

5 To assist families with storm-damaged homes, the government promised to give to the Relief Fund, one hundred times as much as was donated. What did the government give if the donation was:

a $425.00? ______ b $945.00? ______
c $2260.00? ______ d $53.80? ______
e $3580.00? ______ f $214.45? ______

6 Round to the nearest whole number.

a 5·608 ______ b 4·32 ______
c 6·197 ______ d 14·501 ______
e 5·498 ______ f 10·095 ______
g 21·699 ______ h 34·099 ______

7 Continue the pattern. Write the rule.

a 0·245, 2·45, 24·5, ______, ______, ______ Rule: ______
b 0·358, 3·58, 35·8, ______, ______, ______ Rule: ______
c 0·065, 0·65, ______, ______ Rule: ______
d 1·468, 146·8, ______, ______ Rule: ______
e 2·546, 254·6, 25 460 ______, ______ Rule: ______

AC9M6N06 Number **MA3-RN-02** Represents numbers A • Decimals and percentages: Compare, order and represent decimals • **MA3-MR-01** Multiplicative relations B • Select and apply strategies to solve problems involving multiplication and division with whole numbers

Unit 4 Operations using decimals

Addition and Subtraction
Remember – decimal point under decimal point, tenths under tenths, hundredths under hundredths.

Multiplication
$3 \cdot 52$ — two decimal places
$\times\ 3$
$10 \cdot 56$ — two decimal places

Division
Decimal point on decimal point.
$2\overline{)6 \cdot 4}$ = $3 \cdot 2$

1 Estimate then calculate and check.

a 2·58 + 5·08 + 0·65 + 4·88 Est.______

b 3·675 + 2·96 + 3·06 + 2·776 Est.______

2 a 0·704 − 0·5 Est.______

b 6·032 − 4·83 Est.______

c 1·75 − 0·586 Est.______

3 a 4·67 × 5 Est.______

b 3·09 × 8 Est.______

c 2·45 × 7 Est.______

d 0·625 × 4 Est.______

4 a Est.______ $5\overline{)13 \cdot 75}$

b Est.______ $4\overline{)16 \cdot 72}$

c Est.______ $7\overline{)15 \cdot 75}$

d Est.______ $9\overline{)23 \cdot 31}$

5 Add 0·25 to Mr Eagleye's Best Kite Scores on page 13.

______ ______ ______ ______ ______ ______ ______ ______ ______ ______

6 Four children will each run 15·85 km to raise funds for the Starbright Fund. What is the total distance they will run?

Answer ______

Working

7 Miss Beegshot's ranch has sold for $3.475 million while her neighbour's ranch sold for $1 289 000. How much more was Miss Beegshot's ranch?

Answer ______

Working

8 The Daily Star wishes to report the average interest rate this month. Banks' figures are:
Ozzies Own 6·25%, Catchemout 6·8%, Savemup 5·75%, Bandinos 7·2%, Gotcha Bank 6·45%, MCB 5·99% and Go-Lo 4·96%. What is the average interest rate?

Answer ______

Working

Mastery Checklist

I can:
- ☐ order decimals to three places
- ☐ round decimals
- ☐ show decimals on a number line
- ☐ understand place value with decimals
- ☐ multiply decimals by 10 and 100
- ☐ solve problems with decimals.

Unit 5 Fractions, decimals, percentages

WHOLESOME HARRY'S HEARTY PIZZA CAFÉ is different!

1 Complete Harry's Menu Reminder List of equivalent slices/fractions for 1 whole.

a Very Veggie ______ slices = ______ thirds make 1 whole pizza

b Gourmet Goody ______ slices = ______ sixths make 1 whole pizza

c Cheery Chicken ______ slices = ______ quarters make 1 whole pizza

d Texas Tomato ______ slices = ______ eighths make 1 whole pizza

e Meaty Mess ______ slices = ______ fifths make 1 whole pizza

f Double Cheese ______ slices = ______ tenths make 1 whole pizza

You can have as many different fillings as you like, providing your slices add up to a WHOLE PIZZA!

2 Some of Harry's customers like to order half a pizza of one filling and half a pizza of another filling. How many slices of each can they order? What fraction additions does Harry make?

a $\frac{1}{2}$ Texas Tomato (____ slices) + $\frac{1}{2}$ Gourmet Goody (____ slices) $\frac{4}{8} + \frac{3}{6} = 1$ pizza

b $\frac{1}{2}$ Double Cheese (____ slices) + $\frac{1}{2}$ Texas Tomato (____ slices) _____ + _____ = _____

c $\frac{1}{2}$ Gourmet Goody (____ slices) + $\frac{1}{2}$ Double Cheese (____ slices) _____ + _____ = _____

d $\frac{1}{2}$ Cheery Chicken (____ slices) + $\frac{1}{2}$ Double Cheese (____ slices) _____ + _____ = _____

Challenge! Harry has a quiz for children. They get a 10% discount for every correct answer. Will you get a discount?

	True or false?
a $\frac{4}{8}$ Texas Tomato Pizza equals $\frac{2}{4}$ Cheery Chicken Pizza	
b $\frac{3}{5}$ Meaty Mess is more than $\frac{5}{10}$ Double Cheese	
c $\frac{2}{3}$ Very Veggie is more than $\frac{5}{6}$ Gourmet Goody	

Unit 5 Equivalence

1 From Wholesome Harry's Hearty Pizza Café menu on page 18, make a chart of equivalent fractions.

a $\frac{1}{5} = \frac{\_\_}{10}$, $\frac{2}{5} = \frac{\_\_}{10}$, $\frac{3}{5} = \frac{\_\_}{10}$, $\frac{\_\_}{5} = \frac{8}{10}$, $\frac{\_\_}{5} = \frac{10}{10}$

b $\frac{1}{3} = \frac{\_\_}{6}$, $\frac{2}{3} = \frac{\_\_}{6}$, $\frac{3}{3} = \frac{\_\_}{6}$

c $\frac{1}{4} = \frac{\_\_}{8}$, $\frac{2}{4} = \frac{\_\_}{8}$, $\frac{3}{4} = \frac{\_\_}{8}$

d $\frac{1}{2} = \frac{\_\_}{4} = \frac{\_\_}{6} = \frac{\_\_}{10}$

Equivalent fractions

$$\frac{1\ (\times 4)}{3\ (\times 4)} = \frac{4}{12}$$

Multiply the numerator and the denominator by the same number.

2 Complete.

Common Fraction	Fraction	Decimal	Percentage
eg $\frac{1}{2}$	$\frac{5}{10}$	0·5	50%
a $\frac{1}{4}$	$\frac{\_\_}{100}$		
b $\frac{1}{5}$	$\frac{\_\_}{10}$		
c $\frac{2}{5}$	$\frac{\_\_}{10}$		
d $\frac{3}{5}$	$\frac{\_\_}{10}$		
e $\frac{\_\_}{5}$	$\frac{8}{10}$		
f $\frac{9}{10}$			90%
g	$\frac{\_\_}{100}$	0·75	

3 Harry's Friday night menu board gives percentages instead of fractions for choices. Replace all his fractions with percentages of pizzas.

a $\frac{1}{5}$ ______% Meaty Mess + $\frac{8}{10}$ ______% Double Cheese = 100%

b $\frac{1}{2}$ ______% Cheery Chicken + $\frac{3}{6}$ ______% Gourmet Goody = 100%

c $\frac{3}{4}$ ______% Cheery Chicken + $\frac{2}{8}$ ______% Texas Tomato = 100%

d $\frac{4}{8}$ ______% Texas Tomato + $\frac{5}{10}$ ______% Double Cheese = 100%

< **is less than**
> **is greater than**

4 Colour the fraction given for each slab of pizza. Compare the sizes of the fractions coloured, using > and <.

a $\frac{5}{8}$ [| | | | | | |]

b $\frac{5}{6}$ [| | | | |]

c $\frac{7}{10}$ [| | | | | | | | |]

d $\frac{7}{8}$ [| | | | | | |]

e $\frac{5}{8} > \frac{5}{6}$ True or false? ______

f $\frac{5}{6} < \frac{7}{10}$ True or false? ______

g $\frac{7}{8} > \frac{7}{10}$ True or false? ______

h Write the fractions in ascending order.

______

Problem solving

How much left?

1 The Klumpy kids bought a pizza each and ate them in the park. After ten minutes, they compared how much they had left.

Kev Klumpy said he had 60% left, which he thought was the most.

Kathy Klumpy didn't know what percentages were, and she said she had three quarters of hers left.

Kris Klumpy ate quickly and had 0·625 of hers left.

Kollin Krumpy liked to eat slowly and kept as much of his as he could. He had seven eighths left.

a Prove to Kev who had the most left. Draw a diagram for each pizza showing how much was left.

b Complete the table and list the amount of pizza each Krumpy Kid has left.

Is Kev right? ________

Kev's Pizza

Kathy's Pizza

Kris's Pizza

Kollin's Pizza

Kev	
Kathy	
Kris	
Kollin	

I can solve problems by:

☐ understanding percentages, fractions and decimals ☐ drawing diagrams.

AC9M6N03 • AC9M6N05 Number **MAO-WM-01** Working mathematically • choosing and applying mathematical techniques to solve problems • communicating thinking and reasoning coherently and clearly • **MA3-RN-03** Represents numbers B • Decimals and percentages: Make connections between benchmark fractions, decimals and percentages

Unit 5 Decimal equivalents

1 Use a calculator.

Common Fraction	Decimal	Thousandths	Percentage
eg $\frac{1}{8}$	0·125	$\frac{125}{1000}$	12·5%
a $\frac{3}{8}$			
b $\frac{5}{8}$			
c $\frac{7}{8}$			
d $\frac{1}{3}$			
e $\frac{2}{3}$			
f $\frac{1}{6}$			

$\frac{1}{8}$ means 1 ÷ 8

$$8\overline{)1{\cdot}000}$$ = 0·125

$\frac{125}{1000} = \frac{12{\cdot}5}{100} = 12{\cdot}5\%$

2 Count the birds inhabiting the Zoo Wetlands. Note the numbers of each kind.

a Peacocks ☐ b Parrots ☐

c Ducks ☐ d Owls ☐

e Total Birds ☐

What fraction of the total are:

f Peacocks? ☐ g Parrots? ☐

h Ducks? ☐ i Owls? ☐

3 Are the following true or false?

a More than 12·5% of birds in the Zoo Wetlands are owls. ____________

b Parrots and peacocks account for 75% of the bird population here. ____________

c 12·5% of the birds are ducks. ____________

d 60% of the birds are peacocks. ____________

e Owls and ducks together account for 25% of the birds. ____________

4 Write the fractions, decimals and percentages in their correct boxes.

$\frac{2}{8}$, 25%, 0·20, $\frac{333}{1000}$, $\frac{4}{12}$, $\frac{2}{10}$, 33·3%, 0·25, $\frac{20}{100}$, $\frac{250}{1000}$, 20%, $\frac{2}{6}$, 0·2, $\frac{3}{12}$, 0·333

$\frac{1}{3}$	$\frac{1}{4}$	$\frac{1}{5}$

Mastery Checklist I can:
- ☐ use equivalent fractions to make 1 whole
- ☐ match equivalent fractions, decimals and percentages
- ☐ compare fractions using >, < and =.

Unit 6 Frequency

1 A die was thrown 20 times and these were the outcomes.

6, 6, 1, 3, 2, 6, 5, 5, 4, 2, 2, 3, 4, 6, 3, 6, 5, 3, 6, 2

chance experiment

a Present this information in a frequency table.

Score	Tally	Frequency
	Total	

b Which score has the highest frequency? ______

c Which score has the lowest frequency? ______

d Which scores have the same frequency? ______

e Would you have predicted these frequencies? ______

Why? ______

2 Using a die, repeat the above experiment.

a Scores ______

b Fill in the frequency table.

Score	Tally	Frequency
	Total	

c Compare these frequencies with the above experiment and comment on the results.

______

Challenge!

Work with a partner and colour 3 faces of a die red, 2 faces blue and 1 face yellow. Predict the frequencies of each colour after 20 throws.

Draw a frequency table.

Carry out the experiment. How accurate were your predictions?

AC9M6ST01 Statistics **AC9M6P02** Probability **MA3-DATA-02** Data A • Choose and use appropriate tables and graphs • **MA3-CHAN-01** Chance A • List outcomes of chance experiments involving equally likely outcomes and represent probabilities

Unit 6 Probability

Chance

What is the probability that the new girl's birthday will be in April?

It has to be in one of the twelve months so the probability that it is in April is $\frac{1}{12}$ or 0·083 or $8\frac{1}{3}$%.

1 Write a real-life situation where the probability is:

a 50% ______________________________

____

b $\frac{1}{4}$ ______________________________

____

c 0·5 ______________________________

____

d 100% ______________________________

____

2 What is the probability that:

a Mrs Kane's new baby will be a boy? (as a fraction) __________

b I have all the Australian banknotes and one is $5.

(as a percentage) __________

c Mum has 2 apples and 2 oranges and John will choose an apple.

(as a decimal) __________

d Dave has 15 birds and one of them is a cat. (as a percentage) __________

e Emma will open her eyes to see the view. (as a decimal) __________

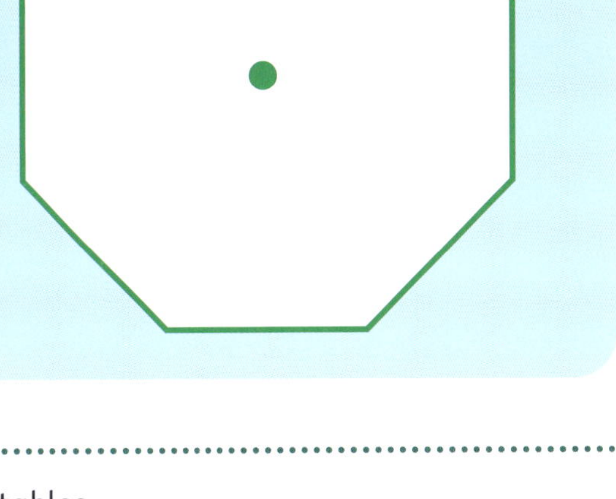

3 This is an eight-sided spinner.

Colour it to show the probability that it will land on:

a red is 25%

b blue is $\frac{3}{8}$

c yellow is 0·125

d black is 0%

e green $\frac{1}{4}$.

Mastery Checklist I can:
- ☐ complete frequency tables
- ☐ compare data sets
- ☐ use fractions and percentages to describe probabilities.

Cubes and their nets

1 Trace and sketch to complete the chart below.

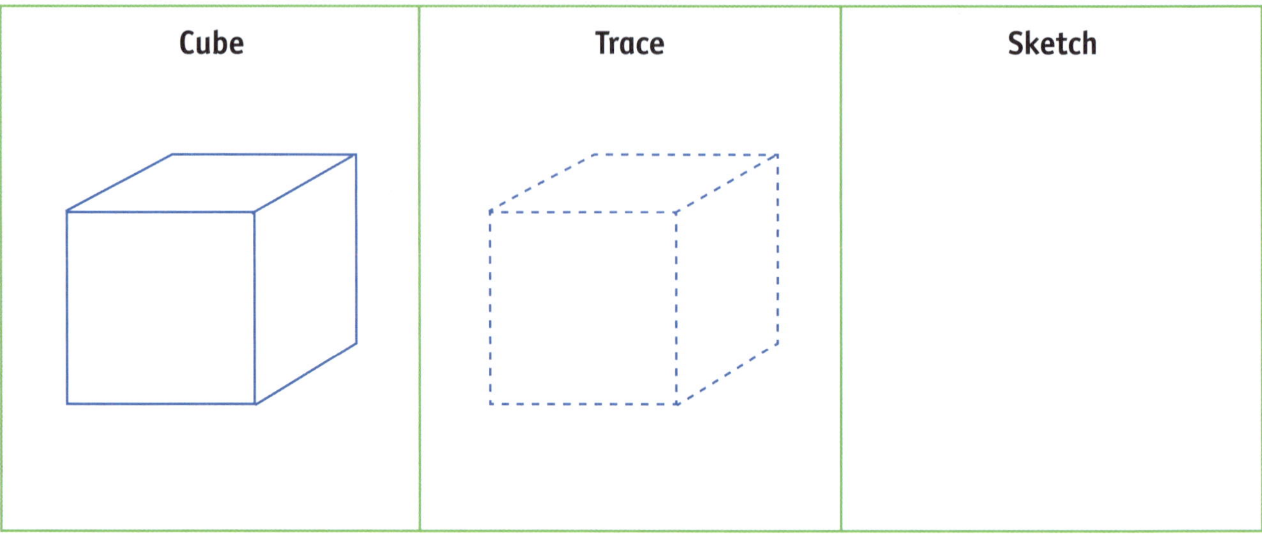

2 Each face of a cube is a ______________.

3 Complete the sentences.

a A cube has ______ edges. b A cube has ______ vertices. c A cube has ______ faces.

4 List 10 real-world objects that are cubes.

______ ______ ______ ______

______ ______ ______ ______

______ ______

5 On the cube below, use blue to trace the edges, draw a dot on each vertex and use green to colour the faces.

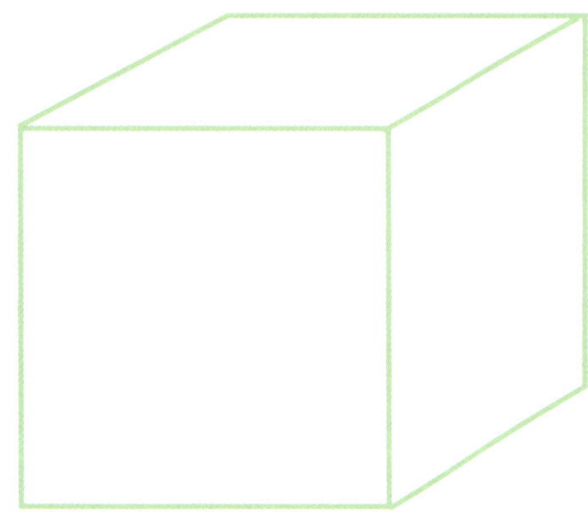

6 If the cube is cut through with the knife, what cross-section would you see? Draw it.

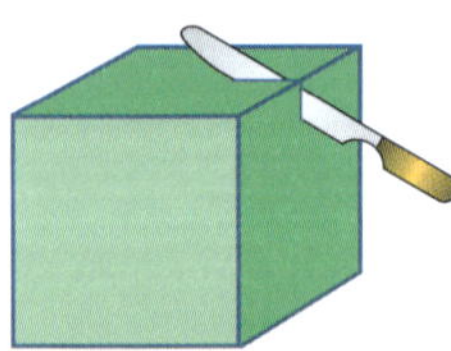

7 Which two other 3D objects could have a cross-section that is a square?

______________ ______________

AC9M6P01 Probability **MAO-WM-01** Working mathematically • choosing and applying mathematical techniques to solve problems • communicating thinking and reasoning coherently and clearly **MA3-3DS-01** Three-dimensional spatial structure A • 3D objects: Connect three-dimensional objects with two-dimensional representations • Three-dimensional spatial structure B • 3D objects: Construct prisms and pyramids

Cubes and their nets

Investigation 1

To test your nets, draw them on a different piece of paper, cut them out and try folding them to make a cube.

8 How many different nets fold to make a cube?
Use the grid paper below to draw them.

9 Did any of your nets fail to fold into a cube? ______
If so, explain why.

____

____

To complete this task, I needed to:

- [ ] identify properties of cubes
- [ ] recall real-world objects that are cubes
- [ ] explore cross-sections of prisms and pyramids
- [ ] use trial and error to investigate different nets that will form a cube.

AC9M6P01 Probability MAO-WM-01 Working mathematically • choosing and applying mathematical techniques to solve problems • communicating thinking and reasoning coherently and clearly
MA3-3DS-01 Three-dimensional spatial structure A • 3D objects: Connect three-dimensional objects with two-dimensional representations • Three-dimensional spatial structure B • 3D objects: Construct prisms and pyramids

Revision

1 **73 685 910**

Shade one bubble.

1 million is added to this number.

Which digit will change?

7	3	6	5
◯	◯	◯	◯

2 What is the value of the **3** in **0·384**?

3	$\frac{3}{10}$	$\frac{3}{100}$	$\frac{3}{1000}$
◯	◯	◯	◯

3 What is the difference between 476 and 389?

87	89	865	515
◯	◯	◯	◯

4 Mr Brodie asked his class to choose a number between 10 and 20, double it and subtract 13.

Zac's answer was 9.

What number did he choose? ☐

Write your answer in the box.

5 This number is to be rounded to the nearest ten thousand.

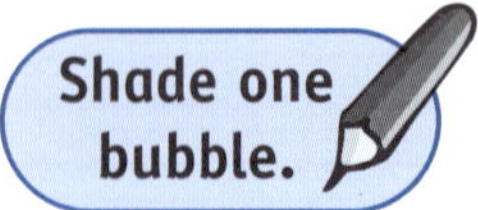

3 417 296

The new number is:

3 400 000	3 420 000	3 417 000	3 500 000
◯	◯	◯	◯

Revision

6 What is the best estimate for:

$$\begin{array}{r} 281 \\ \times \quad 29 \\ \hline \\ \hline \end{array}$$

450	600	4000	9000
◯	◯	◯	◯

7 What is the best estimate for:

$$\begin{array}{r} 2811 \\ \times \quad 29 \\ \hline \\ \hline \end{array}$$

4500	6000	40 000	90 000
◯	◯	◯	◯

8 Shade the arrow which shows 6·23.

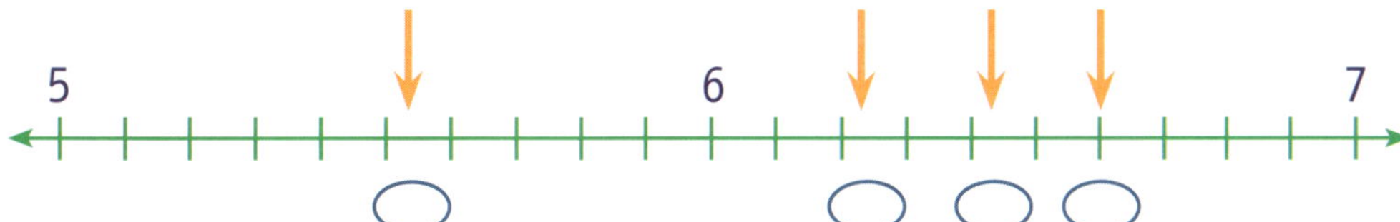

9 What is the remainder when you divide 27 by five?

3	2	6	0
◯	◯	◯	◯

Write your answer in the box.

10 There were 240 library books to sort.

Jasmin sorted $\frac{1}{5}$ of them and Brett sorted 25% of them.

Who sorted the most books? ☐

Unit 7 Constructing number sentences

IN
TRIPLE
INCREASE BY 11
DEDUCT 18
MULTIPLY BY 9
OUT

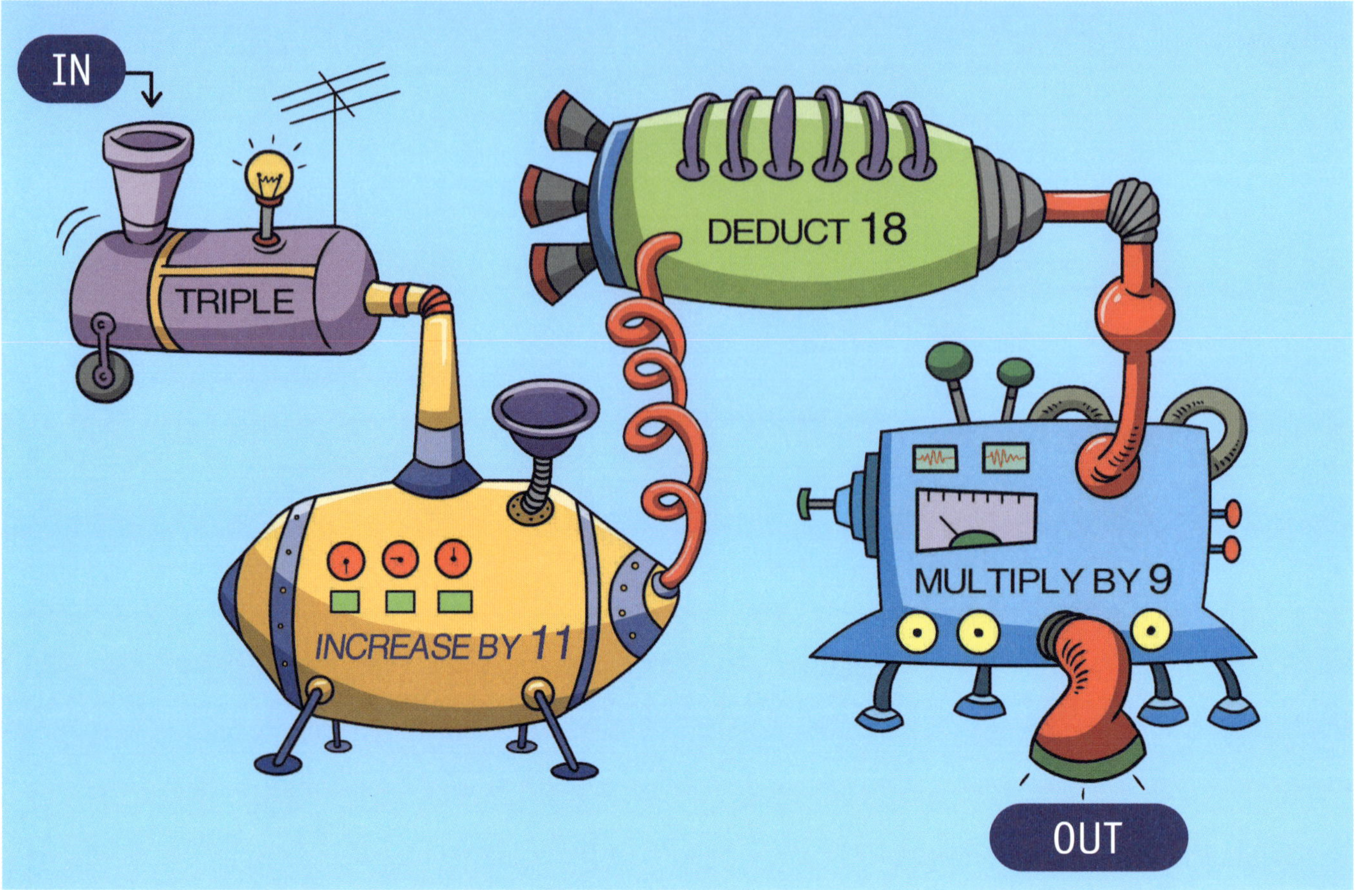

Complete this table for the Number Cruncher's operation.

1 a Complete the first row matching the illustration.

b Choose three numbers to enter into the Number Cruncher. What numbers come out?

IN	× 3	+ 11			OUT

c Write three number sentences.

Equations are number sentences.

____

____

____

d Choose one number sentence and write a story to match it.
Ask a classmate to match your number sentence.

____

____

Unit 7 Number sentence stories

1 Write an inverse operation to help solve each number sentence.
Then write a story to match each number sentence.

eg 84 ÷ 7 = ______ 7 × 12 = 84 The Daring Devils scored 84 goals in their 7 match basketball competition. What was their goal average per match?

a 36 × ______ = 432 ______________ ______________________________
____
____

b ______ − 94 = 291 ______________ ______________________________
____
____

c 75 + ______ + 125 = 289 ______________ ______________________________
____
____

d 120 × ______ = 720 ______________ ______________________________
____
____

e 840 ÷ ______ = 70 ______________ ______________________________
____
____

2 Use sound mathematical knowledge to answer this problem.

a The answer is 254. What might the question be? ______________________________
____

b The answer is 96. What might the question be? ______________________________
____

Challenge!

Use the numbers **5**, **3**, **40** and **50**.

Give directions to a classmate to arrive at the total of **75**.

Problem solving

Tables of values

1 Match the story with the table of values. Complete the table of values and the labels.

Tables

a

Day	1	2	3	4	
	2·5	5	7·5	10	

b

	1	2	3	4	
			11		

c

	1	2	3	4	
		$10			

d

	1	2	3	4	
			210		

e

	1	2	3	4	
		28			

f

	1	2	3	4	
	10				

g

	1	2	3	4	
		11	18		

Stories

The first row uses 5 bricks and each subsequent row uses 1 more brick. How many bricks will it take to build 8 rows of bricks?

I started with 5 ripe tomatoes and three more tomatoes ripened each day. How many ripe tomatoes did I have after 6 days?

I paid $5 for two second-hand books. How much will I pay for ten books?

I drove 210 km in the first three hours of my trip and continued at this rate for seven hours. How far did I travel altogether?

The Getitnow Shoppingtown gave away 10 rewards for the first shopping visit but one less each following time. How many rewards can I collect after a week of shopping?

My builder used 15 tiles in the first row and two less tiles every row as he tiled the roof. How many tiles did he use in 6 rows?

I buy a magazine for $8 and get the next magazine for $2. How much will I pay for nine magazines?

I can solve problems by:

☐ using different operations ☐ creating and completing number sequences.

AC9M6N09 Number **AC9M6A01** Algebra **MAO-WM-01** Working mathematically • choosing and applying mathematical techniques to solve problems • communicating thinking and reasoning coherently and clearly • **MA3-AR-01** Additive relations B • Choose and use efficient strategies to solve addition and subtraction problems • MA3-MR-01 Multiplicative relations B • Select and apply strategies to solve problems involving multiplication and division with whole numbers

Unit 7 Quadrants

Remember, the first number in the pair is read from the *x*-axis and the second number is read from the *y*-axis.

Use these quadrants of the Cartesian number plane to plot a pattern.

1 (0, 0), (1, 2), (2, 1), (3, 3), (4, 2), (5, 4), (6, 3), (7, 5), (8, 4), (9, 6), (10, 5)

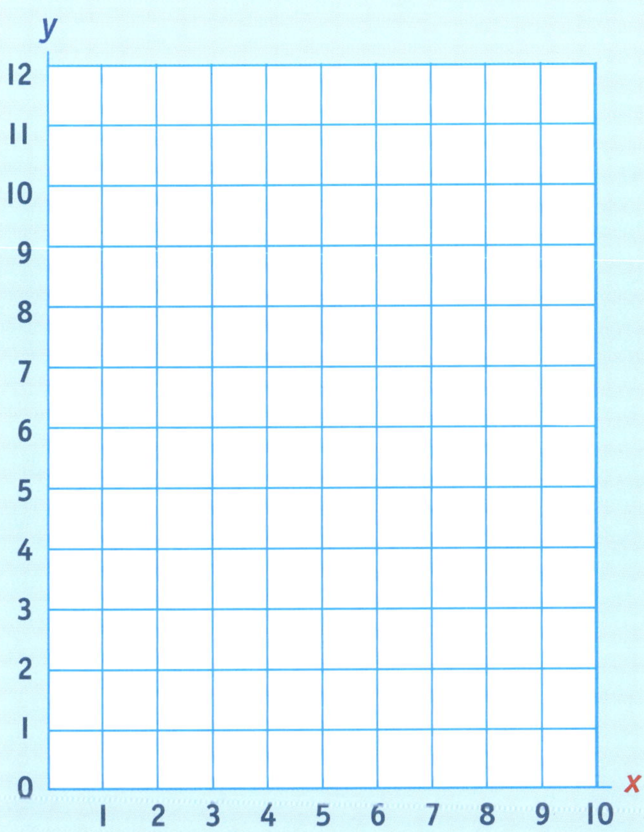

a Join the points to highlight your pattern.

b Describe this pattern.

2 (0, 11), (1, 10), (2, 10), (3, 9), (4, 9), (5, 8), (6, 8), (7, 7), (8, 7), (9, 6), (10, 6)

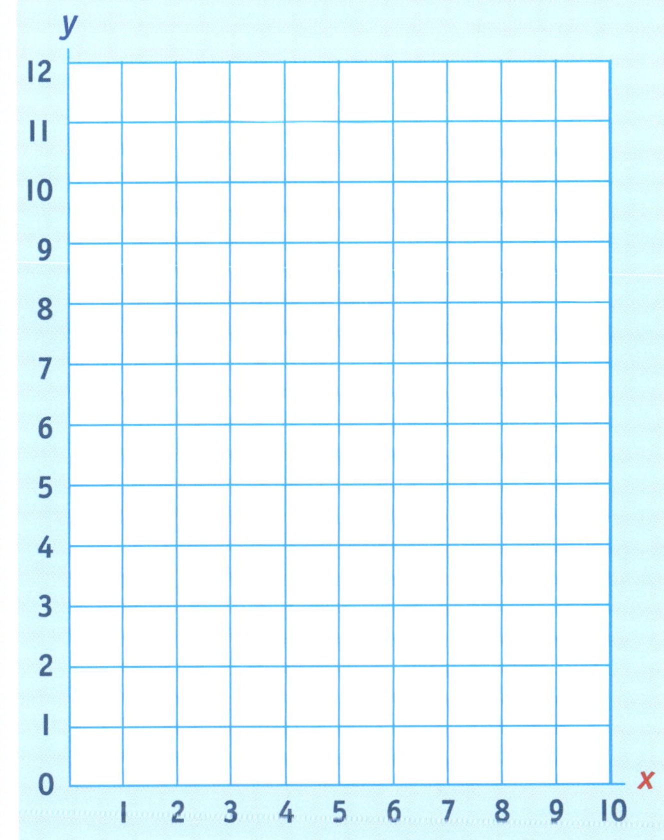

a Join the points to highlight your pattern.

b Describe this pattern.

Unit 7 Your pattern

Position

Work with a partner.

1 a Use this quadrant to plot a pattern.

b Write the points for your pattern on spare paper. Don't let your partner see them.

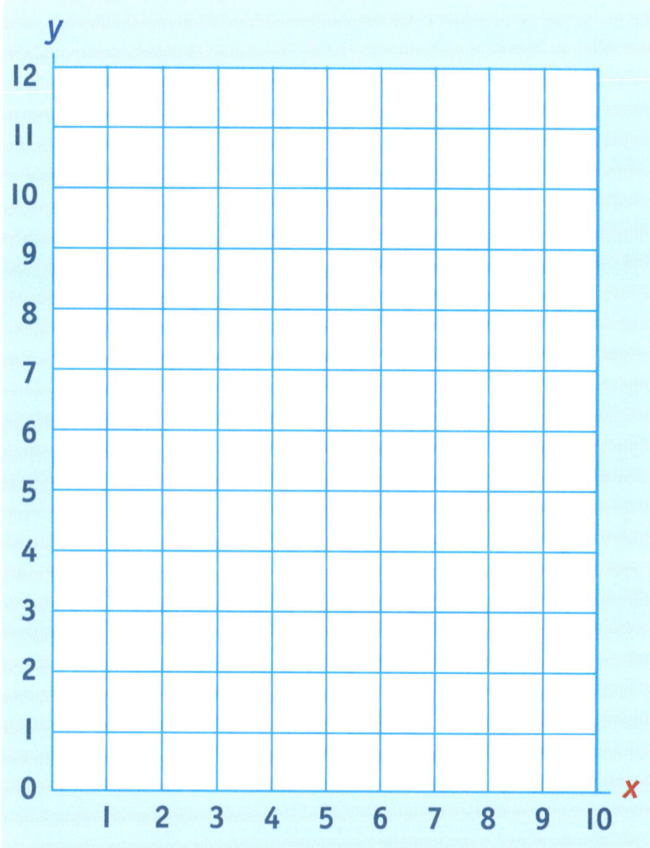

c Describe your pattern.

2 a Swap points with your partner.

b Use this quadrant to plot your partner's pattern.

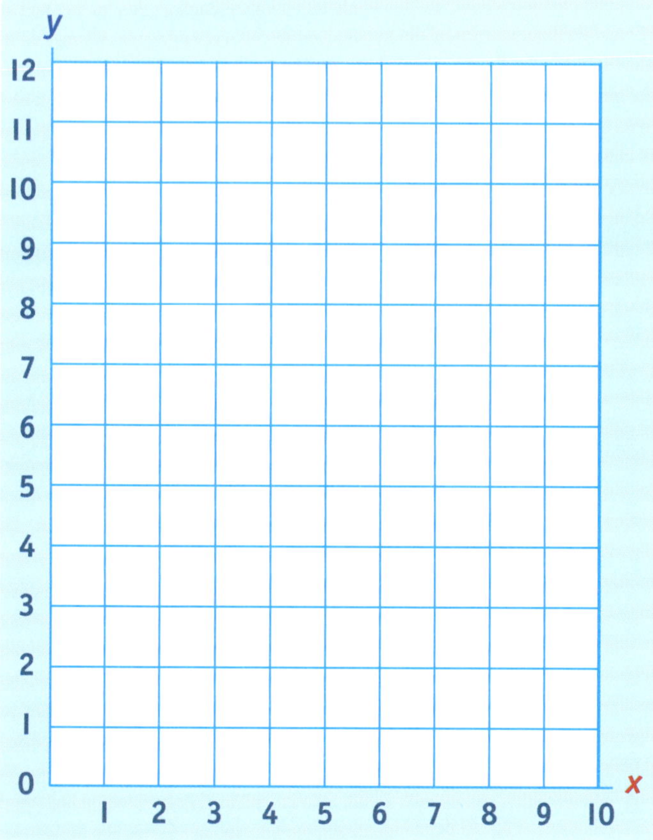

c Describe this pattern.

____

____

____

____

____

____

d Check patterns with each other.

Mastery Checklist

I can:

- ☐ write number sentences
- ☐ write stories for number sentences
- ☐ match a table of values with a number story
- ☐ plot coordinates on a Cartesian number plane
- ☐ make patterns on a Cartesian number plane.

Unit 8 Length in metres

Length 

1 The pool is 50 metres long. What buildings or spaces around your school are 50 m long?

____

2 How many laps of the pool will be swum in the following races?

a 200 m butterfly ____________________ b 800 m butterfly ____________________

c 1500 m freestyle ____________________ d 4 × 100 m relay ____________________

3 The pool is 20 m wide, with 8 lanes. How wide is each lane? ________________

4 a Circle the answer. Making one stroke, a male Olympic freestyle swimmer would swim about:

3 m **20 m** **30 cm** **0·2 km**

b How many strokes for 1 length of the pool? ____________ (approximately)

5 Estimate the height of the diving tower above the level of the water. Circle your answer.

13 m **9·0 m** **93 cm** **3 km**

Unit 8 Length and area

10 mm = 1 cm
100 cm = 1 m
1000 m = 1 km
2800 m = 2·8 km
520 000 cm =
5200 m =
5·2 km

1 Complete:

a 1500 m = 1·5 km
b 2400 m = __________ km
c 2650 m = __________ km
d 1752 m = __________ km
e 350 m = __________ km
f 750 cm = __________ m
g 650 000 cm = 6500 __________ = 6·5 __________
h 384 200 cm = 3842 __________ = 3·842 __________

2 The pool is 50 m long. Convert each training session to kilometres.

Mike's Training Schedule		
MONDAY	30 laps	a kms
TUESDAY	36 laps	b kms
WEDNESDAY	40 laps	c kms
THURSDAY	42 laps	d kms
FRIDAY	48 laps	e kms

3 Using a scale of 1 cm = 5 m, draw the pool in which Mike trains, on separate paper. Trace the pool twice. Label them pool A, B and C. Cut each rectangle various ways and arrange each to make a rectangle with a different perimeter. Note your outcomes here:

a The perimeter of Pool A is __________.
b The perimeter of Pool B is __________.
c The perimeter of Pool C is __________.

Perimeter = distance all around

Area is a square measure.

4 a The surface area of Pool A is __________.
b The surface area of Pool B is __________.
c The surface area of Pool C is __________.

5 Explain the difference in your answers to 3 and 4. ______________________________

____

Challenge! ADD, SUBTRACT, MULTIPLY OR DIVIDE?

Mike's friends also do 2 km freestyle training on Wednesday. However, Jay does 80 laps, Paul does 40 laps, Tim does 50 laps. How long is each boy's training pool?

a Jay's pool [ ] b Paul's pool [ ] c Tim's pool [ ]

Mastery Checklist I can:
- ☐ compare lengths to real-world locations
- ☐ convert between units of length
- ☐ calculate perimeter and area.

Unit 9 Angles in the environment

1 Where can you see two right angles making a straight angle in these buildings? Mark them with right angle symbols.

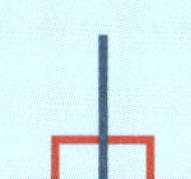

2 Complete.

a The outside of the dog kennel roof forms a ________________ angle.

b The circular stained glass window above the door on the lefthand house contains four angles equal to a ______________________________.

c The yellow angle and the purple angle in the stained glass window together make a ________________ angle.

d The red angle and the green angle in the stained glass window make a ________________ angle.

e The chimney meets the roof and forms a ________________ angle and a ________________ angle.

f The four angles of the corners of the doors add up to ________________ degrees.

3 Draw a circular stained glass window here and make two sets of vertically opposite angles. One pair will be green and yellow. One pair will be red and purple.

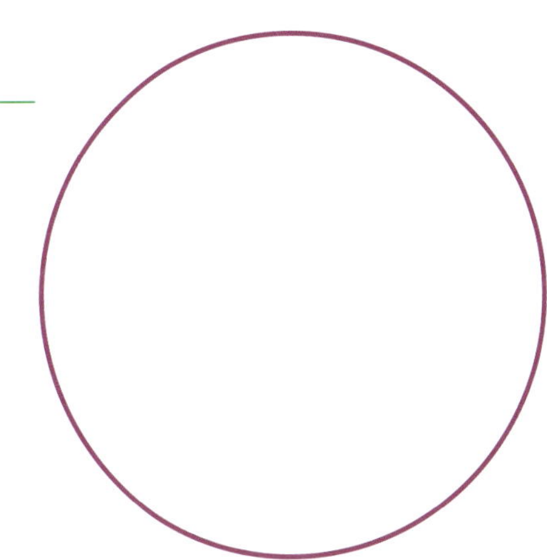

Unit 9 Types of angles

1 Write each angle type.

a

b

c

d
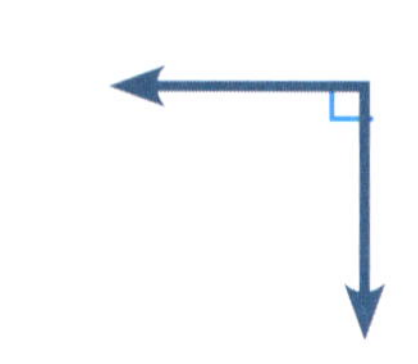

e

f

g
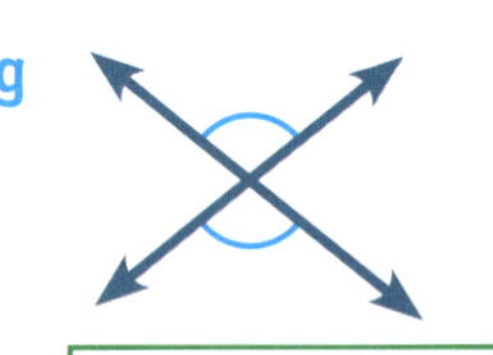

h
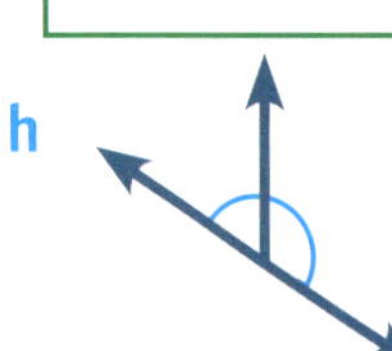

i

j
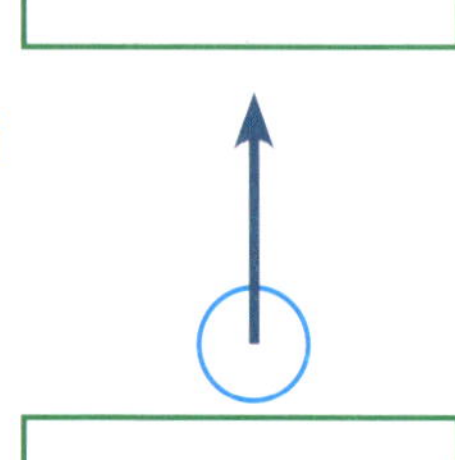

k

l

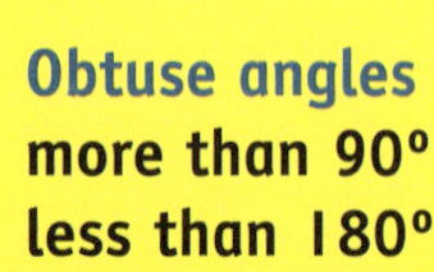

Acute angles less than 90°

Right angles always 90°

Obtuse angles more than 90° less than 180°

Straight angles always 180°

Reflex angles more than 180° less than 360°

Revolutions are always 360°

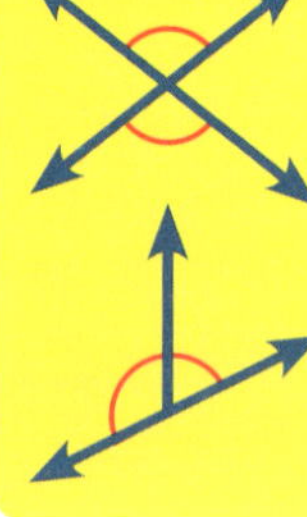

Vertically opposite angles are equal

Adjacent angles together equal a straight angle

2 Draw:

a a reflex angle.

b vertically opposite angles.

c a straight angle.

d an obtuse angle.

e a revolution.

f two adjacent angles.

3 True or false?

a vertically opposite angles = 360° ______

b 360° is a straight angle. ______

c 140° is a reflex angle. ______

d 200° is an obtuse angle. ______

e 90° is a right angle. ______

f two adjacent angles = 180° ______

Unit 9 Drawing angles

1 Draw angles of these sizes on paper or in your workbook.

a 40° b 70° c 30° d 120° e 150° f 110°

2 Draw two intersecting lines from one edge of the ellipse to the opposite edge.

a Colour two vertically opposite angles which you've made, blue.

b Mark two adjacent angles with an x. Measure the adjacent angles.

Their sum should be ________ and it is ________.

3 a Use the axis of symmetry of this ellipse as a starting point to construct the angles of given sizes.

b Construct vertically opposite angles for each one you have drawn.

c Colour each pair of vertically opposite angles to match.

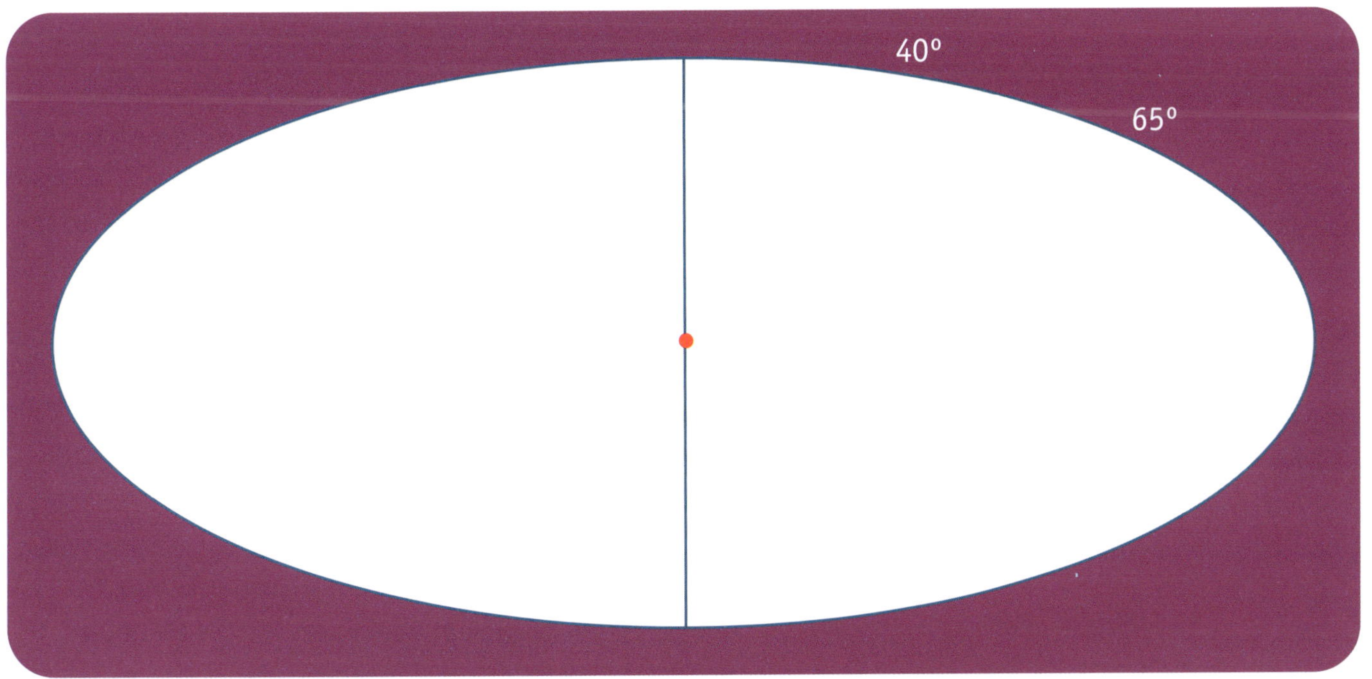

Unit 9 Angle types and measurement

1 These angles have arranged themselves. Tick every one that is correctly grouped.

Adjacent angles here!

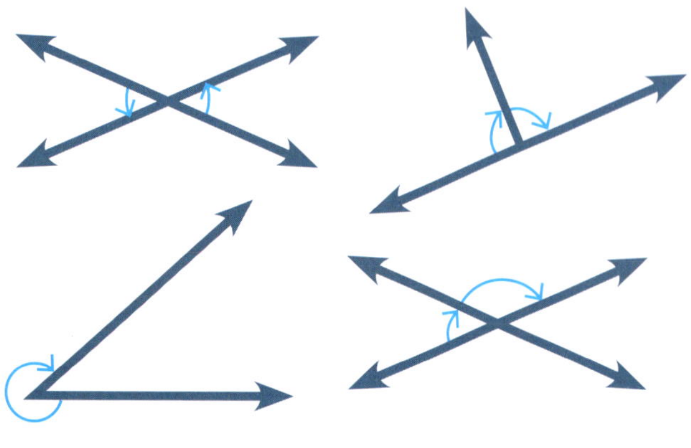

Vertically opposite angles here!

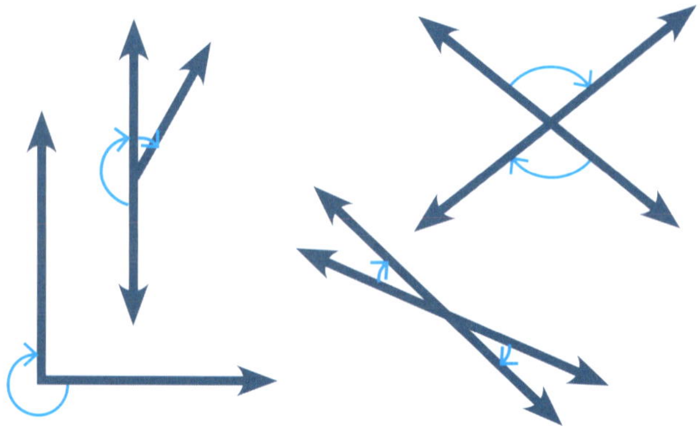

Complete revolutions here!

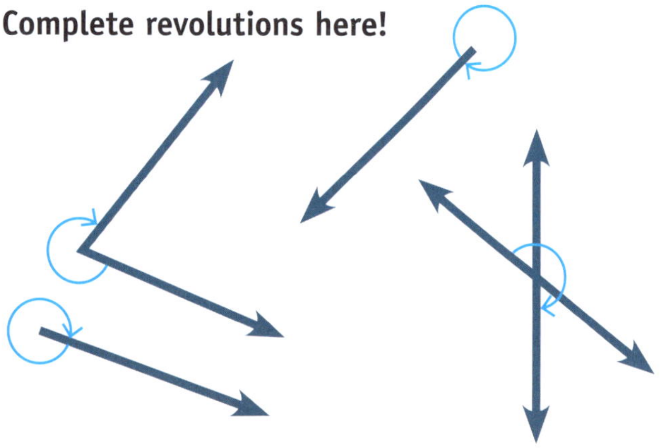

Straight angles here!

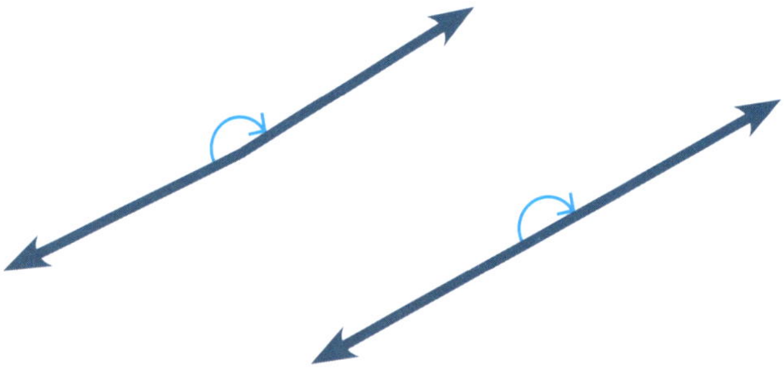

2 Estimate the size of these angles. Label them as adjacent, right, straight, vertically opposite or reflex angles.

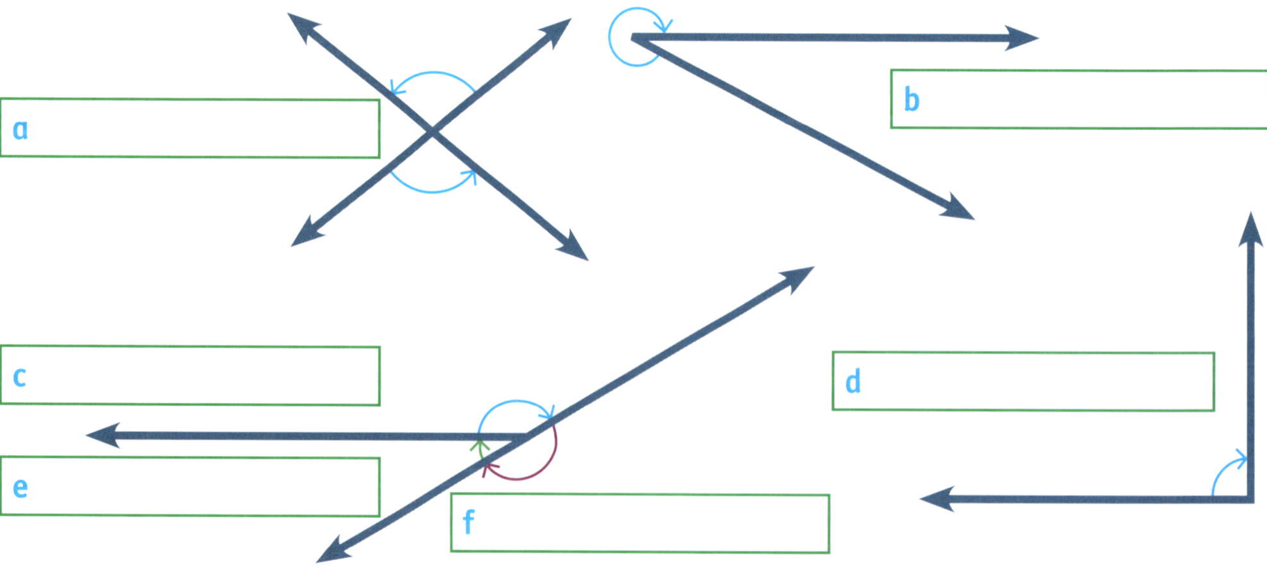

Mastery Checklist I can:
- ☐ recognise angles in the real world
- ☐ recognise and draw different types of angles
- ☐ estimate the size of angles.

Unit 10 Angle sizes and names

On a balloon ride in France, Pia and Frankie look down upon the famous La Belle Gardens where Mari the gardener is working. Study the gardens with Pia and Frankie.

This is a formal garden, where all garden beds are symmetrical and regular in shape.

1 a What size is each inside angle of the hexagonal rose garden? ____________

b What is the total of these angles? ____________

2 How many right-angled triangles are there? ____________

3 a Can there be more than one right angle in a triangle? ____________

b Why? ____________

4 What size are the two equal angles on the right-angled triangles? ____________

5 a What type of triangles are the daisy beds? ____________

b What size is each of their angles? ____________

c What is the size of the outside angles of the hexagon? ____________

d To be sure you are correct, the inside angle and the outside angle should equal ____________.

Why? ____________

6 This garden has ____________ symmetry to the order of ____________.

Unit 10 Drawing 2D shapes

1 On plain paper, use a pencil, ruler and protractor to draw these shapes. Follow the procedures.

a a square
- baseline 5 cm
- label it A B
- angle of 90° at A, arm 5 cm
- repeat at B
- join to make a square
- draw diagonals

b a rectangle
- baseline 10 cm
- label it X Y
- angle of 90° at X, arm 4 cm
- repeat at Y
- join to make a rectangle
- draw diagonals

c an equilateral triangle
- baseline 6 cm
- label it J K
- angle of 60° at J
- repeat at K
- allow arms to cross (intersect)
- draw axes of symmetry

2 List the properties of each shape. Choose from this list.

4 right angles, 3 equal sides, 4 equal sides, 3 angles of 60°, 2 diagonals of equal length, 2 axes of symmetry, opposite sides equal, 4 axes of symmetry, 4 sides, 3 axes of symmetry

a square	**b** rectangle	**c** equilateral triangle

3 Properties of other regular polygons.

Pentagon

a ___ equal sides

___ equal angles of _____°

___ diagonals

___ axes of symmetry

Hexagon

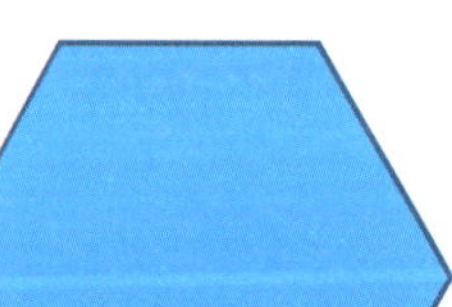

b ___ equal sides

___ equal angles of _____°

___ diagonals

___ axes of symmetry

Octagon

c ___ equal sides

___ equal angles of _____°

___ diagonals

___ axes of symmetry

Challenge! What is the sum of all angles: in a pentagon? ______

in a hexagon? ______

in an octagon? ______

Unit 10 Angle sum

1 To prove that the angles of a triangle add up to 180°, carry out the following investigation.

a On coloured paper, draw any triangle with sides of between 5 cm and 10 cm.

b Mark each angle with letters **A**, **B** and **C**.

c Cut the triangle in three to isolate each angle.

d Place the angles labelled **A**, **B** and **C** side by side to form a straight line on white paper.

e Write a sentence to explain your findings.

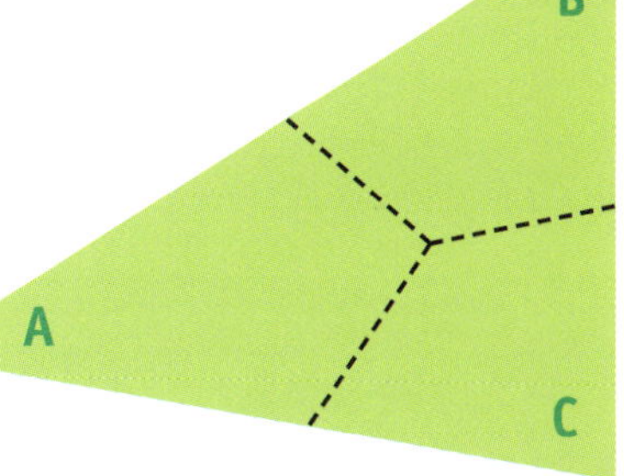

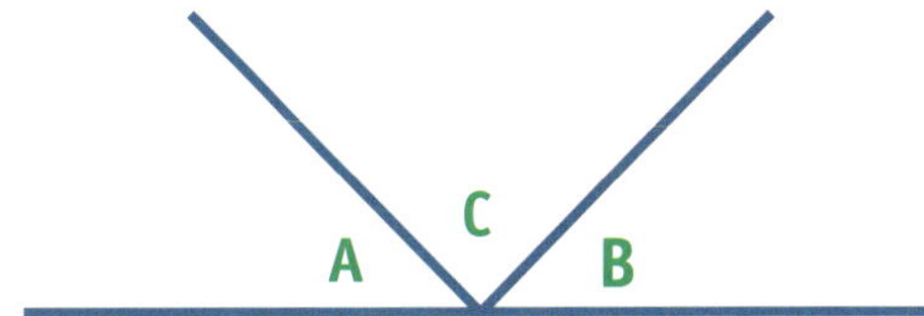

____

____

____

2 Write the size of the missing angle in each triangle.

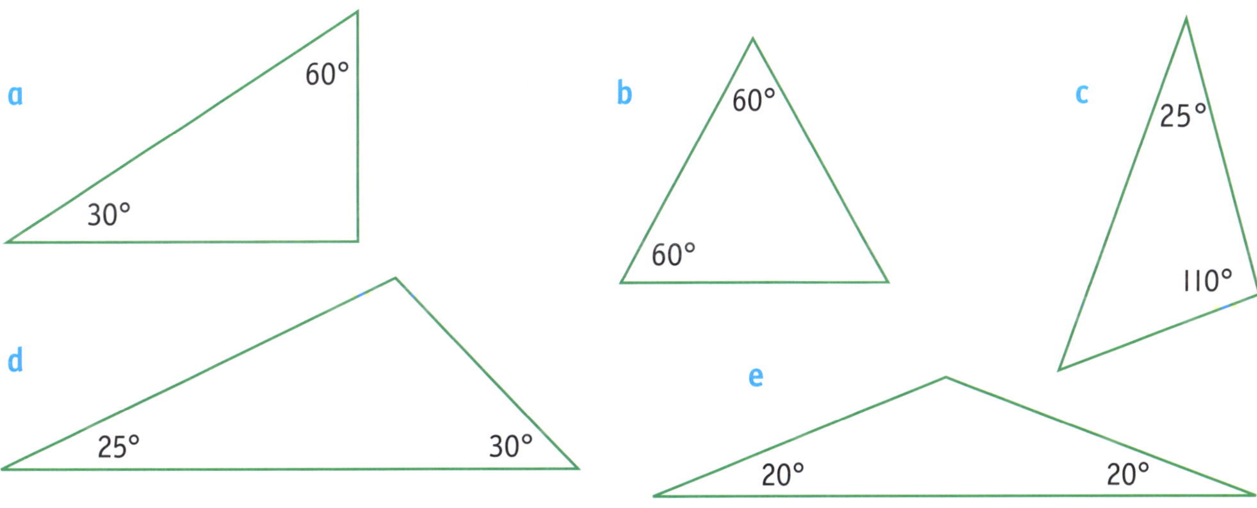

3 Write the size of the missing angles in these quadrilaterals.

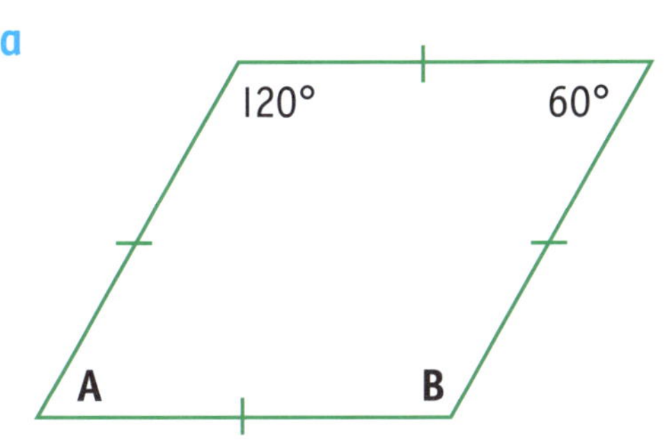

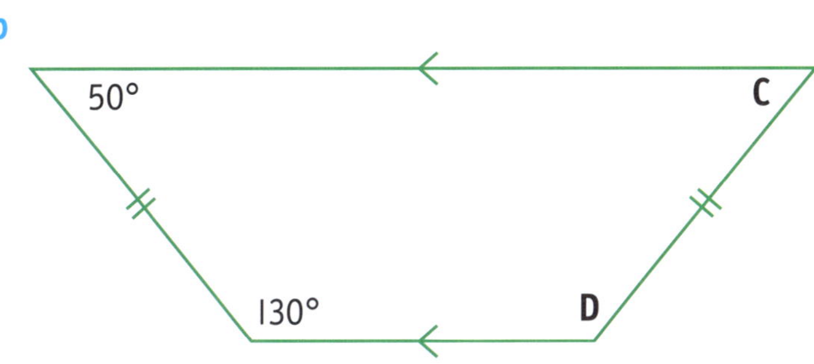

Unit 10 Triangles

1 Name four kinds of triangles.

a has 3 equal sides and three equal angles ______

b has two equal sides and two equal angles ______

c has no equal sides and no equal angles ______

d has one right angle ______

2 Identify the following triangles. Use a ruler and a protractor to measure.

a [ ] b [ ] c [ ] d [ ]

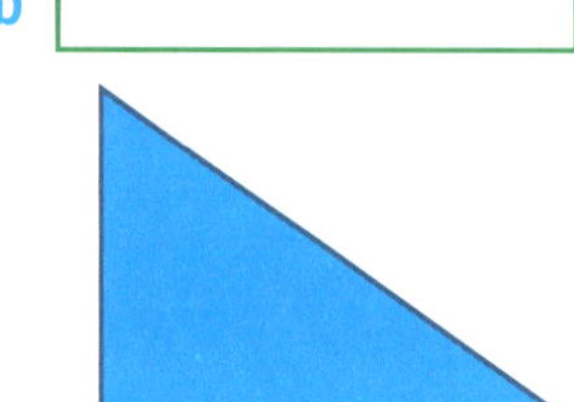

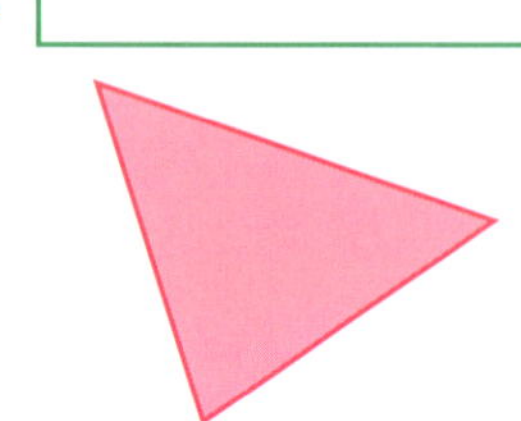

3 Draw a triangle with sides of 4 cm, 4 cm and 5 cm.

a Draw a baseline of 5 cm.

b At one end mark an arc of 4 cm using a compass.

c Repeat at the other end of the base.

d Join compass intersection with end points of baseline. Practise on paper.

4 Find the size of the missing angles. Check with a protractor.

a
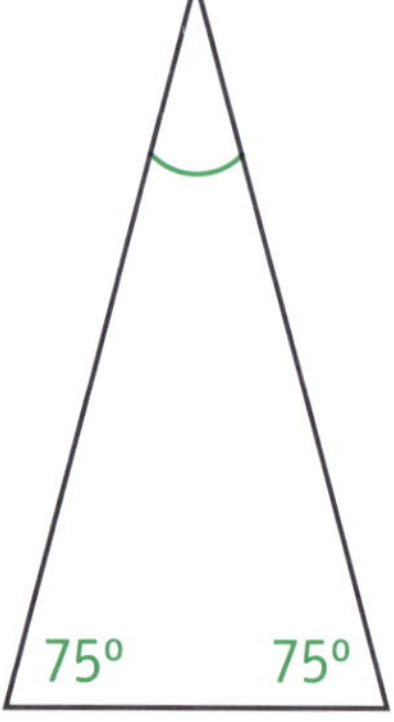

b
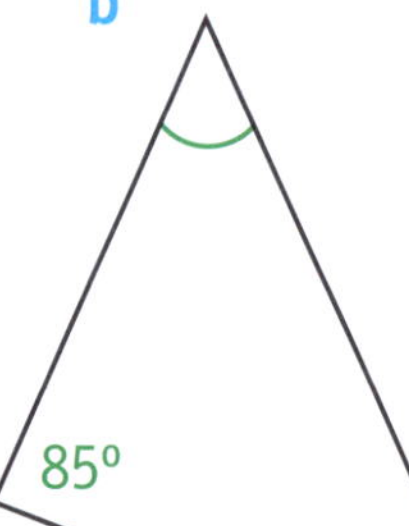

c
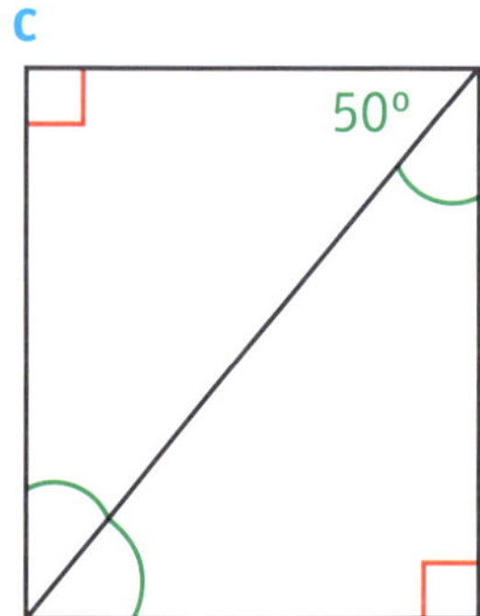

The sum of the angles of a triangle is 180°.

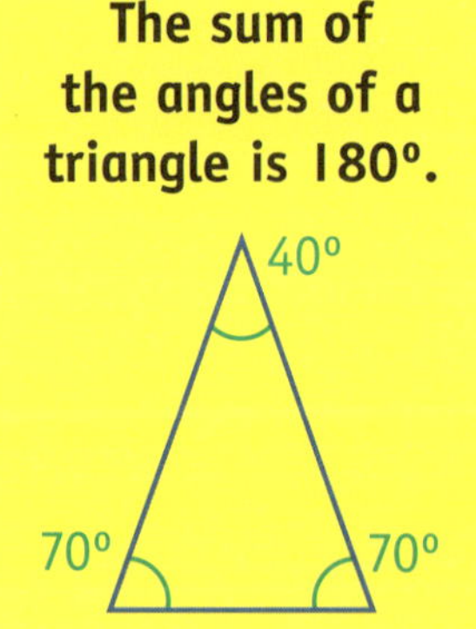

Challenge!

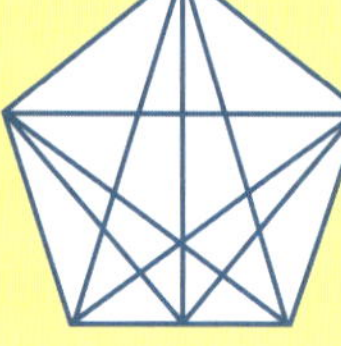

How many triangles can you find in this design? [ ]

Are all types of triangles in this design? [ ]

Mastery Checklist I can:
- [ ] investigate properties of angles
- [ ] investigate properties of 2D shapes
- [ ] find the angle sum of triangles and quadrilaterals
- [ ] use a protractor and a compass.

 AC9M6M04 Measurement **MA3-GM-03** Geometric measure A • Angles: Use a protractor to measure and identify types of angles • **MA3-2DS-01** Two-dimensional spatial structure A • 2D shapes: Classify two-dimensional shapes and describe their properties

Unit 11 Two-way tables

At school camp, teachers split students up into two groups.
Below is the data they collected from their time away. Study these tables.

On time	Yellow team	Red team
Breakfast	32	26
Lunch	24	40
Dinner	26	42

Meals	Yellow team	Red team
Chicken	60	52
Pasta	48	62
Salad	55	55

Task	Yellow team	Red team
Bed-making	40	40
Tables	50	32
Washing-up	36	46

Drinks	Yellow team	Red team
Water	50	48
Juice	56	58
Milk	45	45

Tick the one best answer.

1 a What do the tables tell us?

- ☐ The teachers were stricter on the yellow team than the red team.
- ☐ The yellow team were better behaved than the red team.
- ☐ The red team were better behaved than the yellow team.
- ☐ The red team and yellow team were different in most aspects of camp.

b Yellow and red were the same at:

- ☐ drinking milk, bed-making and eating salads.
- ☐ bed-making, eating salads and drinking juice.
- ☐ drinking water, washing up and eating salads.
- ☐ being on time, drinking milk and bed-making.

c Which statement is true?

- ☐ Red are better at completing set tasks.
- ☐ Red are better at being on time.
- ☐ Red drink more fluids than yellow.

d The teachers said that the red team and yellow team were equally well behaved.

Can you tell that from these tables? Why? ______________________________

____

____

____

Unit 11 Two-way column graphs

Label each column graph to match a two-way table on page 43.

1 a

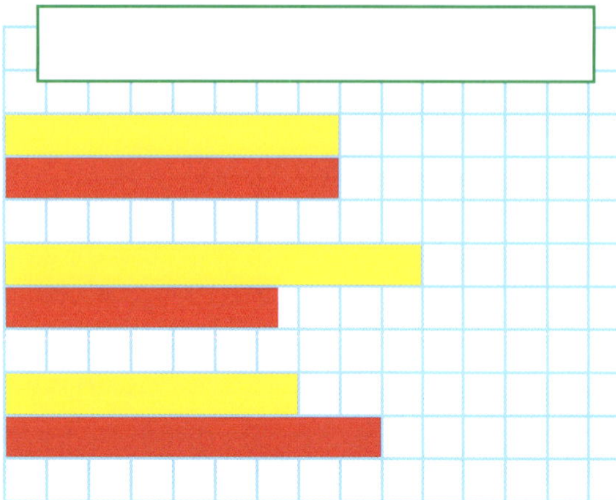

b

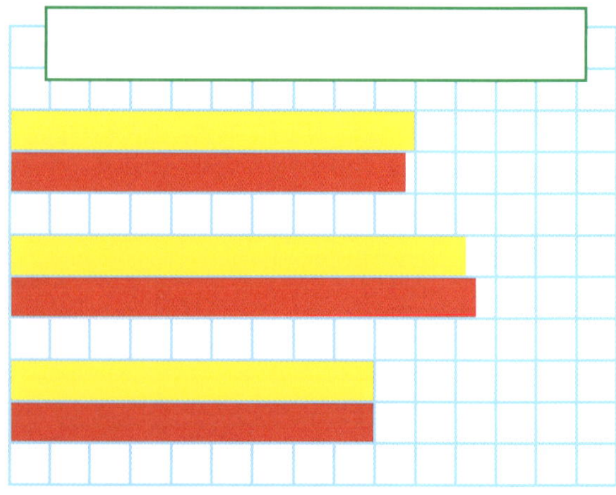

c

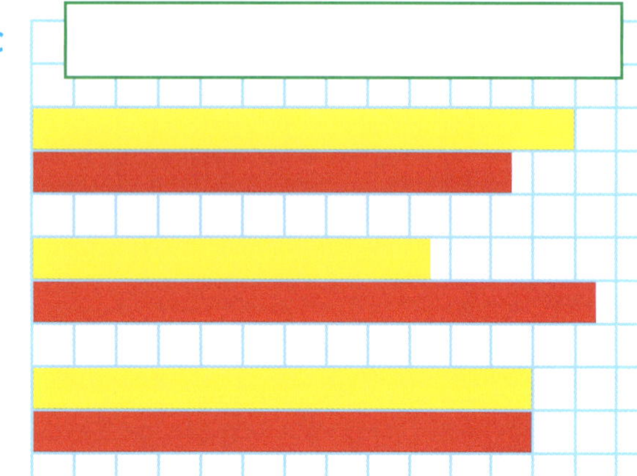

d

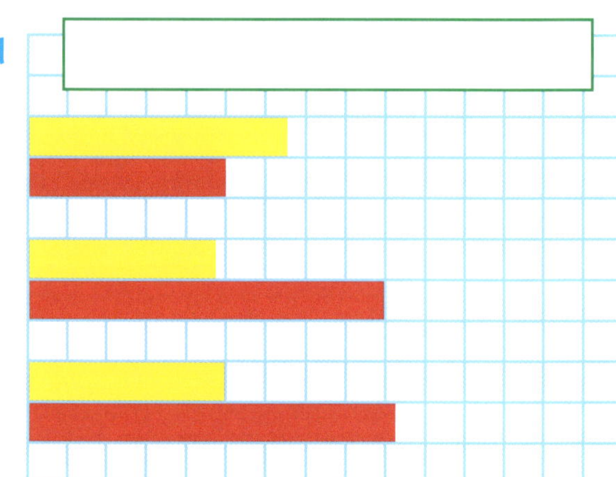

2 In which category is there the greatest difference between the yellow team and the red team?

____

3 In which category is the result for yellow and red closest? _______________

4 Which set of data is easiest to interpret, column graphs or two-way tables? _______________

Why? _______________

____

5 Make a horizontal side-by-side column graph from this two-way table.

Height	Men	Women
Over 170 cm	8	5
150 to 170 cm	7	10

Unit 11 Misleading graphs

1 What is misleading about these graphs? Explain.

Redraw the graph more correctly.
Hint: Draw a scale.

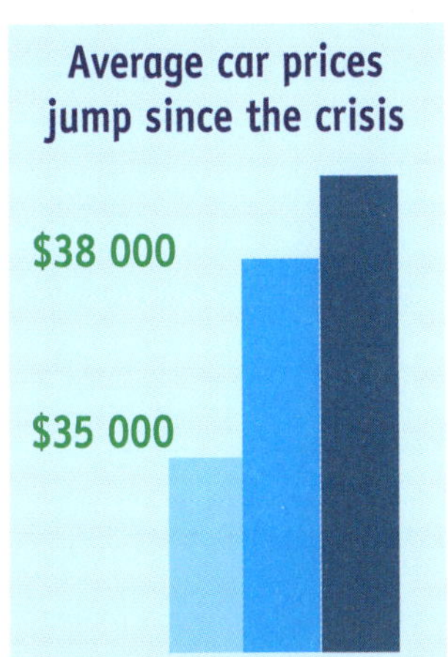

a

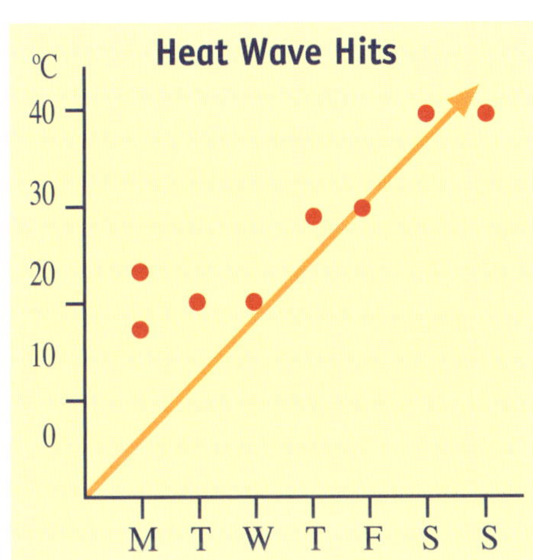

b

Pets in Year 6
Each symbol = 10 children

CATS
DOGS
FISH
SNAKES

c

2 Write another reason for finding a graph misleading.

a Graph is not labelled correctly.

b No title or axis labels.

c Incorrect scale used.

d Images in picture graphs the wrong size.

e

Unit 11 Media claims and graphs

Study the graphs below and decide if the news item is telling the story correctly.

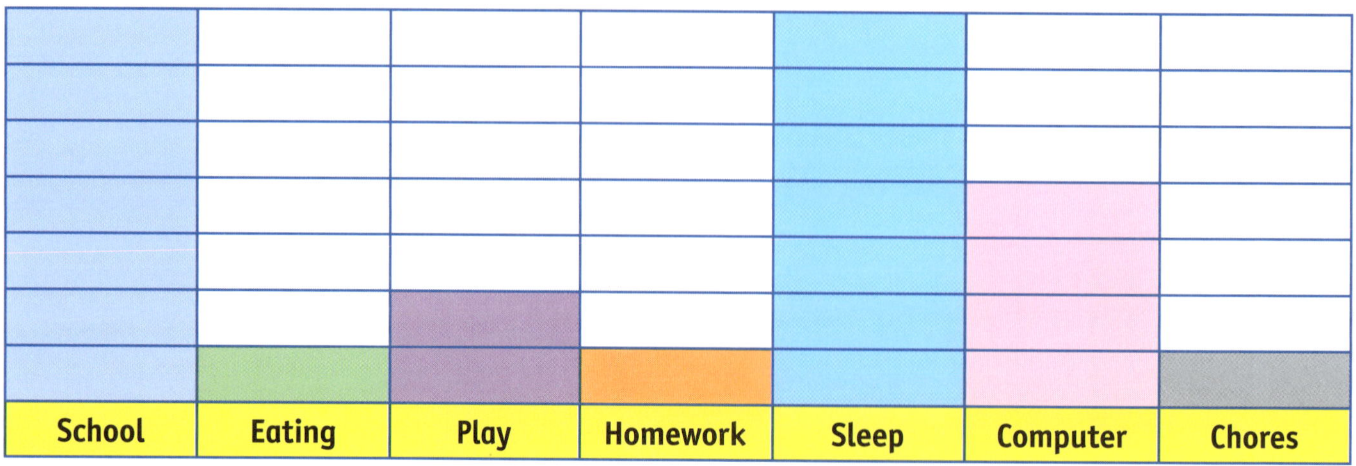

1 Researchers have issued a report stating that children are spending more time in front of a computer. This is reducing the amount of sleep they have, which affects their school work.

Comment: ______________________________

____

____

____

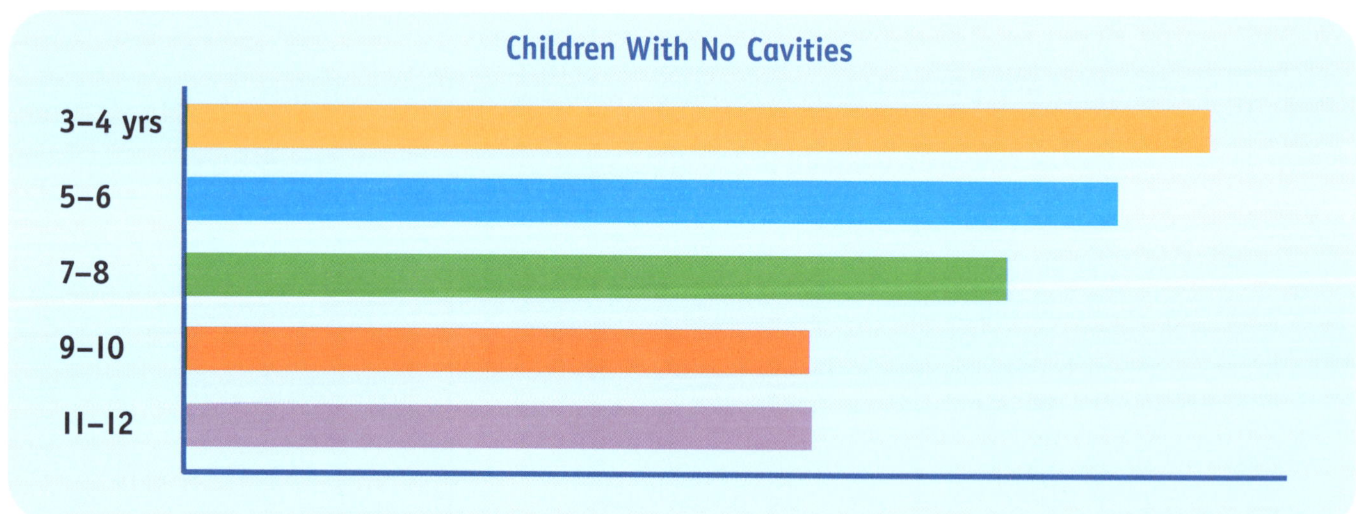

2 Research into dental health shows that children in younger age groups have better teeth than children in older age groups.

Comment: ______________________________

____

____

____

Unit 11 Reviews on iBuy

Graphs 1 & 2

starsella

Shop

About

Feedback

$22.10

iBuy Reviews

★	14
★★	20
★★★	20
★★★★	22
★★★★★	20

1 Use the information above to complete the two-way table.

Star rating	bowwow	starsella	Total
1★			
2★			
3★			
4★			
5★			
Total			

2 The mode is the most common result.
What is the mode for the sellers' reviews?

a bowwow ________ b starsella ________

3 The range is the difference between the highest result and the lowest result.
What is the range for the sellers' reviews?

a bowwow ________ b starsella ________

4 Present the data as a column graph.
Use red for starsella and blue for bowwow.

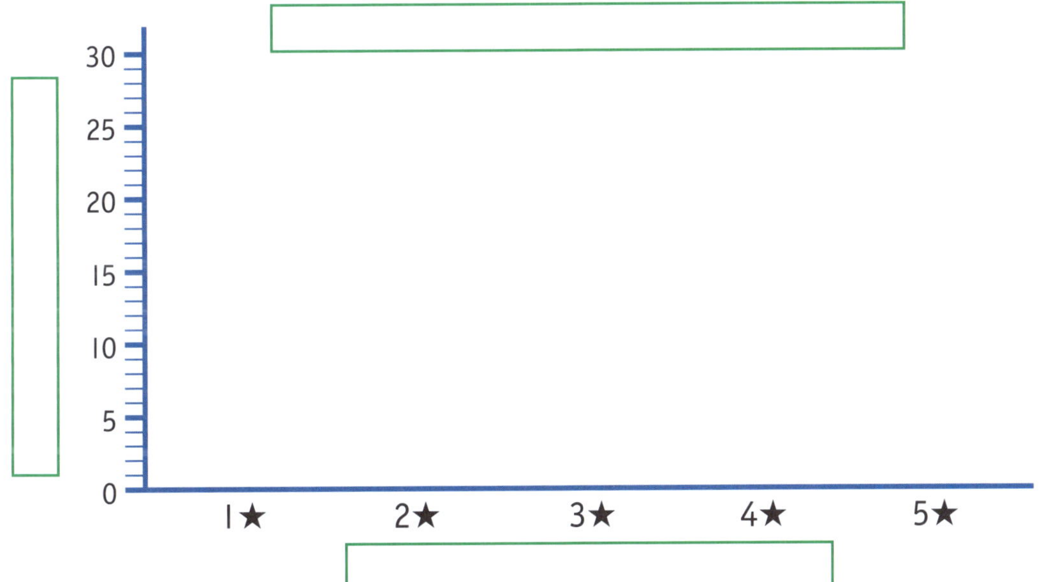

5 Which seller would you buy from? Why? ________________

6 Is it easiest to interpret the star chart, two-way table or column graph? ________________
Give a reason for your answer.

____

Mastery Checklist

I can:

- ☐ interpret two-way tables
- ☐ match two-way tables to graphs
- ☐ graph data from a two-way table
- ☐ identify how graphs can be misleading
- ☐ decide if statements accurately reflect data
- ☐ find the mode and the range.

Revision Term 1

1 94 538 267 p 2

a Round to the nearest 10 million. ______

b How many thousands? ______

c Which digit is in the millions place? ______

d Which digit will change if 10 000 is added? ______

e Which digit has the least value? ______

2 Complete. p 6

a +

49	52	
38	67	
		☐

b −

86	37	
49	27	
		☐

3 Complete. p 9

×	6	8	4	13	20	53
7						
4						
9						

4 How much? p 9

$1.80

a 3 hamburgers = ______

b 4 pizza slices = ______

$2.35

c 7 hot dogs = ______

d one of each = ______

e 9 pizza slices + 3 hot dogs = ______

$2.15

5 Complete. p 9

Factor	70	12		80
Factor	4		15	3
Product		84	90	

6 Write remainders as fractions. p 10

a $7\overline{)58}$ b $8\overline{)39}$ c $6\overline{)46}$

7 Estimate and calculate. p 12

a

$$\begin{array}{r} 817 \\ \times\ 64 \\ \hline \end{array}$$

Estimate: ______

b

$$\begin{array}{r} \$3.89 \\ \times\ 28 \\ \hline \end{array}$$

Estimate: ______

8 Write in ascending order. p 13

9·4, 8·99, 9·39, 9·6, 9·09

______ ______ ______ ______ ______

9 Write as a decimal. p 14

a $7\frac{4}{10}$ ______ b $11\frac{3}{100}$ ______

10 p 16

a 74 × 10 = ______

b 8·9 × 10 = ______

c 16 × 100 = ______

d $3.59 × 100 = ______

11 Round to 1 decimal place. p 16

a 9·55 ______ b 2·327 ______

c 1·08 ______ d 25·949 ______

12 Complete. p 19

a $\frac{3}{5} = \frac{\square}{10}$ b $\frac{3}{4} = \frac{6}{\square}$

c $\frac{1}{3} = \frac{\square}{9} = \frac{4}{\square} = \frac{\square}{30}$

13 Write as percentages. p 19

a $\frac{1}{4}$ ______ % b $\frac{3}{4}$ ______ %

c $\frac{1}{10}$ ______ %

Revision Term 1

14 Complete the table. p 21

Common fraction	Decimal	Thousandths	Percentage
$\frac{3}{8}$			
$\frac{5}{8}$			
$\frac{1}{6}$			
$\frac{5}{6}$			

15 a Present this information in the frequency table: p 22

5, 5, 2, 4, 3, 5, 4, 4, 3, 1, 1,
4, 5, 5, 2, 5, 6, 4, 5, 1

Score	Tally	Frequency

16 Plot the points on the number plane. p 31

a A (1, 1) b B (4, 6) c C (3, 0)

d D (0, 7) e E (2, 5) f F (5, 1)

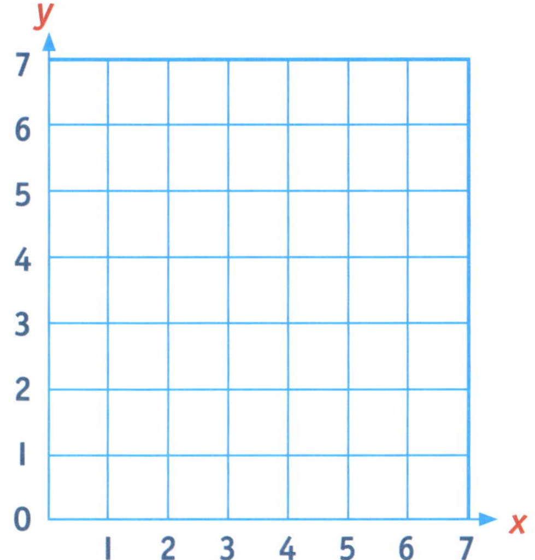

17 Write the operation that will help solve each problem. Then solve the problems. p 29

a 72 − _____ = 68 ____________

b 7 × _____ = 80 + 4 ____________

c _____ ÷ 6 = 42 − 6 ____________

d 250 − _____ = 238 ____________

18 Find the perimeter. p 34

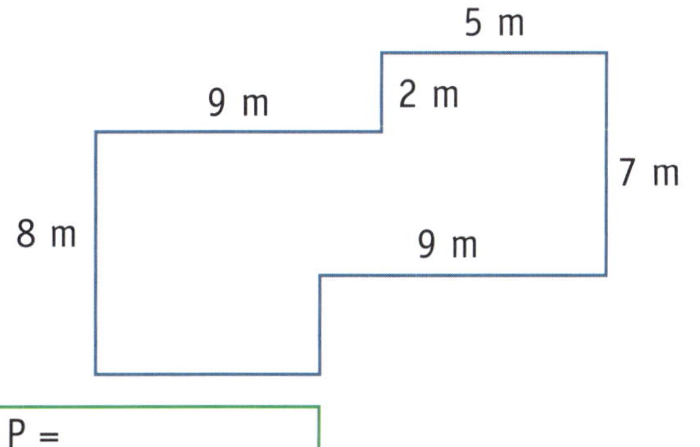

P =

19 Find the size of the missing angles. Name them. p 36

a
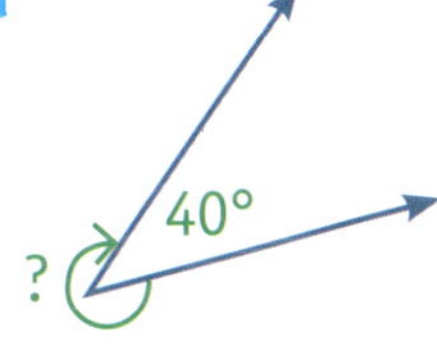

b
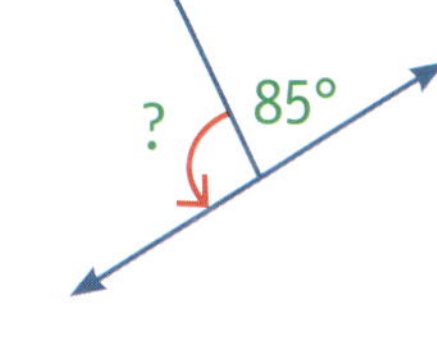

____________ ____________

____________ ____________

20 Write the size of the missing angle. p 41

a
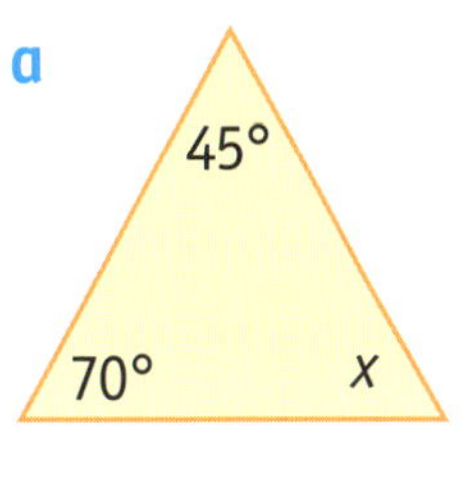

b
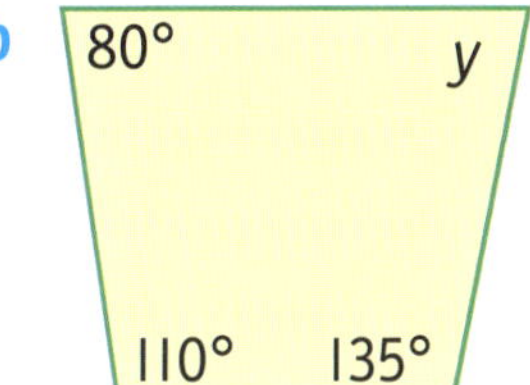

x ________ y ________

c Can there be two right angles in a triangle? ________

Why? ____________________

NAPLAN* practice

This is a test to see how well you understand what you have learnt.

Instructions

Read each question carefully. There are three different ways to show your answer:

- Shade the bubble next to the correct answer.
- Write a word in a box.
- Write a number in a box.

Use a pencil. DO NOT use a pen. If you make a mistake, rub it out and try again.

Write your answer in the box.

1

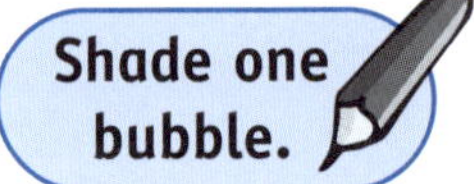

2 How many thousands in **134 568**?

1	134	34	4
◯	◯	◯	◯

3 A higher temperature than **−4 °C** is

−5 °C	−8 °C	0 °C	−6 °C
◯	◯	◯	◯

4

$$\begin{array}{r} 94 \\ 8\overline{)752} \end{array}$$

To check this answer, which inverse operation would you use?

8 × 752	752 ÷ 8	94 × 8	752 × 94
◯	◯	◯	◯

5 I am thinking of a two-digit number that is three more than a square number. The difference between its digits is 4. What is the number?

51	37	84	26
◯	◯	◯	◯

* This is not an officially endorsed publication of the NAPLAN program and is produced independently of Australian governments.

Test practice

6 What is the size of this reflex angle?

Write your answer in the box.

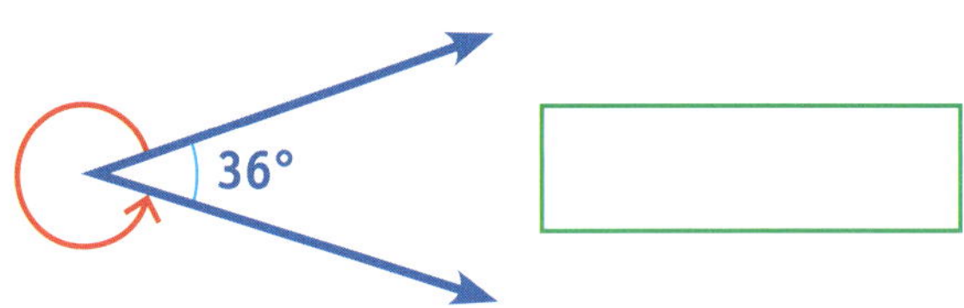

7 What distance is Murray from Franco?

	Murray	Franco
Dendy	165 km	238 km
Nimbull	171 km	98 km

8 What label will suit the vertical axis on this graph?

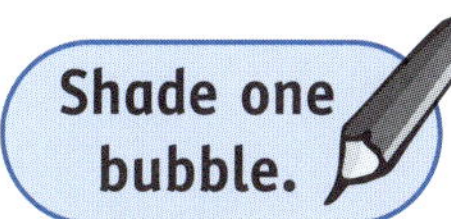

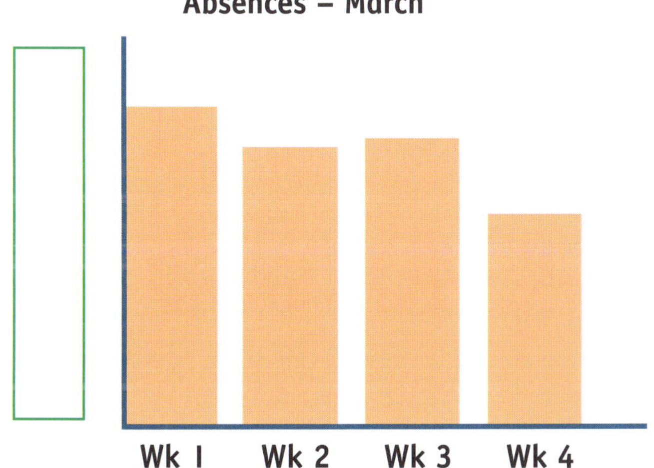

- Days absent ◯
- Weeks ◯
- Students ◯
- Classes ◯

9 The population of a country is about 64 million people.
Which of these numbers could it be?

64 657 900 ◯   63 478 890    64 375 000    63 089 456 ◯

Test practice

10 Which division algorithm is correct?

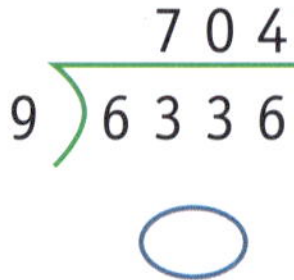

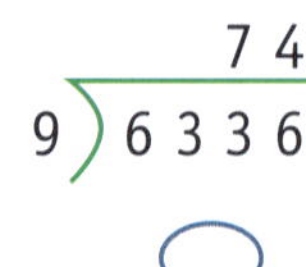

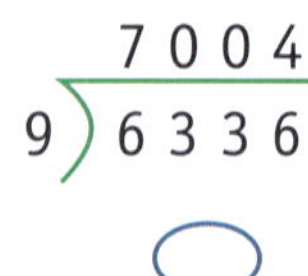

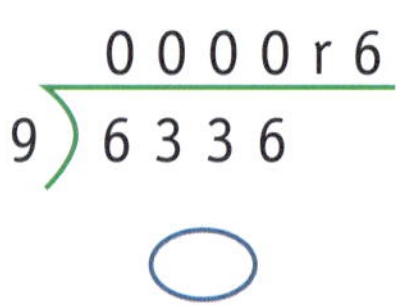

11 When 1 000 000 is added to 47 853 100, the new number is

57 853 100 

47 953 100 ◯

47 853 100 ◯

48 853 100 ◯

12 Kev's father drives between towns in his job. Here is his travel log.
What is his average daily distance travelled for the week?

Monday 327 km	**Tuesday** 318 km
Wednesday NO TRAVEL	**Thursday** 265 km
Friday 385 km	

291 km ◯ 323 km ◯ 259 km ◯ 265 km ◯

13 Which decimal amount is out of ascending order?

Write your answer in the box.

6·04 kg, 6·124 kg, 6·242 kg, 6·046 kg, 6·42 kg

[ ]

14 Kerry explained that her light was shaped like a triangular pyramid.
Which diagram matches her description?

◯

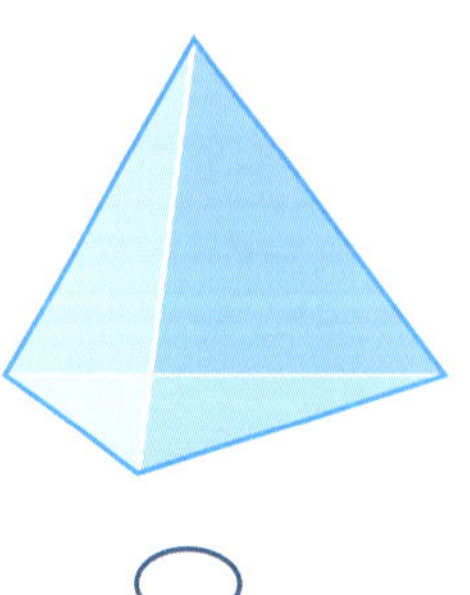
◯

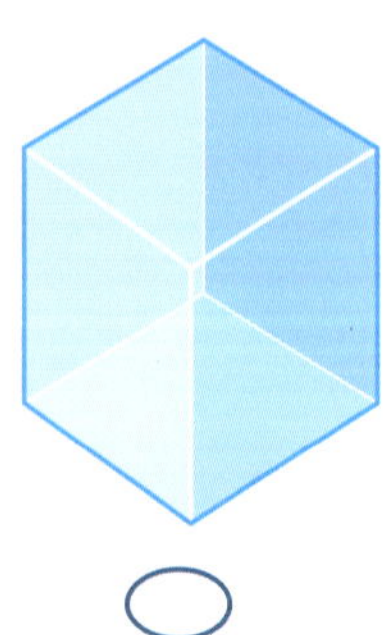
◯

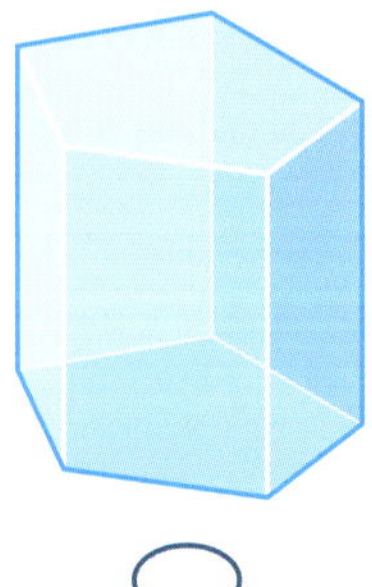
◯

Test practice

15 Toby chose a pizza which was $\frac{1}{2}$ veggie, $\frac{1}{4}$ chicken and 25% cheese and sausage. Which pizza did he choose?

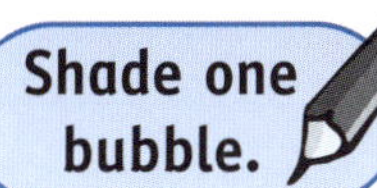

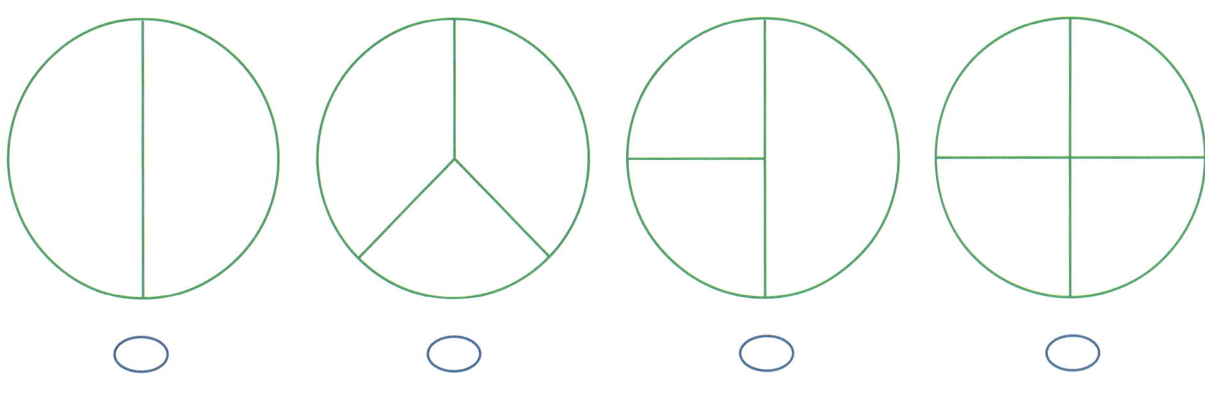

16 Which sign will make this statement true?

37 584 006  **35 784 006**

–	>	=	<

17 Which result is missing from the two-column graph?

Write your answer in the box.

Average test scores – June

Marks	Spelling	Tables	Grammar	Vocab	Maps
Year 5	9	10	7	8	7
Year 6	10	9	9	9	7

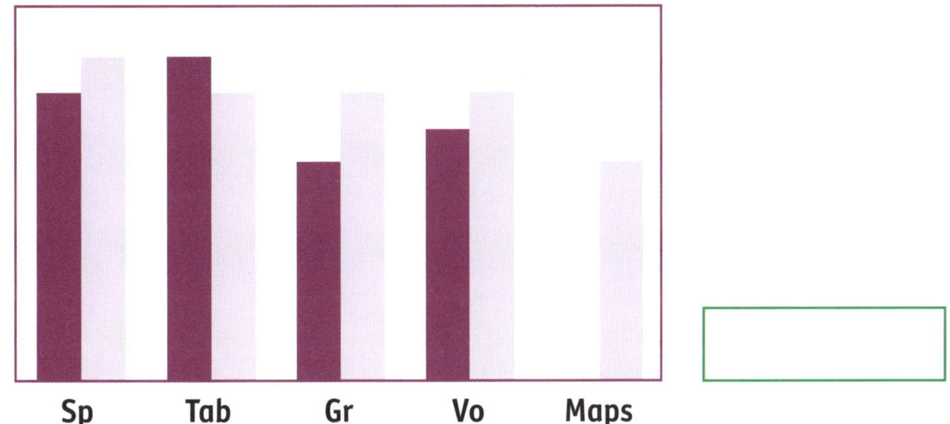

Test practice

18 Maya plotted the following points on the number plane.

(1, 4) (2, 3) (4, 3) (5, 4) (6, 5)

Which is her correct effort?

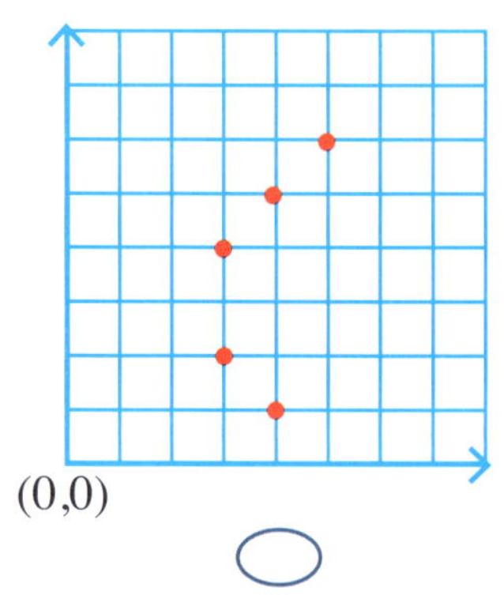

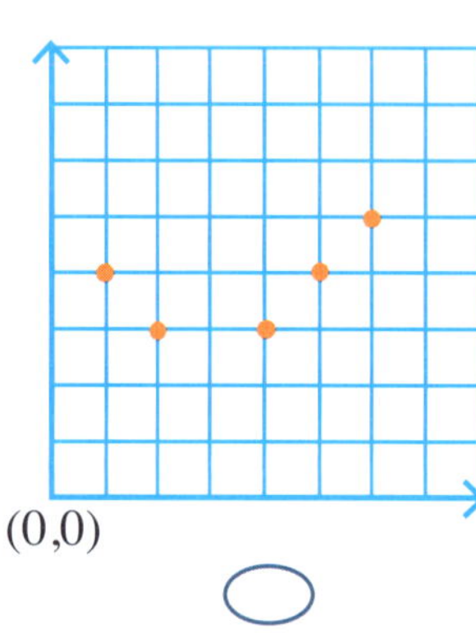

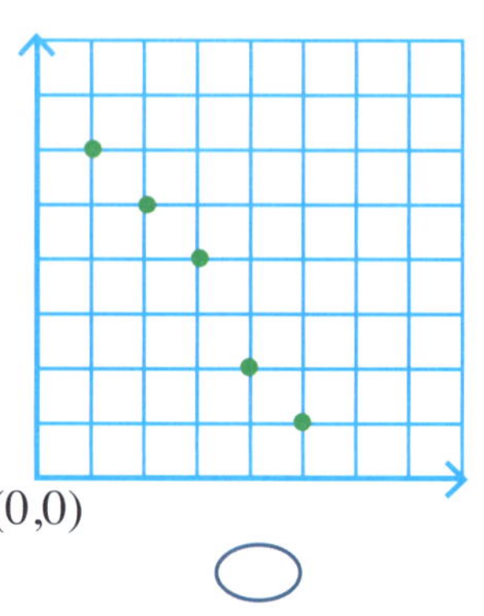

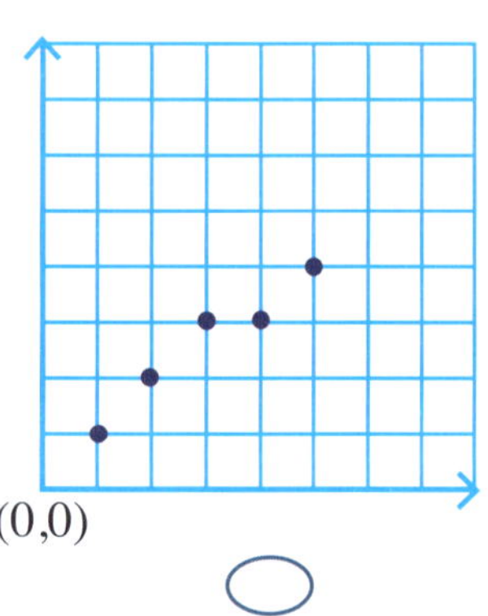

19 The class had to build a 3D object with 42 cubes.
What dimensions would be best?

6 cubes × 3 cubes × 4 cubes

7 cubes × 3 cubes × 2 cubes

8 cubes × 4 cubes × 10 cubes

8 cubes × 4 cubes × 2 cubes

20 Which angle is adjacent to angle **B**?

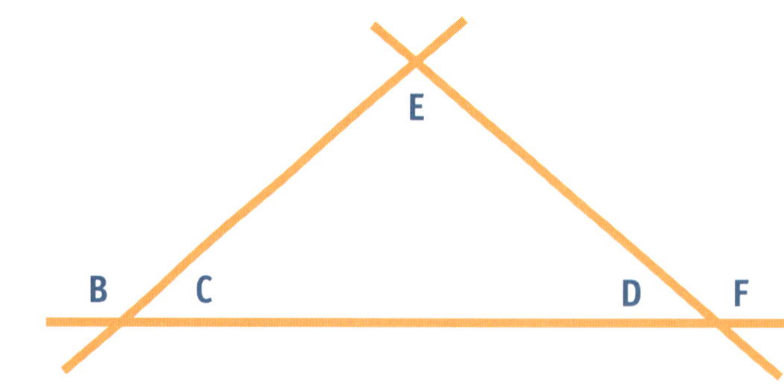

C ◯ **D** ◯ **E** ◯ **F** ◯

Test practice

21 The chess players fitted 3 games into 2 hours.

They had two breaks of 6 minutes each.

How long for each game?

Write your answer in the box.

22 Which line graph is telling us that children's average height is remaining stable this year?

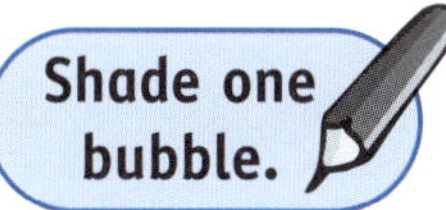

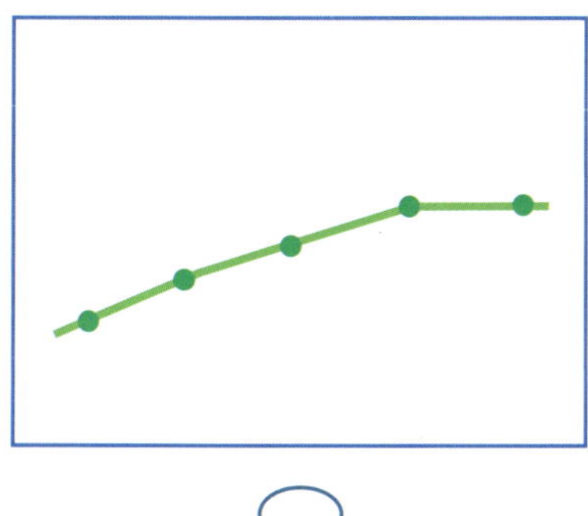

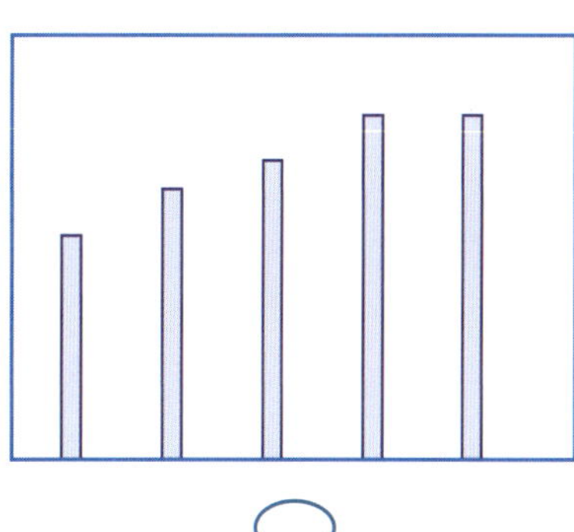

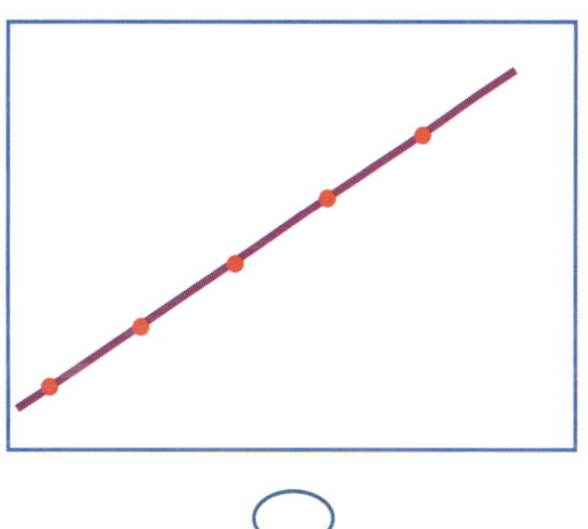

23 Which polygon has correctly drawn diagonals?

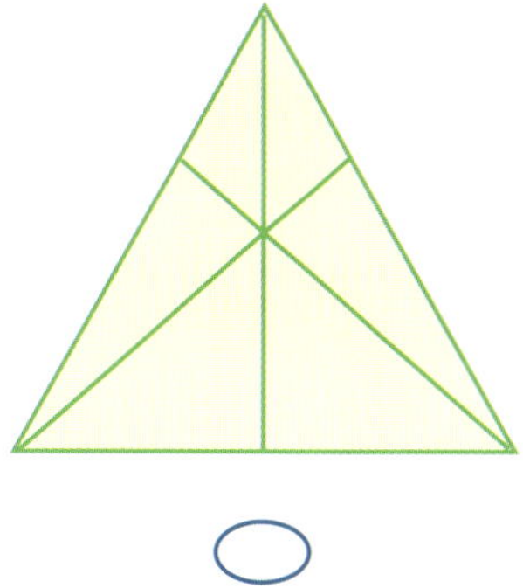

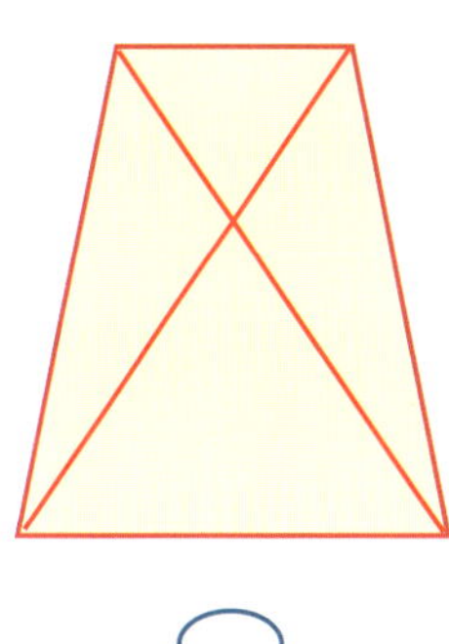

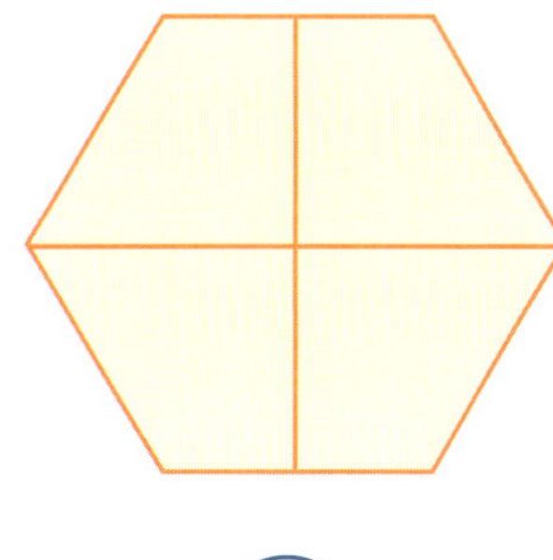

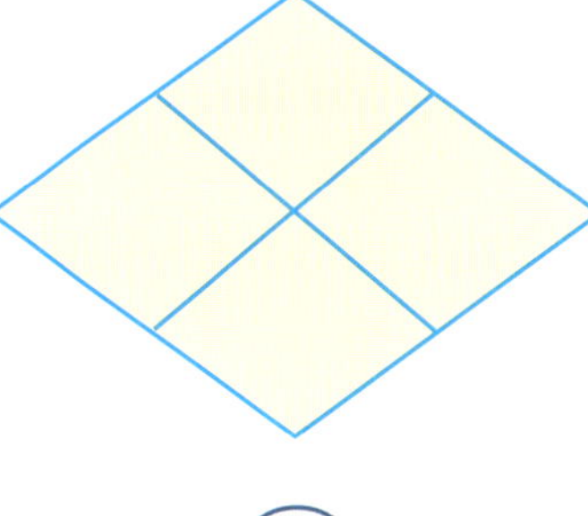

Test practice

Shade one bubble.

24 Jenny has eaten $\frac{3}{5}$ of her fruit and Chloe has eaten 35% of hers.
Van has eaten 0·5 of his and Lily has eaten 75% of hers.
Who has eaten the smallest amount of their fruit?

Jenny  **Chloe**  **Van**  **Lily**

25 Which unfolded paper cut-out started as this?

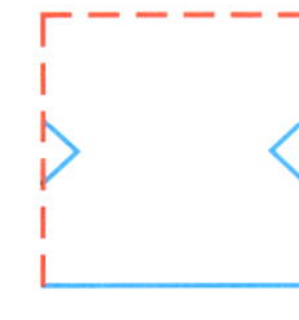

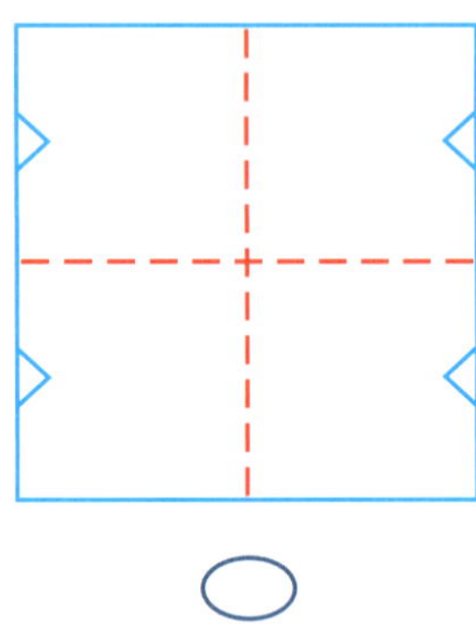

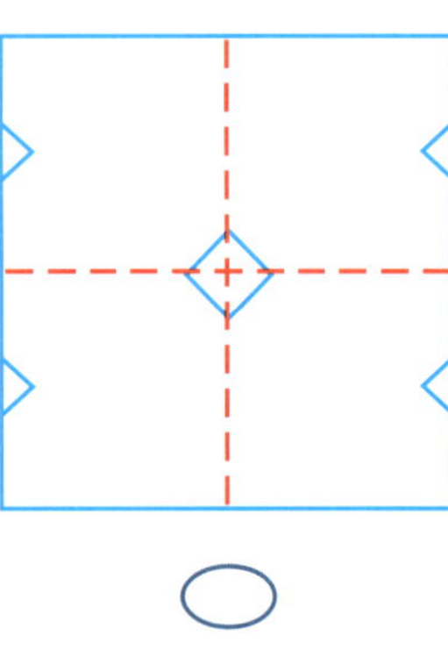

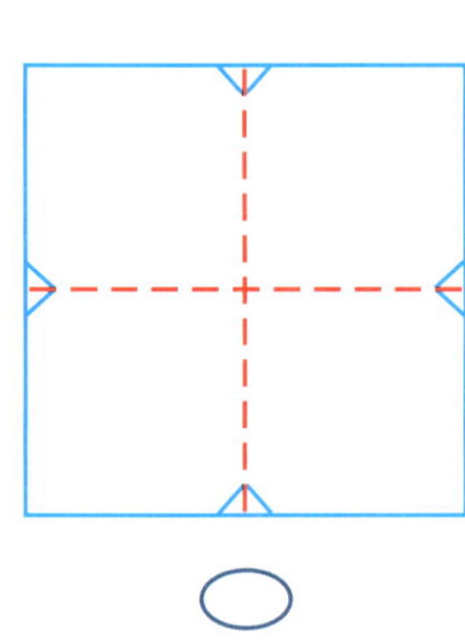

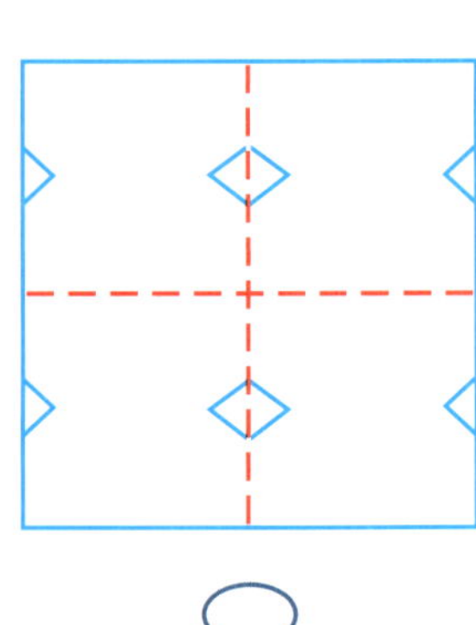

26 Jiro bought 5 kg of sausages at $11.98 per kg.

Rounded to the nearest dollar, how much did that cost?

$55 | $60 | $59.90 | $59

27 Rounded to two decimal places, which is the largest decimal number?

3 · 6 7 3 | 3 · 6 3 7 | 3 · 6 7 7 | 3 · 7

Test practice

28 Before I downloaded an app to my phone, I had \$25 credit. The app cost \$3.99. How much credit do I now have?

\$28.99 ◯ \$22.99 ◯ \$22 ◯ \$21.01 ◯

29 How many diagonals does a pentagon have?

8 ◯ 4 ◯ 20 ◯ 5 ◯

30 What is the missing term in this pattern?

30, 29·44, 28·88, ________ , 27·76

28·22 ◯ 27·23 ◯ 28·32 ◯ 27·56 ◯

31 The doctor ordered that I eat a whole packet of cranberries each day. I have eaten $\frac{5}{12}$ of a packet today. How much do I still have to eat? Which number sentence will help me to solve this question?

$1 - \frac{1}{12} =$ _____ ◯ $\frac{5}{12} - 1 =$ _____ ◯ $\frac{5}{12} +$ _____ $= 1$ ◯ $\frac{5}{12} - \frac{5}{12} =$ _____ ◯

32 Which 3D object will this net make?

a triangle ◯ a triangular pyramid ◯

a triangular prism ◯ a triangular polygon ◯

Unit 12 Prime numbers

Prime numbers have only two factors – themselves and 1.

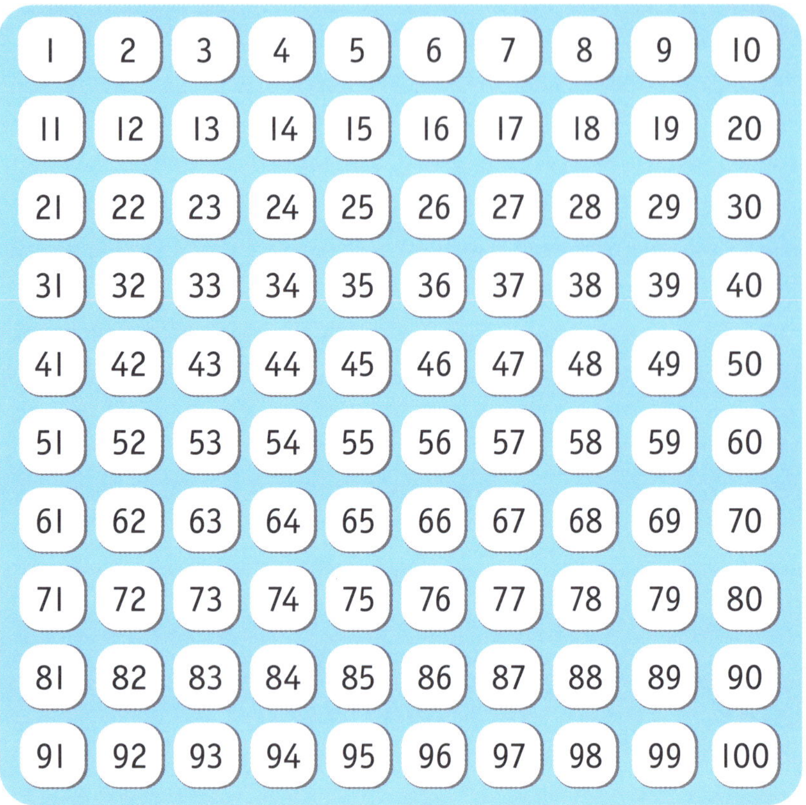

1	2	3	4	5	6	7	8	9	10
11	12	13	14	15	16	17	18	19	20
21	22	23	24	25	26	27	28	29	30
31	32	33	34	35	36	37	38	39	40
41	42	43	44	45	46	47	48	49	50
51	52	53	54	55	56	57	58	59	60
61	62	63	64	65	66	67	68	69	70
71	72	73	74	75	76	77	78	79	80
81	82	83	84	85	86	87	88	89	90
91	92	93	94	95	96	97	98	99	100

1 a Cross off 1.

b Circle 2, then cross off all multiples of 2.

c Circle 3, then cross off all multiples of 3.

d Circle 5, then cross off all multiples of 5.

e Circle 7, then cross off all multiples of 7.

f Highlight the circled numbers and all remaining numbers. They are the prime numbers less then 100.

Write them here: ______________________________

2 Prime numbers are multiples of 1 and themselves only. They have no other f______________.

3 Which numbers are prime? Circle them.

87	2	129	104	71	217

4 True or false? All prime numbers are odd. ______________ Why? ______________

____

5 Write the prime and odd numbers 0 to 50 in the diagram.

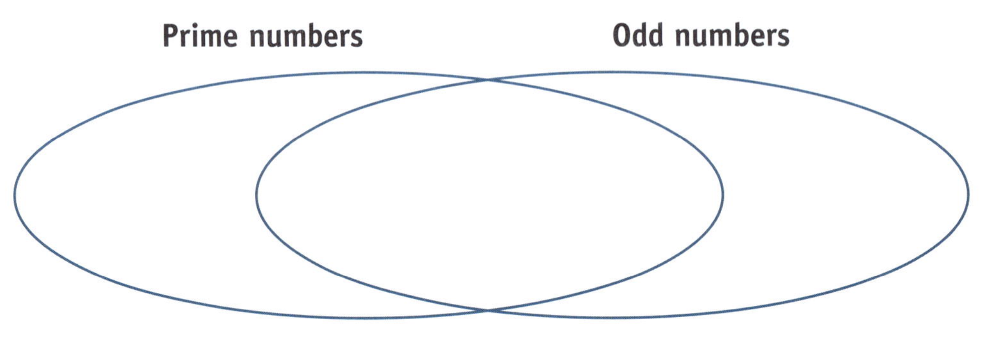

Unit 12 Composite numbers

Composite numbers have more than two factors.
eg 4 is composite.
Its factors are 1, 2, 4.

1 What are the composite numbers >50 and <80?

____

____

2 What is the smallest composite number larger than zero? ________

3 Describe each set of numbers.

eg 5, 10, 15, 20, 25 — Multiples of 5 <30

a 6, 12, 18, 24, 30, 36, 42, 48 ______________________

b 25, 30, 35, 40, 45 ______________________

c 21, 28, 35 ______________________

d 82, 84, 86, 88 ______________________

e 32, 40, 48, 56, 64 ______________________

4 This array illustrates some factors of 72.
Draw three more arrays to show different factors of 72.

a

$18 \times 4 =$ ______

b

c

d

Challenge!

Place the numbers to and including 25 in the boxes so that the numbers match the row and column headings.

Some of the numbers can go in more than one box.

	Multiples of 3	Prime numbers	Multiples of 5	Square numbers
<10				
Factors of 18				
>15				
Factors of 30				

Unit 12 Integers

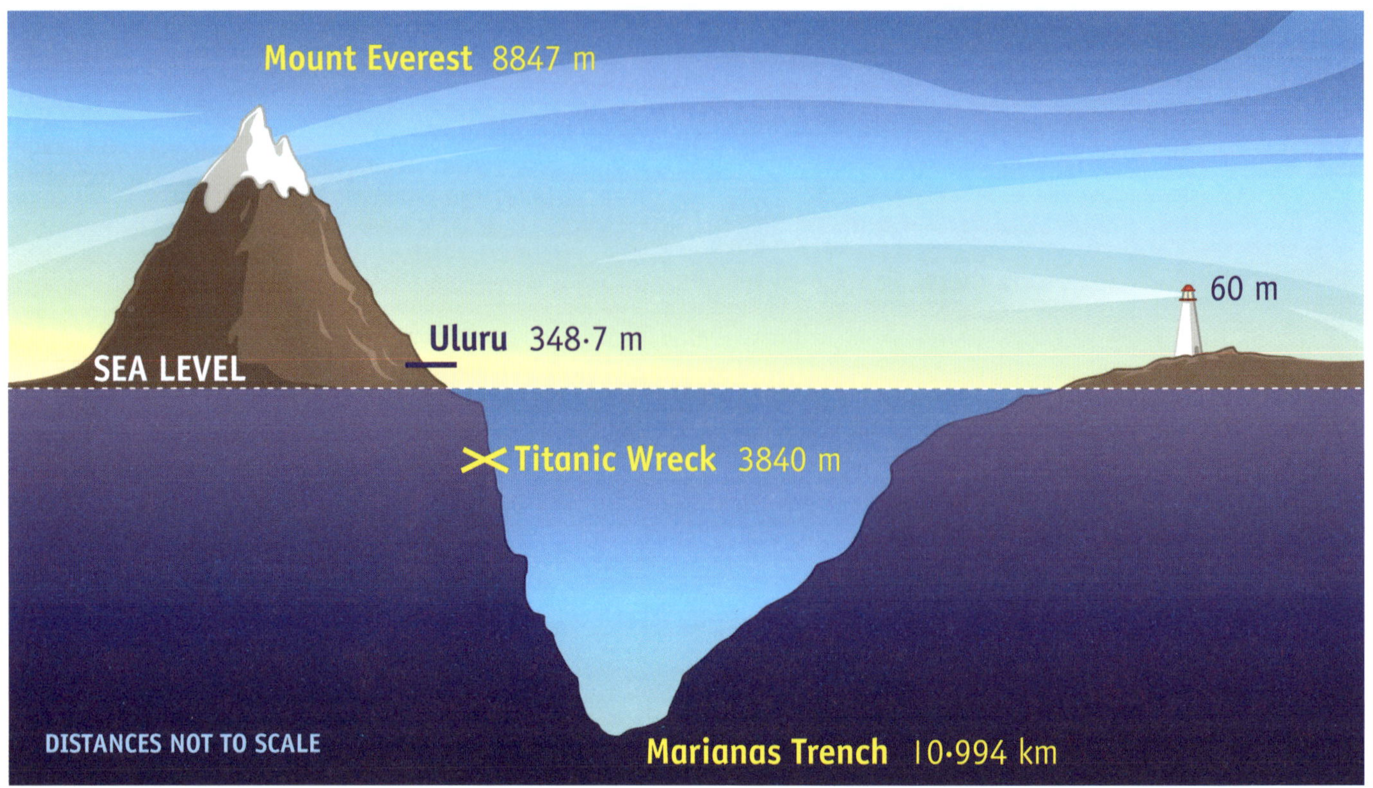

We can write a height above sea level as +4357 m. We can write a depth below sea level as –2460 m.

1 Write the height of Mt Everest to indicate metres above sea level. ______

2 Write the height of Uluru to indicate metres above sea level. ______

3 Write the depth of the wreck of the Titanic to show metres below sea level. ______

4 Place an x at the spot –55 m where you estimate a sunken submarine off Sydney Harbour lies.

5 Place a K at the spot +2228 m where you estimate the top of Mt Kosciusko reaches.

6 How many metres between:

a the Titanic wreck and the top of Uluru? ______

b the Marianas Trench and the top of the lighthouse? ______

c Explain how you worked out these answers. ______

______

7 a Enter 5 into a calculator. Subtract 1. Write the answer. ____
Continue to subtract 1, writing the answer each time.

____, ____, ____, ____, ____, ____, ____, ____, ____

b Describe the pattern you found. ______

8 a Enter 9 into the calculator. Subtract 2. Write the answer. ____
Continue to subtract 2, writing the answer each time.

____, ____, ____, ____, ____, ____, ____, ____

b Describe the pattern you found. ______

9 Explain this pattern. ______

 AC9M6N01 • AC9M6N09 Number **MA3-RN-01** Represents numbers B • Whole numbers: Locate and represent integers on a number line • **MA3-AR-01** Additive relations A • Apply efficient mental and written strategies to solve addition and subtraction problems

Unit 12 Integers

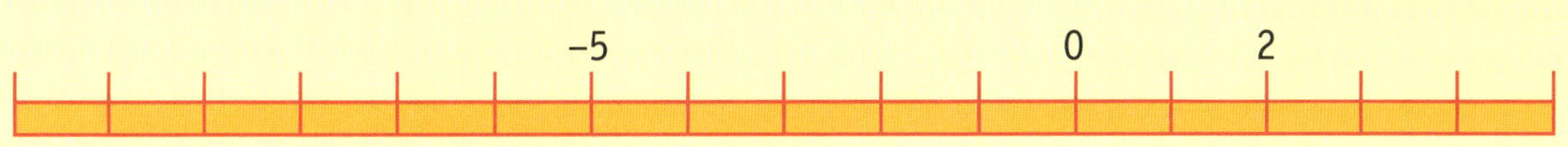

Negative numbers are below zero. −3 = minus 3 and means 3 below zero.

1 Complete the number line using positive and negative numbers.

−5 0 2

2 −8 °C 0 °C 8 °C

a Write in the temperatures below zero.

b If the temperature falls by 5 °C, what is the new temperature? ____________

c If the temperature rises by 3 °C, what is the new temperature? ____________

d By how much does the temperature have to rise to show 10 °C? ____________

e If the thermometer shows −5 °C in one hour's time, by how much has it fallen? ____________

3 Put each set of numbers in ascending order.

a 3, −3, 1, −4, 0, −2, −5, −1, 2 ____________

b −10, 0, 5, −5, 10, 15, −15 ____________

c −2, −4, 6, 2, 0, 4 ____________

4 Use a calculator for the following. Illustrate the number sentence on the number line.

eg 56 − 64 = ________

a 124 − 154 = ________

b 498 − 672 = ________

c 306 − 390 = ________

d How can you check your calculation? ____________

____

Mastery Checklist I can:
- ☐ recognise prime numbers
- ☐ recognise composite numbers
- ☐ show positive and negative numbers on a number line
- ☐ use positive and negative numbers in real-world situations.

Unit 13 Order of operations

Let me see!
That's 21 × 4.
That's 84!

16 + 5 × 4?

I know!
That's 16 + 20!
That equals 36!

20 ÷ 5 – 1

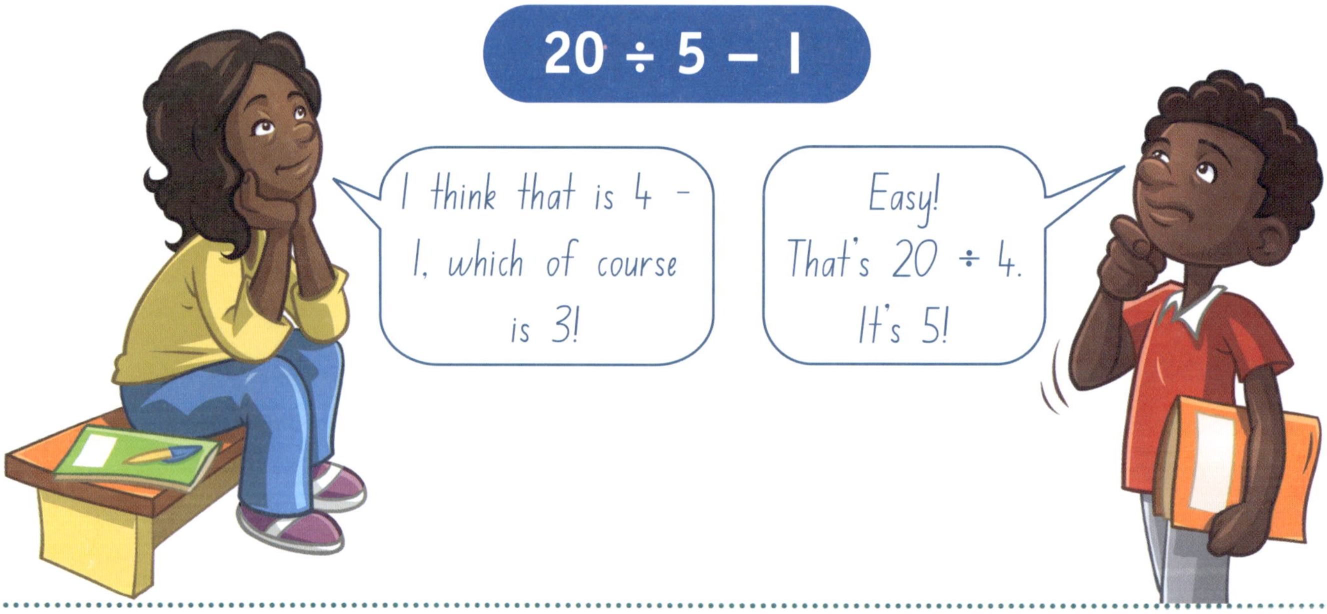

I think that is 4 – 1, which of course is 3!

Easy!
That's 20 ÷ 4.
It's 5!

Who is correct? Use the correct order to work operations and your answers will be correct.

Work out these.

1 a 15 + 7 × 3 = ________

b 64 ÷ 8 + 12 = ________

c 25 + 46 + 18 ÷ 3 = ________

d 98 – 34 + 15 – 9 × 2 = ________

e 100 – 32 + 8 – 4 × 16 = ________

f 7 × 25 + 1500 – 250 × 2 = ________

First: work grouping symbols ( )
Then × and ÷ left to right.
Lastly
+ and – left to right.

5 + (9 × 4) + 6 ÷ 2 – 4
5 + 36 + 3 – 4 = 40

Unit 13 Order of operations

Grouping symbols are brackets.

There are two kinds.

1 ( ) Brackets, ordinary brackets, round brackets

2 [ ] Square brackets

Solve the innermost set first.

1 a $7 + 6 \times 3 =$ ______ b $24 \div 6 - 4 =$ ______

c $23 - 10 \div 2 =$ ______ d $(3 + 8) \times 6 =$ ______

e $48 \div (18 - 12) =$ ______ f $16 \div 4 + 8 =$ ______

g $(4 + 7) \times (13 - 8) =$ ______ h $17 - (2 + 3) =$ ______

2 Put in the brackets to make these true.

a $7 + 8 \div 3 = 5$ b $19 - 6 + 2 = 11$ c $6 \times 4 + 2 = 36$

d $18 \div 9 - 3 = 3$ e $7 + 9 \div 4 = 4$ f $18 \div 6 \div 3 = 9$

3 Set these out to show the steps.

a $5 + 11 \times 2 - 16$ = 5 + 22 - 16
= ______

b $16 \div 4 + (10 - 3)$ = ______
= ______

c $36 - [20 + 2 \times 2]$ = ______
= ______

d $(5 + 7) \div 3 + 8$ = ______
= ______

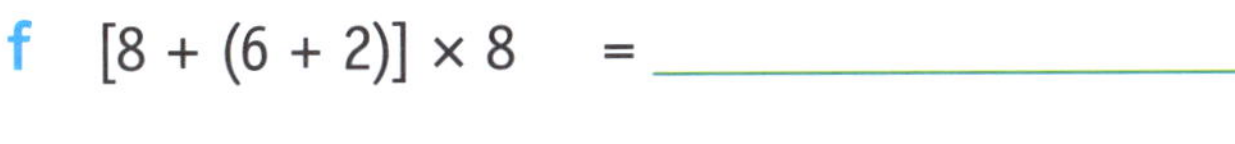

e $9 \times 7 - 30 \div 10$ = ______
= ______

f $[8 + (6 + 2)] \times 8$ = ______
= ______

g $24 \div 8 \times 2 + 34$ = ______
= ______

h $6 + 8 - 7 \times 2$ = ______
= ______

i $[(50 + 60) \div 5] \div 2$ = ______
= ______

j $(9 + 3) \times (18 - 15)$ = ______
= ______

4 Make up 4 examples for a friend to work out.

Make sure you know the answers.

a ______ = ______
= ______

b ______ = ______
= ______

c ______ = ______
= ______

d ______ = ______
= ______

5 Was that difficult? ______ Explain your answer. ______

______

______

Unit 13 Order of operations

Brackets 

The same set of numbers can have a different outcome when expressed differently.
eg **(62 – 15) × 2 = 94, 62 – (15 × 2) = 32**

1
a $6 \times 4 + 5 =$ _____
b $7 + 8 \times 3 =$ _____
c $3 \times (5 + 8) =$ _____
d $8 \times 9 - 12 =$ _____
e $15 - 16 \div 4 =$ _____
f $24 \div (10 - 4) =$ _____
g $(32 + 16) \div 8 =$ _____
h $(5 + 3) \times 6 + 2 =$ _____
i $15 - 15 \div 15 =$ _____
j $(120 - 25) \div 5 =$ _____
k $7 \times 2 \times 2 + 16 =$ _____
l $12 + 4 \times 9 - 10 =$ _____
m $(3 \times 4) + (7 \times 6) =$ _____
n $10 - 36 \div 9 \times 2 =$ _____
o $5 \times 6 \div 3 + 18 =$ _____

2 Solve, showing your working.

a $(27 \div 3) \times (3 + 6) =$ __________
b $27 \div (3 \times 3) + 6 =$ __________
c $27 \div 3 \times 3 + 6 =$ __________
d $(36 - 4) \times (3 \times 2) + 8 =$ __________
e $(36 - 4) \times 3 \times (2 + 8) =$ __________
f $[(36 - 4) \times 3] \times 2 + 8 =$ __________
g $12 \times (7 + 3 - 2) =$ __________
h $[(8 \times 9 + 4) - 12] \div 4 =$ __________
i $(15 \div 15 \times 2) - 2 =$ __________

3 Write and answer your own equations using 5 numbers and no brackets.

a __________ b __________
c __________ d __________

4 Add brackets to make the same numbers come to a different answer.

a __________ b __________
c __________ d __________

5 Add brackets in a different way to make different outcomes again.

a __________ b __________
c __________ d __________

6 Add brackets to make these equations true.

a $3^2 + 5 \times 2 = 4 \times 3 + 4$
b $16 - 8 + 8 \times 4 = 17 + 3 + 5 \times 4$

Challenge!

Choose 4 of these numbers.
How many different equations can you make with them?

5 3 8 2 0
6 4 1 9 10 12

Mastery Checklist

I can:
- ☐ use the correct order of operations
- ☐ understand the use of brackets
- ☐ write equations with brackets.

AC9M6A02 Algebra **MA3-MR-02** Multiplicative relations B • Explore the use of brackets and the order of operations to write number sentences

Unit 14 Zero in multiplication and division

ZERO IS A VERY IMPORTANT NUMERAL.
IT MAKES A DIFFERENCE! IT MAY BE A BIG DIFFERENCE!

Circle the correct answer for each equation.

1 304 × 6	2 509 × 7	3 2804 ÷ 4	4 56 014 ÷ 7
204	483	71	802
1824	3563	701	8002
324	763	74	8200

5 603 × 4	6 306 × 3	7 505 × 6	8 900 × 6
252	9018	3030	5040
2412	98	3005	5400
2434	918	330	540

9 3224 ÷ 8	10 3645 ÷ 9	11 2135 ÷ 7	12 912 ÷ 3
43	45	306	302
403	445	35	304
423	405	305	34

Unit 14 Multiplication

Zeroville Council wishes to resurface its car park after the fair. How many square metres will be needed for the job if the car park is 107 m long and 48 m wide?

```
  107
×  48
  856
 4280
 5136
```

Estimate: 100 × 50 = 5000 m **Answer =** 5136 m

Remember: Zero is a very important digit. It keeps other digits in their correct places.

Estimate all answers first.

1 a 309 × 52 Est. ______ b 508 × 74 Est. ______ c 760 × 83 Est. ______ d 405 × 96 Est. ______

2 a \$2.08 × 54 Est. ______ b \$6.70 × 36 Est. ______ c \$9.40 × 29 Est. ______ d \$6.03 × 75 Est. ______

3 a The car park contains 209 sections of 27 car spaces each.
Joe: "That's 783 altogether!" Sol: "No, that's 5643 spaces!" Bud: "I get 2943!"
Who is correct? ______

b Asphalt costs \$29 per square metre. How much will it cost to lay 5136 m^2?
Est. ______ Cost ______

c Will took 575 photos at the fair but only 490 turned out. At 58 cents per photo, how much money did he lose? Est. ______ Cost ______

d The post office received 36 sheets of stamps, each sheet containing 108 stamps.
How many stamps is that? Est. ______ Stamps ______

Challenge!

Write a problem for \$3.05 × 26 and find the answer.
Compare your problem with a friend's.

AC9M6N09 Number MA3-MR-01 Multiplicative relations A • Select and apply mental and written strategies to multiply 2- and 3-digit numbers by 2-digit numbers • Use estimation and rounding to check the reasonableness of answers to calculations

Unit 14 Operations with zero

When zero is multiplied, the answer is always zero.
eg 6115 × 0 = 0   0 × 1·7 = 0

1 Fill in the missing digits and the answer.

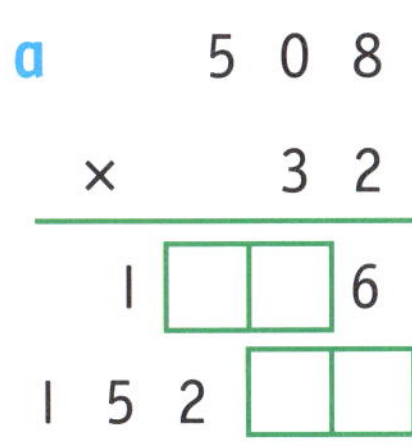

a
```
      5 0 8
  ×     3 2
  ---------
    1 □ □ 6
  1 5 2 □ □
  ---------

```

b
```
      □ 0 7
  ×     4 □
  ---------
    2 1 4 9
  1 2 □ □ 0
  ---------

```

c
```
      8 0 □
  ×     6 7
  ---------
    □ □ □ 6
  □ □ □ □ 0
  ---------

```

d
```
      □ 0 □
  ×     9 6
  ---------
    5 □ □ 2
  8 1 1 □ 0
  ---------

```

2 Work these mentally.

Item	Number per pack	Packs per box	Total
Tacks	3020	8	a
Nails	2400	6	b
Nuts	2055	8	c
Bolts	905	5	d

3 Zeros are high fliers too.
These prices are return air fares from Sydney:

Perth $1405   **Adelaide** $780   **Darwin** $1035   **Hobart** $705

What would be the total cost for each group to travel?

a 8 to Perth ______   b 12 to Adelaide ______

c 9 to Darwin ______   d 24 to Hobart ______

4 Zeros are into scale model building. Complete the table.

Building	Scale	Height of model	Height of building
CMC Tower	1 cm = 405 cm	72 cm	a
BBC Bridge	1 cm = 350 cm	27 cm	b
JR Centre	1 cm = 202 cm	58 cm	c

5 a 7 × 0 × 6 = ______   b 13 × 4 × 0 = ______   c 23 × 4 × 0 = ______

d 0 × 16 × 3 = ______   e (5 + 6 + 2) × 0 = ______   f (13 − 9) × 0 = ______

g 0 × 500 = ______   h 1000 × 6 × 0 = ______   i (18 ÷ 6) × (5 − 5) = ______

Trial and error

3 7 0 4 9

Using the digits, make a three-digit number and a two-digit number.
Find the largest possible product and the smallest possible product.

Unit 14 Division with zeros

1 Remember the zero in the answer.

> **Zeros have to keep digits in their place!**
>
> **9)12654 = 1406**
>
> **(Without zero, the answer would be 146!)**

a 4)1208   b 9)7209   c 5)3500

d 6)4212   e 6)1812   f 3)1527

g 7)8414   h 8)6448   i 9)2745   j 7)4956

k 4)3224   l 5)3045   m 8)8344   n 5)6045

2 Write the remainders as fractions.

a 5)3527   b 3)311   c 7)3528   d 8)4059

e 4)4141   f 4)1230   g 5)3400   h 9)13520

i 2)3014   j 6)48554   k 5)9904   l 7)2946

3 a Six farmers bought 12 024 sheep together.
How many sheep will each farmer have?

Est. ____________ Answer ____________

b I have paid $1260 for health insurance for one year.
My brother pays $816 for 8 months. Who has the better monthly rate?

Est. ____________ Answer ____________

c Nine batsmen make a total of 1036 runs in 3 cricket test matches. 64 runs are sundries.
What is the average runs scored by the batsmen in the 3 match series?
HINT: Take away the sundries first.

Est. ____________ Answer ____________

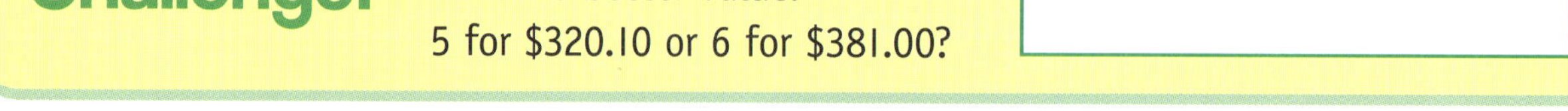

Challenge! Which is better value:
5 for $320.10 or 6 for $381.00?

Mastery Checklist I can:
- ☐ understand the role of 0 when dividing and multiplying
- ☐ estimate and multiply to check
- ☐ solve multiplication word problems
- ☐ solve division word problems.

Unit 15 Fractions

A $\frac{8}{12}$ m

B 0·2 m

C $\frac{2}{10}$ m

D $\frac{2}{6}$ m

E $\frac{3}{12}$ m

F $\frac{4}{8}$ m

G 0·75 m

H $\frac{4}{12}$ m

I $\frac{6}{12}$ m

J 0·25 m

K $\frac{6}{8}$ m

L $\frac{4}{6}$ m

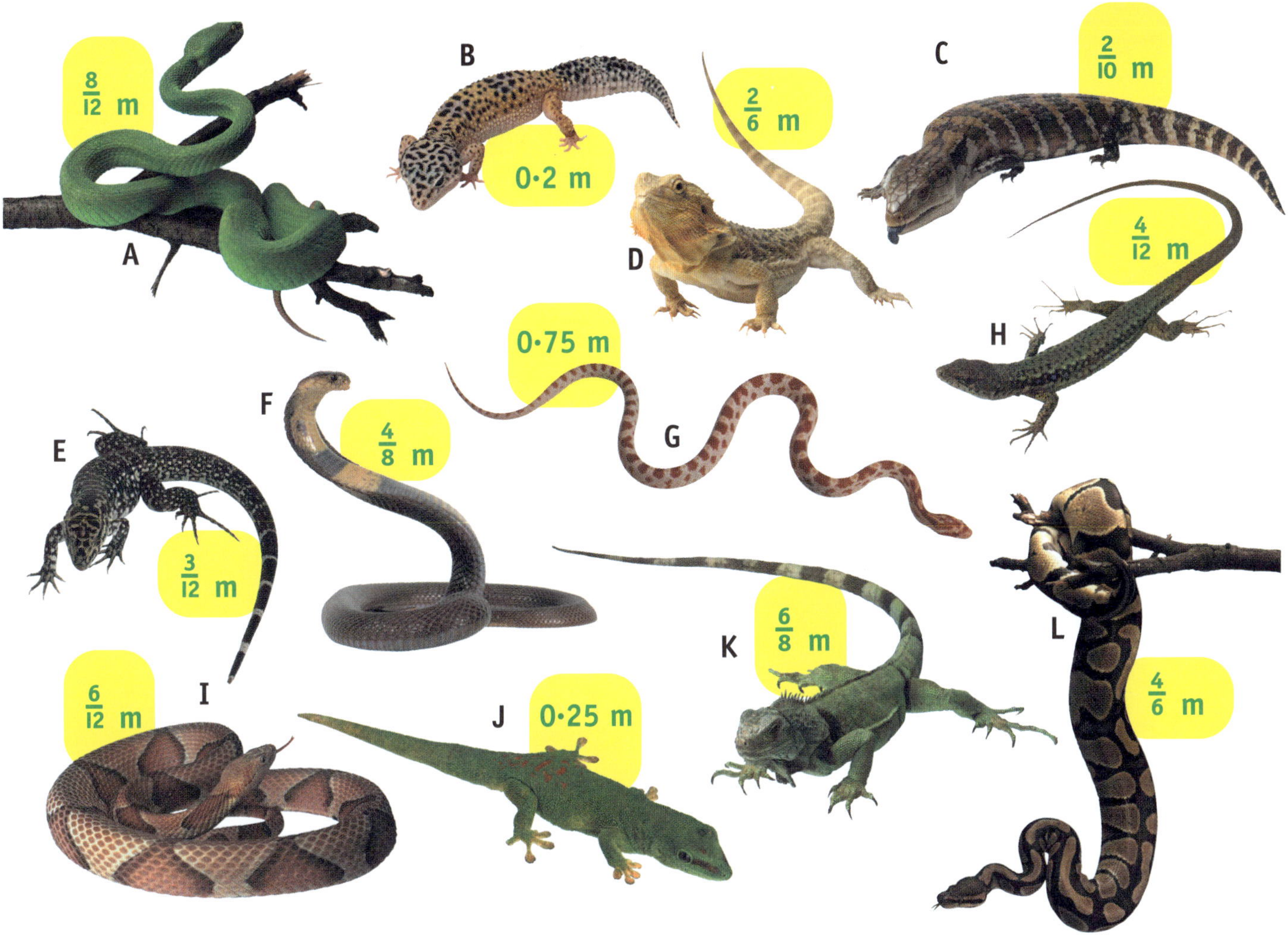

The zoo has a major problem. Some reptiles have escaped.
They are usually grouped according to size.

1 Help Zena the zookeeper put them in their right cages.

a $\frac{1}{4}$ m	b $\frac{1}{3}$ m	c $\frac{1}{5}$ m	d $\frac{1}{2}$ m	e $\frac{3}{4}$ m	f $\frac{2}{3}$ m

2 Which reptiles have these length labels?

eg $\frac{3}{6}$ = F, I

a $\frac{4}{8}$ = ______

b $\frac{6}{12}$ = ______

c $\frac{2}{8}$ = ______

d $\frac{2}{6}$ = ______

e $\frac{3}{12}$ = ______

f $\frac{2}{10}$ = ______

g $\frac{9}{12}$ = ______

h $\frac{8}{12}$ = ______

i $\frac{6}{8}$ = ______

j 0·25 = ______

k $\frac{75}{100}$ = ______

Unit 15 Adding and subtracting fractions

1
a $\frac{3}{4} - \frac{1}{4} =$ ______
b $\frac{3}{4} + \frac{1}{4} =$ ______
c $\frac{5}{6} - \frac{3}{6} =$ ______
d $\frac{2}{3} + \frac{1}{3} =$ ______
e $\frac{7}{8} - \frac{3}{8} =$ ______
f $\frac{7}{8} - \frac{1}{8} =$ ______

To + or –, make the denominators the same.

$\frac{1}{4} + \frac{1}{8} = \frac{2}{8} + \frac{1}{8} = \frac{3}{8}$

$\frac{2}{5} - \frac{3}{10} = \frac{4}{10} - \frac{3}{10} = \frac{1}{10}$

2 Colour each fraction a different colour on the bar.

eg $\frac{1}{4} + \frac{3}{8} = \frac{2}{8} + \frac{3}{8} = \frac{5}{8}$

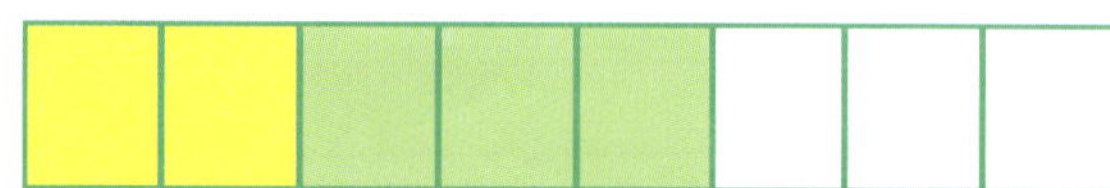

a $\frac{1}{3} + \frac{1}{6} =$ ______

b $\frac{1}{2} + \frac{1}{8} =$ ______

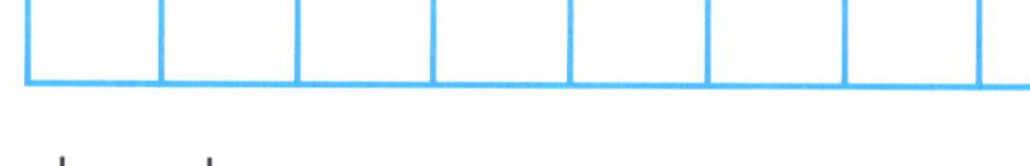

c $\frac{1}{6} + \frac{5}{12} =$ ______

d $\frac{1}{4} + \frac{1}{8} =$ ______

e $\frac{1}{4} + \frac{1}{12} =$ ______

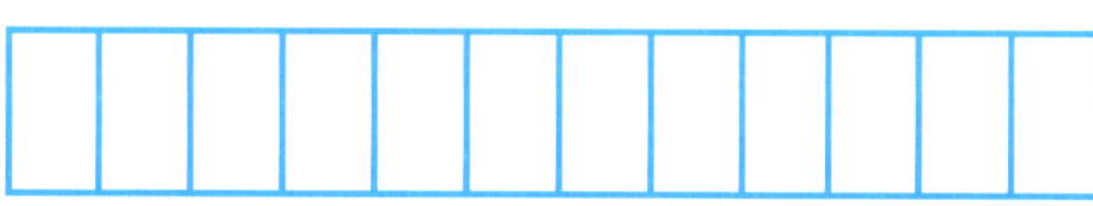

f $\frac{3}{8} + \frac{1}{2} =$ ______

3 Show subtraction by shading the fraction to take away. Write the fraction left.

a $1 - \frac{3}{8} =$ ______

b $1 - \frac{7}{12} =$ ______

c $1 - \frac{5}{6} =$ ______

d $1 - \frac{1}{3} =$ ______

Draw a diagram

Draw diagrams to show:

a $\frac{3}{5} - \frac{1}{10}$
b $\frac{1}{4} + \frac{1}{3}$
c $\frac{2}{6} + \frac{1}{4}$
d $\frac{2}{3} - \frac{5}{12}$

Unit 15 Adding fractions to more than 1

1 Add and write the answer as a mixed numeral.

eg $\frac{4}{5} + \frac{3}{5}$
$= \frac{7}{5} = 1\frac{2}{5}$

a $\frac{3}{10} + \frac{9}{10}$ ______

b $\frac{3}{4} + \frac{3}{4}$ ______

c $\frac{3}{8} + \frac{7}{8}$ ______

d $\frac{7}{12} + \frac{11}{12}$ ______

e $\frac{2}{3} + \frac{2}{3}$ ______

2 Kerry had two Crunchy Bars. Beatle ate seven tenths of one of them and Little Beatle ate nine tenths of another one. How much Crunchy Bar must they give back to Kerry?

______ Answer ______

3 Use equivalent fractions. Add, and answer as mixed numerals.

eg $\frac{3}{8} + \frac{3}{4}$
$= \frac{3}{8} + \frac{6}{8}$
$= \frac{9}{8} = 1\frac{1}{8}$

a $\frac{3}{4} + \frac{7}{8}$ ______ ______

b $\frac{2}{3} + \frac{5}{6}$ ______ ______

c $\frac{7}{10} + \frac{1}{2}$ ______ ______

d $\frac{1}{4} + \frac{7}{8}$ ______ ______

e $\frac{7}{12} + \frac{1}{2}$ ______ ______

4 Simon met a pie man and took some pieces of pie. He took $\frac{4}{5}$ of an apple pie, $\frac{3}{10}$ of a blackberry pie and $\frac{1}{2}$ of a peach pie. How much pie was Simon guilty of stealing?

______ Answer ______

5 When changing both fractions to equivalent fractions with the same denominator, use the lowest common multiple (LCM) of the denominators, eg LCM of 2 and 4 is 4.

a LCM of 4 and 3 = ______
b LCM of 2 and 6 = ______
c LCM of 2 and 4 = ______
d LCM of 3 and 2 = ______
e LCM of 5 and 2 = ______
f LCM of 4 and 5 = ______

6 Use the LCM to make equivalent fractions and add.

eg $\frac{1}{4} + \frac{1}{3}$
$= \frac{3}{12} + \frac{4}{12}$
$= \frac{7}{12}$

a $\frac{1}{4} + \frac{2}{3}$ ______ ______

b $\frac{3}{4} + \frac{2}{3}$ ______ ______

7 Doing a building job for his friends, Toby worked for $\frac{1}{2}$ a day on Monday, $\frac{3}{4}$ of a day on Tuesday and finished the job with $\frac{5}{8}$ of a day on Wednesday. How many days work did Toby do?

______ Answer ______

Mastery Checklist I can:
- ☐ identify equivalent fractions
- ☐ use equivalency to add and subtract fractions
- ☐ use mixed numerals
- ☐ find the lowest common multiple.

Unit 16 Fractions of a quantity

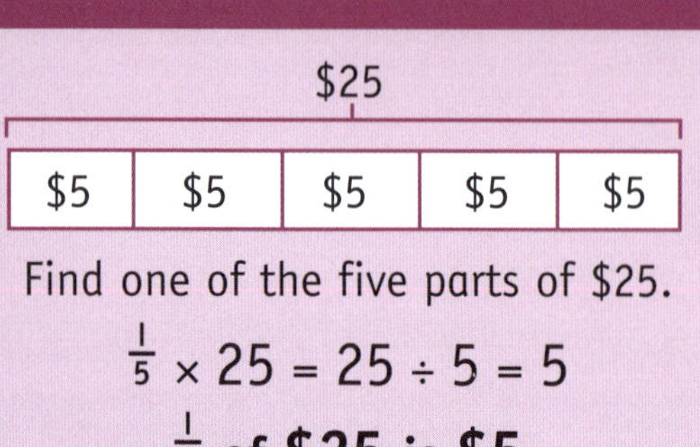

Find one of the five parts of $25.

$\frac{1}{5} \times 25 = 25 \div 5 = 5$

$\frac{1}{5}$ of $25 is $5

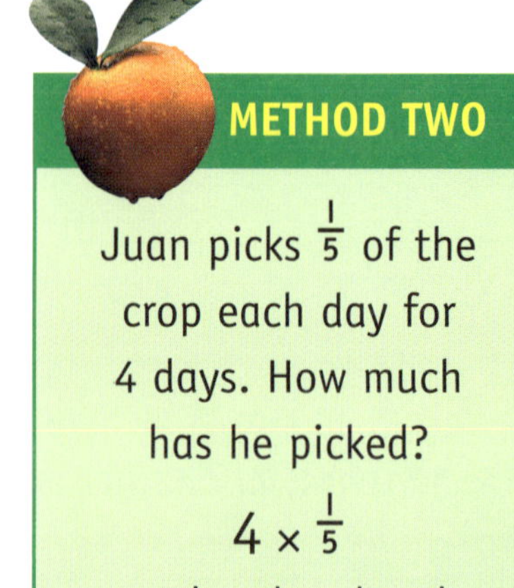

Juan picks $\frac{1}{5}$ of the crop each day for 4 days. How much has he picked?

$4 \times \frac{1}{5}$

$= \frac{1}{5} + \frac{1}{5} + \frac{1}{5} + \frac{1}{5}$

$= \frac{4}{5}$

WPS NEWSLETTER

Year 6 has been raising $\frac{1}{10}$ of their target total dollars for their Canberra trip every day for 7 days! Mr Snape is very pleased and says that experience w

720 children asked. $\frac{1}{4}$ found to have March birthdays.

House Painting

Guaranteed speedy completion!

Mrs Pinke reports that our painters covered $\frac{1}{10}$ of the job every hour for 5 hours …

What is the value of each amount?

1 Draw the diagram first.

a $\frac{1}{5}$ of $80 (price of jeans)

$80

______

b $\frac{1}{4}$ of 720 children

720

______

c $7 \times \frac{1}{10}$

targeted total

______

d $5 \times \frac{1}{10}$

time to complete task

______

AC9M6N07 Number **MA3-RFQ-02** Representing quantity fractions B • Find fractional quantities of whole numbers (halves, quarters, fifths and tenths)

Unit 16 Working with fractions

1 a $\frac{1}{2}$ of 28 = ______ b $\frac{1}{4}$ of 36 = ______ c $\frac{1}{5}$ of 40 = ______ d $\frac{1}{10}$ of 40 = ______

e $\frac{1}{2}$ of 56 = ______ f $\frac{1}{4}$ of 28 = ______ g $\frac{1}{5}$ of 35 = ______ h $\frac{1}{5}$ of 55 = ______

2 Work the following problems and colour the bar to show the answer.

a Jan ate $\frac{1}{5}$ of the pizza which had cost $25.
What was the value of the eaten piece?

$\frac{1}{5}$ × $25

= $5

b Bob has spent $\frac{1}{4}$ of his money on food.
How much of his $200 budget has he spent?

______

______

c Lou's Mum took 24 of his toys when he was rude.
She gave him back $\frac{1}{4}$ the next day.
How many of his toys did she give back?

______

______

3 a $\frac{1}{2}$ × 24 + 7

= ______

b $\frac{1}{5}$ × 55 − 4

= ______

c 18 − $\frac{1}{4}$ × 48 − 3

= ______

d 20 − $\frac{1}{10}$ × 30

= ______

1 day

6 × $\frac{1}{10}$ of a day.

$\frac{1}{10} + \frac{1}{10} + \frac{1}{10} + \frac{1}{10} + \frac{1}{10} + \frac{1}{10} = \frac{6}{10}$ of a day.

REDUCE → $\frac{3}{5}$ of a day.

4 a 3 × $\frac{1}{4}$ hour

= $\frac{1}{4} + \frac{1}{4} + \frac{1}{4}$

= ______

b 4 × $\frac{1}{2}$ year

= ______

= ______

c 6 × $\frac{1}{10}$ my money

= ______

= ______

d 3 × $\frac{1}{5}$ hour

= ______

= ______

e 7 × $\frac{1}{4}$ day

= ______

= ______

f 5 × $\frac{1}{10}$

= ______

= ______

Trial and error

Which is the largest?

$\frac{1}{10}$ of $50 $\frac{1}{5}$ of $30 $\frac{1}{4}$ × $40

Unit 16 Mixed numerals

Mixed numerals have a whole number and a fraction, eg $3\frac{1}{4}$

1 Write as mixed numerals.

a $\frac{5}{2}$ ______ b $\frac{7}{3}$ ______ c $\frac{12}{5}$ ______

d $\frac{5}{3}$ ______ e $\frac{6}{5}$ ______ f $\frac{9}{4}$ ______

g $\frac{13}{4}$ ______ h $\frac{3}{2}$ ______ i $\frac{11}{8}$ ______

2 Find the missing numeral.

a $\frac{\square}{2} = 3\frac{1}{2}$ ______ b $\frac{\square}{5} = 1\frac{3}{5}$ ______ c $\frac{\square}{4} = 1\frac{3}{4}$ ______ d $\frac{\square}{3} = 1\frac{2}{3}$ ______

3 Multiply using repeated addition and write the answer as a mixed numeral.

a $\frac{1}{4} \times 7$

= ______

= ______

b $\frac{1}{5} \times 9$

= ______

= ______

c $\frac{1}{2} \times 11$

= ______

= ______

d $6 \times \frac{1}{5}$

= ______

= ______

$\frac{1}{3} \times 7$

$= \frac{1}{3} + \frac{1}{3} + \frac{1}{3} + \frac{1}{3} + \frac{1}{3} + \frac{1}{3} + \frac{1}{3}$

$= \frac{7}{3}$ or 7 thirds

$= 2\frac{1}{3}$

4 Draw diagrams to show your answers.

a Henry and his four brothers ate one third of a pizza each. How many pizzas did they eat altogether?

______

b Eight children are given $\frac{1}{4}$ m of ribbon each. How many metres of ribbon were used?

______

c One fifth of each of 6 apples has been nibbled away. How many apples are gone?

______

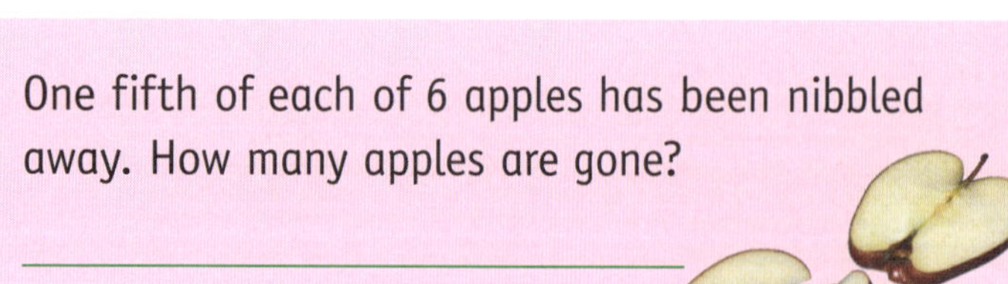

Mastery Checklist I can:
- ☐ find fractions of quantities
- ☐ use repeated addition to multiply
- ☐ solve fraction word problems with mixed numerals.

Problem solving

Using fractions

Show the solution of each problem by **drawing a diagram** and **writing a number sentence**.

1 Yan has 50 cards in his collection of endangered animal cards. He swapped $\frac{1}{10}$ of them for cards of dangerous beasts. How many cards did he swap?

2 There are 60 days left until the boat departs. We spend $\frac{1}{2}$ of that time waiting for our tickets to arrive. How many days did we wait?

3 Two fifths of my class will go away for a holiday. Of the class of 30, how many students will go on a holiday?

4 We collected 85 old cans on the side of the road. Daisy, our youngest helper collected $\frac{2}{5}$ of that total. How many cans did the rest of the team collect?

5 My marks in the end-of-year maths exam were 150. My teacher said that $\frac{1}{10}$ of that total came from fractions questions. How many marks did I get for fractions questions?

6 A water tank holds 200 L of water. In a week we use $\frac{1}{4}$ of it on the garden and $\frac{1}{5}$ of it to wash the windows. How much water is left in the tank?

I can solve problems by:

☐ understanding fractions ☐ writing number sentences and drawing diagrams.

Unit 17 Percentages

Percentage means 'out of 100'.
75% = $\frac{75}{100}$ or $\frac{3}{4}$ or 0·75.

1 Arrange these percentages in ascending order.

____

2 Match a percentage from above to each set of equivalent fractions.

a $\frac{20}{100}$, 0·2 or $\frac{1}{5}$ = ____________

b $\frac{25}{100}$, 0·25 or $\frac{1}{4}$ = ____________

c $\frac{30}{100}$, 0·3 or $\frac{3}{10}$ = ____________

d $\frac{35}{100}$, 0·35 = ____________

e $\frac{50}{100}$, $\frac{1}{2}$ or 0·5 = ____________

f $\frac{75}{100}$, $\frac{3}{4}$ or 0·75 = ____________

g $\frac{85}{100}$ or 0·85 = ____________

3 Shade 25% and write the answers.

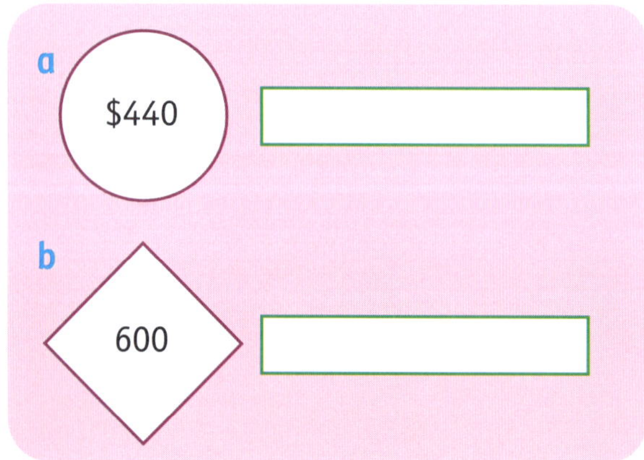

4 Shade 20% and write the answers.

a $1000 ____________

b 30 ____________

 AC9M6N07 Number **MA3-RN-03** Represents numbers B • Decimals and percentages: Make connections between benchmark fractions, decimals and percentages

Unit 17 Calculating percentages

1 Use equivalent percentages and fractions to calculate the following.

a 25% of $40
= $\frac{1}{4}$ of $40
= ______

b 10% of $50
= ______
= ______

c 10% of $60
= ______
= ______

d 50% of $120
= ______
= ______

e 25% of 1 day
= ______
= ______

f 10% of 1 metre
= ______
= ______

g 25% of 1 hour
= ______
= ______

h 50% of 1 km
= ______
= ______

2 Use equivalent decimals and fractions to calculate the following.

a 0·1 of 10
= ______
= ______

b 0·25 of 24
= ______
= ______

c 0·1 of 50
= ______
= ______

d 0·5 of 1 day
= ______
= ______

3 What is the discount in each case?

a $65
10% discount
[ ]

b $80
50% discount
[ ]

c $100
25% discount
[ ]

d $200
25% discount
[ ]

DISCOUNT IS ALWAYS SUBTRACTED

4 What is the price after the discount has been deducted?

a

[ ]

b

[ ]

c
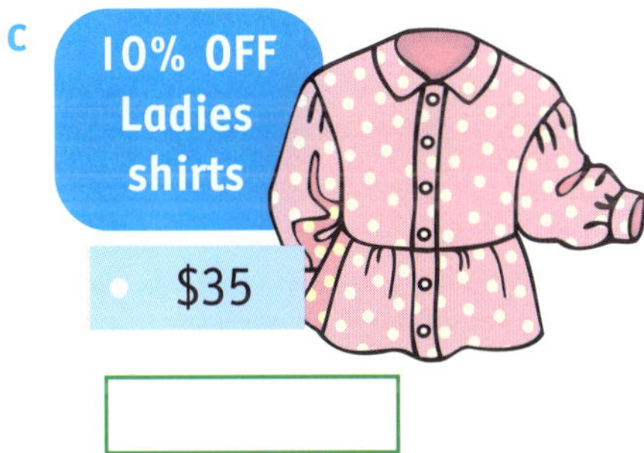

[ ]

5 The Smiths are shopping for a new chair. They are confused by the deals offered.
Help them choose the cheapest chair. Which one do you estimate? ______

a

Cost ______

b

Cost ______

c

Cost ______

Unit 17 Percentages of amounts

1 Complete these price tags.

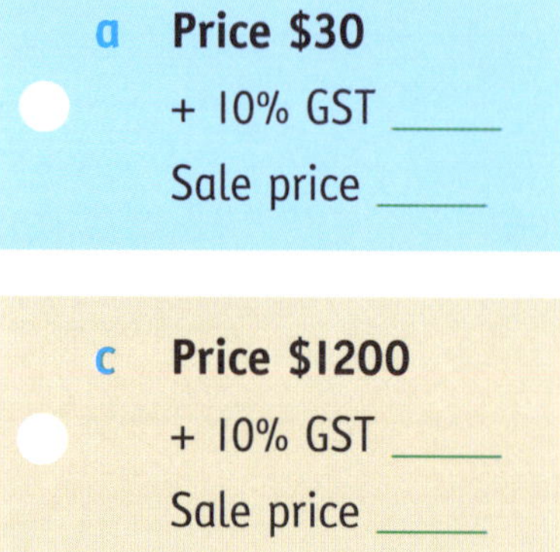

a Price $30
+ 10% GST _____
Sale price _____

b Price $75
+ 10% GST _____
Sale price _____

Add GST

Cost Price	$40
10% GST	+$4
Total	$44

c Price $1200
+ 10% GST _____
Sale price _____

d Price $500
+ 10% GST _____
Sale price _____

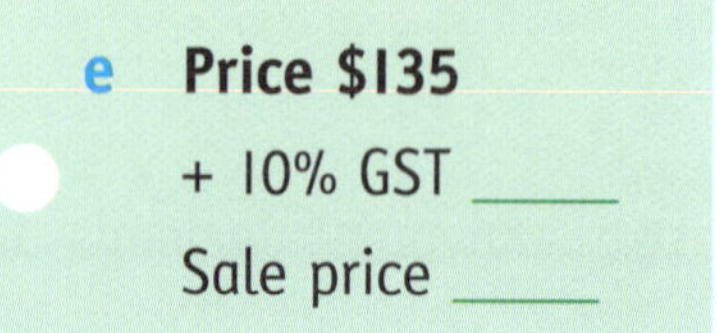

e Price $135
+ 10% GST _____
Sale price _____

2 These are the Faro family's monthly bills. They wish to reduce every one by 25%.
What will be the new amount for each?

a Telephone $120 _____

b Dining out $350 _____

c Food $600 _____

d Dog food $80 _____

e Maintenance $500 _____

f Car expenses $320 _____

3 How much would the Faro family save each month? _____

Unit 17 Working with percentages

1 Colour an amount in each column to make a set of three, eg 50% of 300 is 150.
Use a different colour for each set of three.

A	B	C
50%	75	300
25%	100	750
10%	5	1000
10%	4	16
50%	100	400
25%	150	10

2 Ren made 60 runs in the cricket match and Jesse made 20 fewer than Ren.

a How many runs were made altogether? ______________________

b Who made 40% of the run total? ______________________

3 There are 10% more cats than dogs in the street. If there are 2 more cats than dogs, how many cats and dogs are there? ______________________

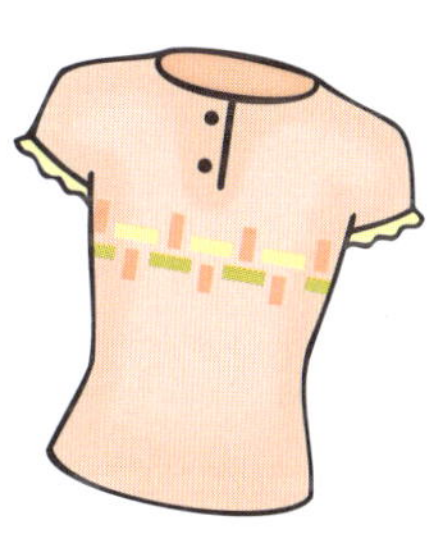

4 Alene spent 25% of her money on a T-shirt. She now has $75 left.
How much did she have to begin with? ______________________

5 Last year 1500 people attended the school fete. This year 1800 attended.
By what percentage did the attendance increase? ______________________

Challenge! Write each set of cards in ascending order.

0·5, 41%, $\frac{36}{100}$, 0·39 ______________________

0·18, $\frac{8}{10}$, 81%, 0·83 ______________________

Mastery Checklist I can:
- ☐ match percentages, decimals and fractions
- ☐ shade diagrams to show percentages
- ☐ calculate discounts
- ☐ solve percentage word problems.

Investigate angles

Investigation 2

1 Study this analogue clock face.

a How many 90° angles using whole numbers on the clock face are there? ________

b How big is the angle between the hands of the clock at any five-minute interval, eg between 5 past and 10 past? ________

c How many 30° angles are there around the clock? ________

d How many 60° angles are there around the clock? ________

e Draw a forty-five degree angle on the clock.

f If a hand of the clock moved clockwise from twenty past to ten past, what angle does it move through? ________

2 Join the 2 and the 8, the 3 and the 9 with straight lines.
Use this diagram to prove that vertically opposite angles are equal.

____

3 Make up two more questions about the movement of the hands of a clock on the clock face.

____

____

4 Find north using an analog clock face.

a Outside in the sun, point the 12 on your clock face towards the sun. Hold it there.

b Bisect the angle between the 12 and the hour at that moment, eg at 20 past three, bisect the angle between the 12 and the 3.

c That line points north.

d Draw a diagram to illustrate this method.

Investigate angles

Investigation 2

1 Study this semaphore flag signalling system.

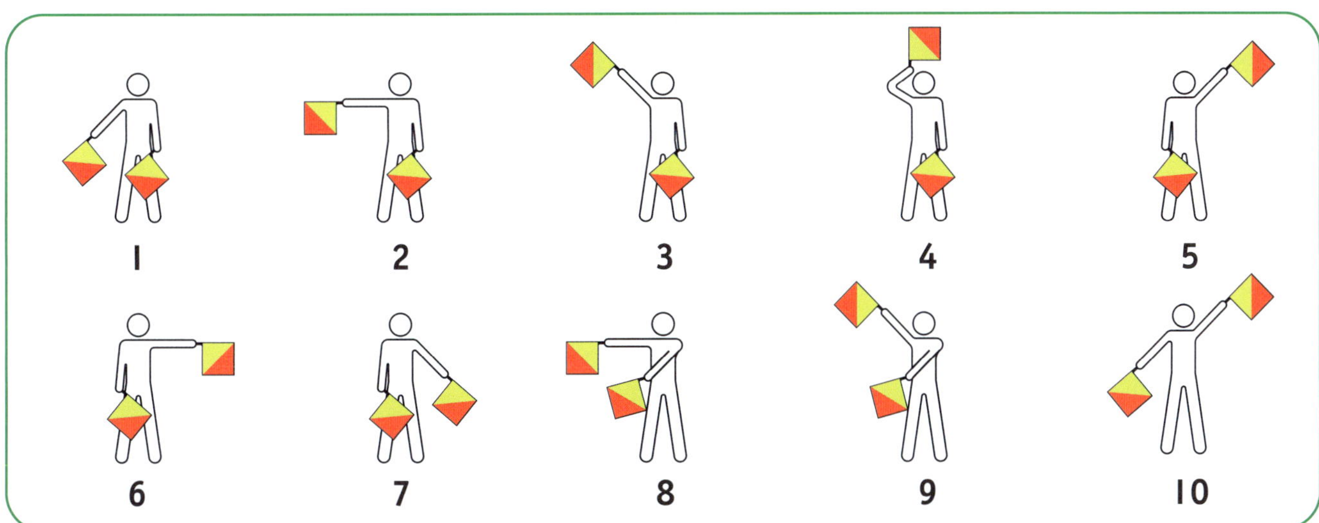

2 What pattern can you see in the position of the flags?

____

3 Place a blue dot in each of the 45° angles, a green dot in the 90° angles and a pink dot in the 135° angles.

4 Explain how to remember the signals and the numbers they stand for.

____

____

____

5 Make up a code using angles and signs you can make with hands or arms. Illustrate it.

To complete this task, I needed to:

- ☐ recognise different types of angles in the environment
- ☐ use diagramming skills
- ☐ describe and represent mathematical situations in a variety of ways.

I enjoyed this task!

Revision

1 Four students had different answers to this question.

$$5 + 4 \times 6 - 4$$

Who is correct?

Ren 50 ◯ Jarrah 25 ◯ Lucy 30 ◯ Sam 18 ◯

2

$$\frac{3}{4} \bigstar \frac{3}{5}$$

Which sign can replace the star to make the sentence true?

◯

◯

= ◯

◯

3

$$6\overline{)360 \cdot 12}$$

60·2 ◯ 6·02 ◯ 60·02 ◯ 6·002 ◯

---

4 What price will you pay? [ ]

Write your answer in the box.

Revision

5

Write your answer in the box.

0·17 | 71% | $\frac{7}{10}$ | 0·72

If these cards are written in descending order, which card is first?

6 The shaded numbers are all:

Shade one bubble.

20	21	22	**23**	24
25	26	27	28	**29**
30	**31**	32	33	34
35	36	**37**	38	39
40	**41**	42	**43**	44

composite 

prime 

factors of 100 

multiples of 3

7

I multiply a number by 3, then subtract 7 to get an answer of 11.
Which equation can be used to find the number?

$\frac{1}{3} \times ★ - 7 = 11$ 

$3 \times 11 - 7 = ★$

$3 \times ★ - 7 = 11$ 

$★ - 7 = 11 \times 3$

8 Colour each fraction a different colour on the bar to add.

$\frac{1}{6} + \frac{7}{12}$

$\frac{8}{18}$ $\frac{8}{12}$ $\frac{9}{12}$ $\frac{10}{12}$

Unit 18 Area

$10\,000 \text{ m}^2 =$ 1 hectare (1 ha)

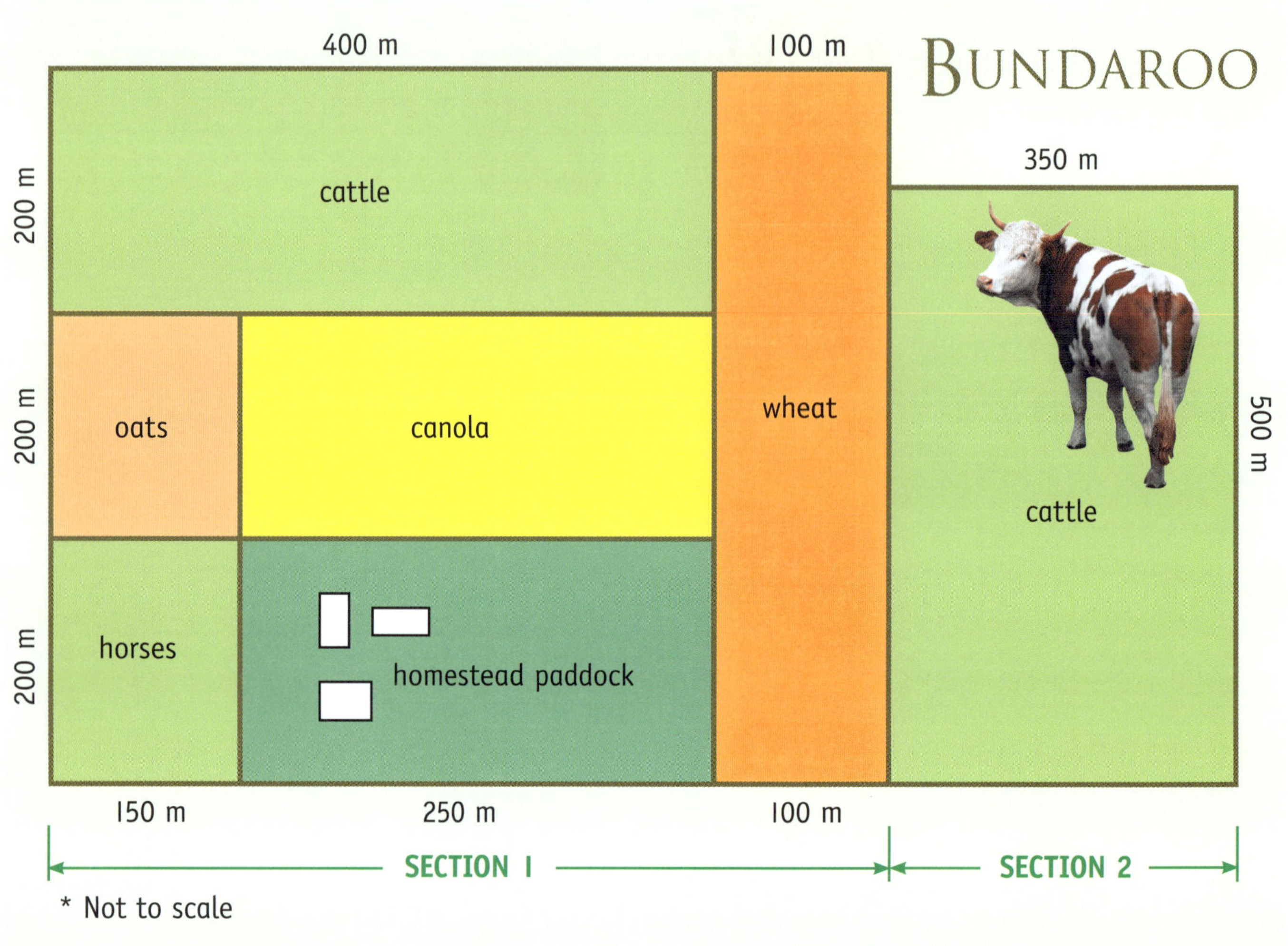

BUNDAROO

400 m | 100 m

350 m

200 m | cattle

200 m | oats | canola | wheat | cattle | 500 m

200 m | horses | homestead paddock

150 m | 250 m | 100 m

SECTION 1 | SECTION 2

* Not to scale

The property, Bundaroo, is for sale. This plan has been used to advertise it. The advertisement gives some details.

1 Fill in the details on the FOR SALE sign.

2 Estimate how many hectares in the:

a small cattle paddock. ____________

b wheat paddock. ____________

c homestead paddock. ____________

d horse paddock. ____________

3 Which two paddocks together are about 6 ha?

____

____

BUNDAROO

FOR SALE

SEE COLOUR MAP

Small cattle paddock:		m ×		m
Wheat:		m ×		m
Horses:		m ×		m
Oats:		m ×		m
Homestead:		m ×		m

Good Land, Great Improvements!

Unit 18 Hectares

Area is a square measure.
Rectangle Area = Length × Width

1 Record the measurements and find the exact areas of the paddocks of Bundaroo.

Paddock	Length (m)	Width (m)	Area (m^2)	Hectares (ha)
a Horse				
b Small cattle				
c Wheat				

2 Study the map on page 84. Bundaroo has two sections.

Write the dimensions for each section.

a Section 1 ________________ b Section 2 ________________

3 Use a calculator to find the area of each section. Add them together.

Total area = ________________

4 Circle the areas which would be measured using hectares.

a a local park
b a high school
c a suburb
d my backyard
e a parking lot
f a suburban garden
g two football fields
h a shopping plaza

5 How many will fit into a hectare? Circle your guess.

a suburban house blocks	3	5	10	20
b soccer fields	1	2	5	10
c classrooms	25	100	160	250

Draw a diagram

How many ways can you measure a hectare?

Using a scale of 1 cm = 20 m, measure this shape and check that it equals 1 hectare.

On separate paper, make other scaled sketches of 1 hectare. How many different ways can you show 1 ha?

Unit 18 Perimeter and area

1 Draw 4 rectangles or squares that have a perimeter of 24 cm using the cm grid paper.

2 Label each shape with its dimensions of length and width.

3 Write the area of each shape inside it, eg area = 36 cm^2.

4 What did you find out about shapes with the same perimeter?

5 Write the area of each shape as a multiplication number sentence.

6 Use this grid to investigate perimeters of shapes with the same area.

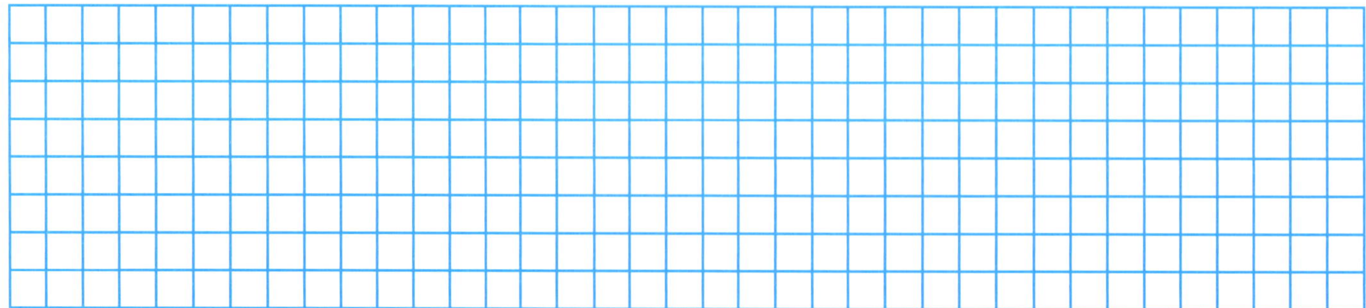

AC9M6M02 Measurement MA3-GM-02 Geometric measure A • Length: Measure lengths to find perimeters • MA3-2DS-02 Two-dimensional spatial structure A • Area: Calculate the areas of rectangles using familiar metric units

Unit 18 Large areas

1 Colour the rectangles that have an area of 1 hectare.

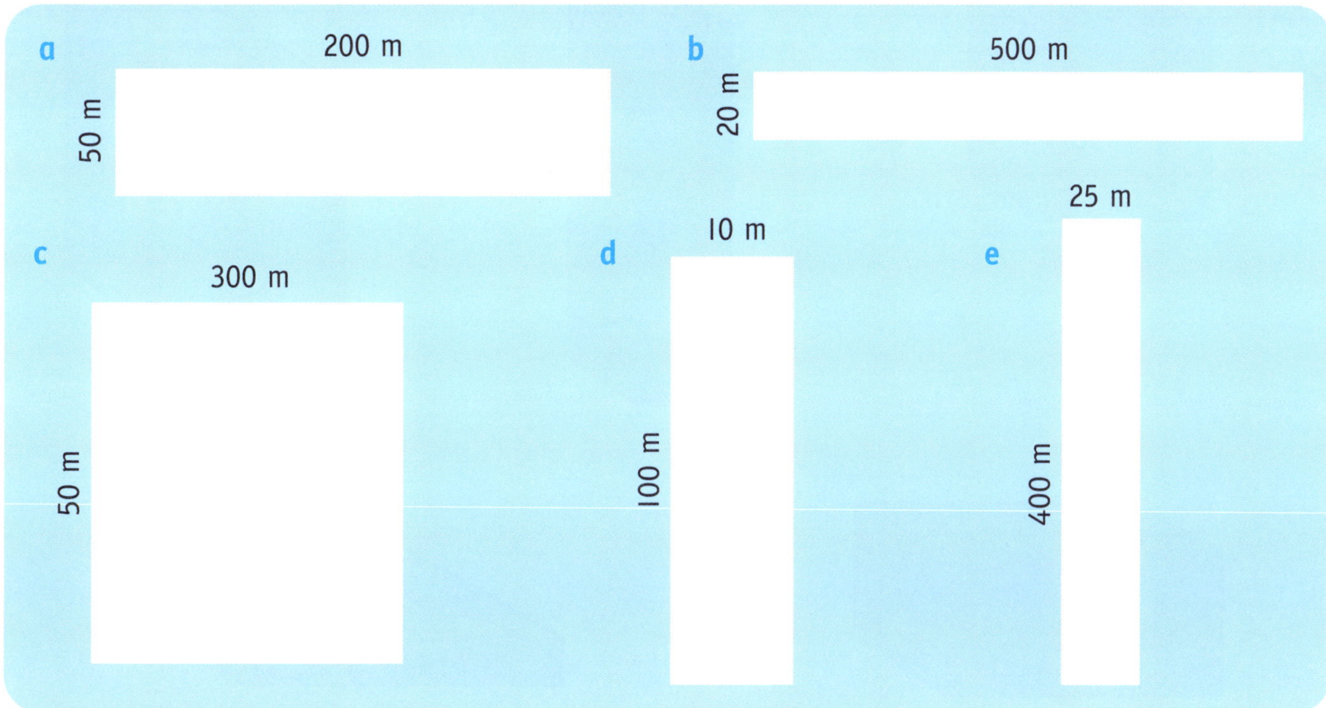

2 What is the perimeter of each hectare shape from question 1 above?

Shape	Length	Width	Perimeter

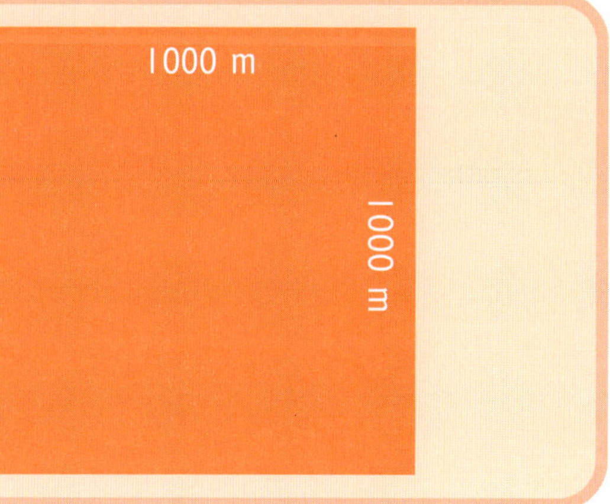

3 True or false?

a Shapes with the same perimeter have the same area. ____________

b Shapes with the same area can have different perimeters. ____________

Trial and error

Trace this scale sketch of 1 km^2.

Cut it out and reassemble it to form a regular shape with the largest perimeter possible.

Is it still 1 km^2?

Discuss your findings.

1000 m

1000 m

Mastery Checklist I can:

- ☐ estimate area and calculate to check
- ☐ understand hectares
- ☐ convert between hectares and square metres
- ☐ explore how changing perimeter affects area.

Unit 19 Volume

A

4 cm

4 cm

2 cm

B

8 cm

2 cm

2 cm

C

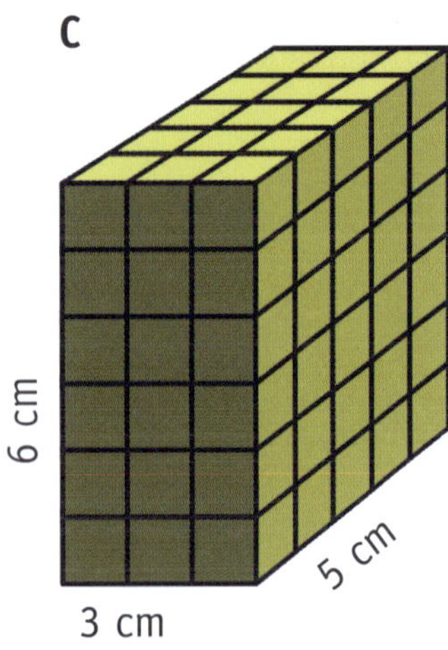

D

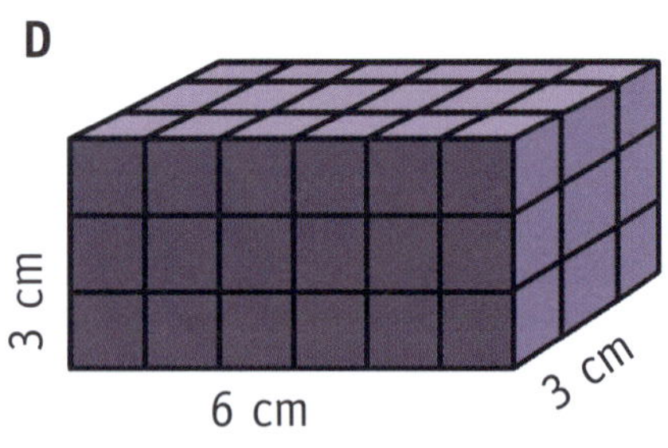

E

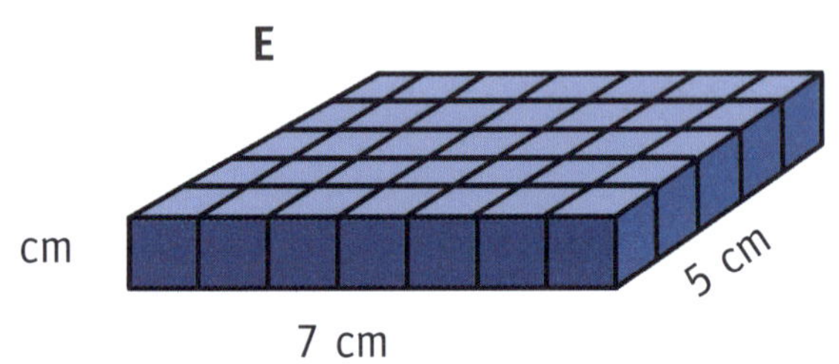

1 a What is the volume?

A ________ B ________ C ________ D ________ E ________

b List the volumes in descending order.

________ ________ ________ ________ ________

2 What is the difference in volume between:

a Objects C and E? ________

b Objects A and B? ________

c Objects D and E? ________

d Objects C and D? ________

3 Draw objects with these volumes.

a 12 cm^3	b 6 cm^3	c 8 cm^3

AC9M6M01 Measurement MA3-3DS-02 Three-dimensional spatial structure B • Volume: Find the volumes of rectangular prisms in cubic centimetres and cubic metres

Unit 19 Capacity, volume and mass

Capacity is the amount of fluid a container can hold.

Remember: 1 mL = 1 cm³

1 Collect the objects listed in the table below.

a Order them according to your estimate of their volume:

____

____

b Use a two-litre container which is clearly marked in millilitres to measure the volume of each object, using the 'water level' method.

Objects	Original water level (mL)	Water level with object added (mL)	Difference in water level (mL)	Volume of object (cm^3)
a stone				
a Base 10 flat				
an apple				
a cube block				
a plasticine ball				
Choose your own object:				

c Now order the objects according to their measured volumes:

____

d Compare your estimates with your results. Suggest reasons for the differences.

____

____

____

2 a Now order your objects according to your estimate of their mass.

____

b Use balance scales to measure the mass of your objects in grams. Record your results in the table.

c Now order the objects according to their measured masses:

____

____

d Compare your mass results with your volume results. Suggest reasons for the differences.

____

____

____

Objects	Mass (grams)
a stone	
a Base 10 flat	
an apple	
a cube block	
a plasticine ball	
Choose your own object:	

Problem solving

For water:
1 mL = 1 cm^3 = 1 g

Mass of water

1 Find out what a litre of water weighs.

You will need scales, a litre measure, water and a large empty container. Prove your outcomes by weighing the water in different containers. Keep a record of your findings.

Mass of container	Mass of container + 1 L water	Mass of 1 L water

2 Find the weight of the following amounts of water in the same way.

a 1500 mL ____________ b 650 mL ____________

c 3 L ____________ d 2·4 L ____________

e Explain what you have found. ________________________________

3 a The mass of 10 mL of water = ________ b The mass of 100 mL of water = ________

The volume of 10 mL of water = ________ The volume of 100 mL of water = ________

4 Give the volume (cm^3), capacity (mL) and mass (g) of the water in the following:

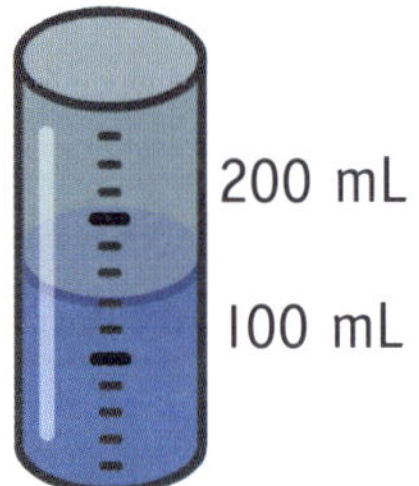

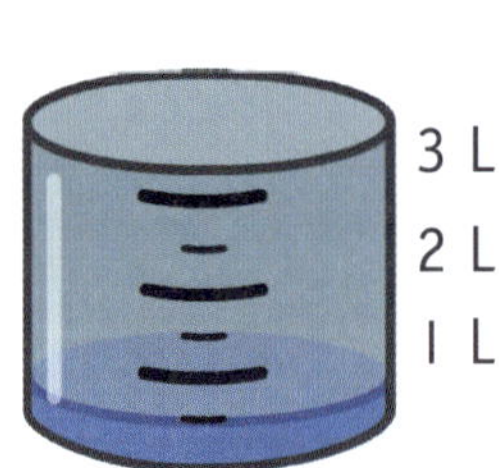

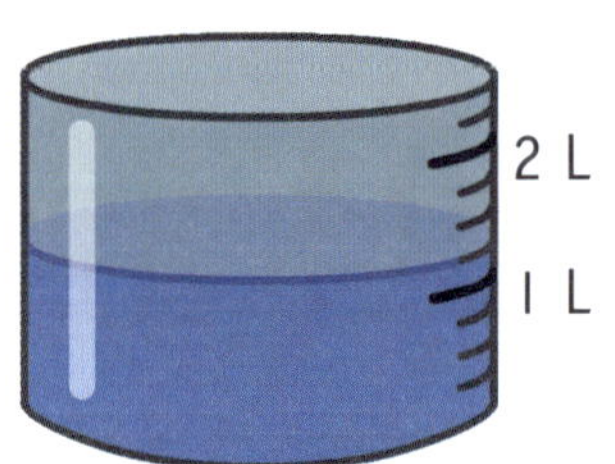

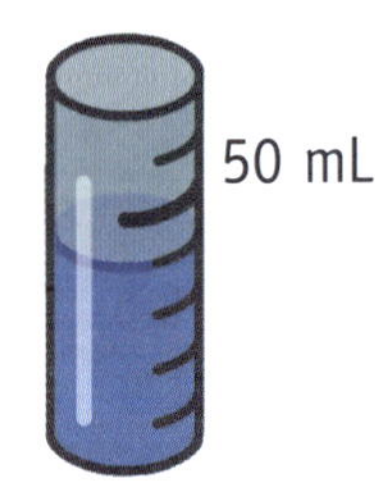

a Volume = ☐ Capacity = ☐ Mass = ☐

b Volume = ☐ Capacity = ☐ Mass = ☐

c Volume = ☐ Capacity = ☐ Mass = ☐

d Volume = ☐ Capacity = ☐ Mass = ☐

5 Complete the tables.

Litres	Millilitres
a 0·2 L	
b 0·6 L	
c	850 mL

Capacity	Mass
a 2500 mL	
b	300 g
c 2·5 L	

I can solve problems by:

☐ understanding volume ☐ converting measurements.

 AC9M6M01 Measurement **MAO-WM-01** Working mathematically • choosing and applying mathematical techniques to solve problems • communicating thinking and reasoning coherently and clearly • **MA3-3DS-02** • **MA3-NSM-01** Three-dimensional spatial structure A • Volume: Connect decimal representations to the metric system

Unit 19 Capacity and volume

Wilde Water Aquariums

Wonders under water
see it all here

Remember!
Volume = length × width × depth
1 m^3 holds 1000 L water
1·5 m^3 holds 1500 L water
1 L water weighs 1 kg

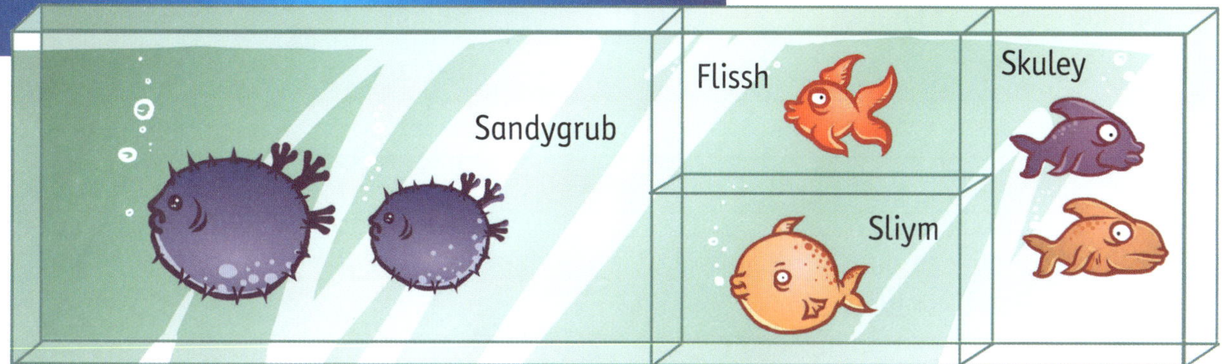

1 Kenny the Keeper is very proud of his exhibits. He needs help understanding the amount of water to keep in each tank. Help him by filling in the table. Use a calculator.

Tank	Length	Width	Depth	m^3	Capacity L	Note
a SANDYGRUB	1·5 m	1 m	1·2 m			large eater
b FLISSH	0·8 m	1 m	0·8 m			friendly
c SLIYM	0·8 m	1 m	0·7 m			rare
d SKULEY	0·7 m	1 m	1·2 m			dangerous

2 What is the mass of the water in each tank?

a Sandygrub ________ b Flissh ________ c Sliym ________ d Skuley ________

3 If the depths of water are reduced by 10 cm in each tank, how much water will be needed to fill them again? **Flissh Tank: 0·8 m × 1 m × 0·1 m = 0·08 L = 80 L**

a Sandygrub Tank:	b Sliym Tank:	c Skuley Tank:

Mastery Checklist I can:
- ☐ compare volumes of rectangular prisms
- ☐ use displacement to calculate the volume of an object
- ☐ explore the differences between mass and volume.

AC9M6M01 Measurement **MA3-3DS-02** Three-dimensional spatial structure B • Volume: Recognise the multiplicative structure for finding volume • Volume: Find the volumes of rectangular prisms in cubic centimetres and cubic metres

Problem solving

Finding volume

1 Use centimetre cubes to build three different rectangular prisms with a volume of 36 cm³.

Volume	Length	Width	Height
a 36 cm³			
b 36 cm³			
c 36 cm³			

Volume
is the amount of space something occupies.

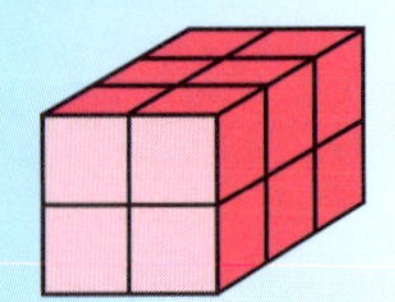

Dimensions = 2 × 2 × 3
Volume = 12 cubic units

If a swimming pool popped out of the ground, it would look like this. The pool has no deep or shallow end.

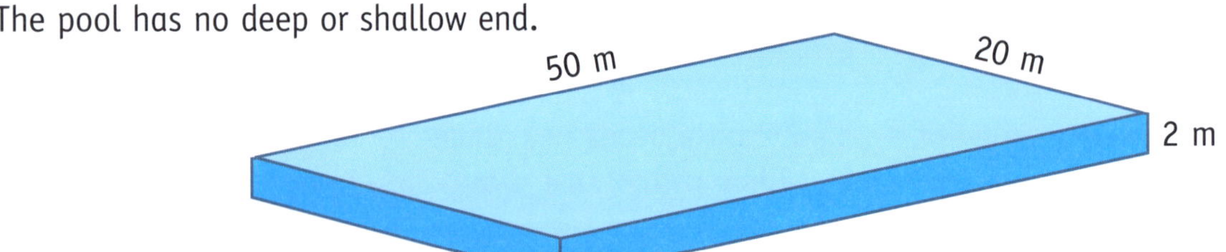

2 Write the dimensions of the pool here. ______

3 Use Base ten blocks to build a model of the pool where 1 flat = 100 m³.

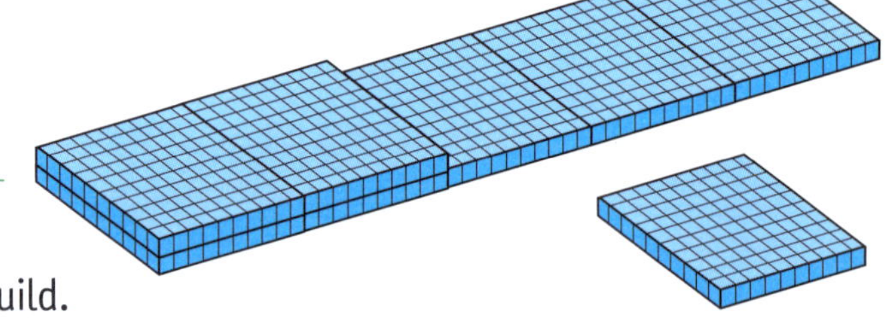

a What is the volume in m³? ______

b Using the same number of flats, find the dimensions of other pools which you can build.

______

4 What are the dimensions of a pool which has the surface area of the original pool?

______

5 What are the volumes of the following irregular 3D objects?

a

b

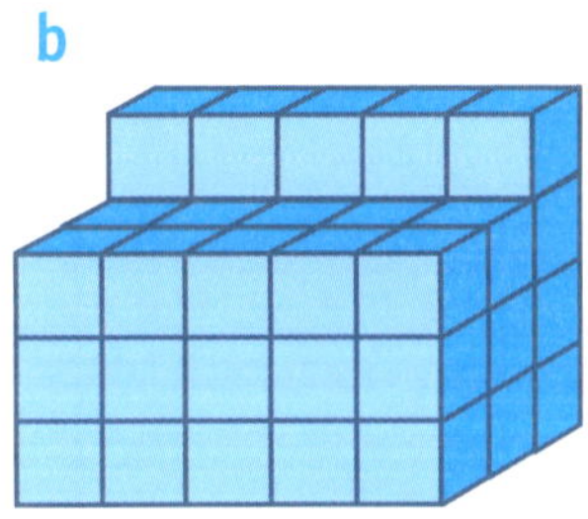

c

d

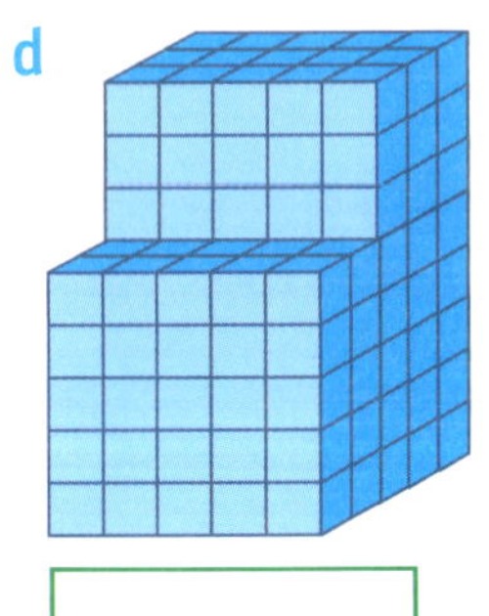

I can solve problems by:

☐ understanding volume ☐ writing equations.

 AC9M6N09 Number **AC9M6M02** Measurement **MAO-WM-01** Working mathematically • choosing and applying mathematical techniques to solve problems • communicating thinking and reasoning coherently and clearly • **MA3-3DS-02** Three-dimensional spatial structure B • Volume: Find the volumes of rectangular prisms in cubic centimetres and cubic metres

Unit 20 24-hour time

AIRPORTTRANS TIMETABLE

Central to Terminal 1

Central	Beltone	Daytown	Jacksville	Terminal 1
1410	1427	1439	1450	1458
1420	1437	1449	a	b
1415	1432	1444	c	d
1425	1442	1454	1505	1513
1430	1447	1459	e	f
1445	1502	1514	1525	1533

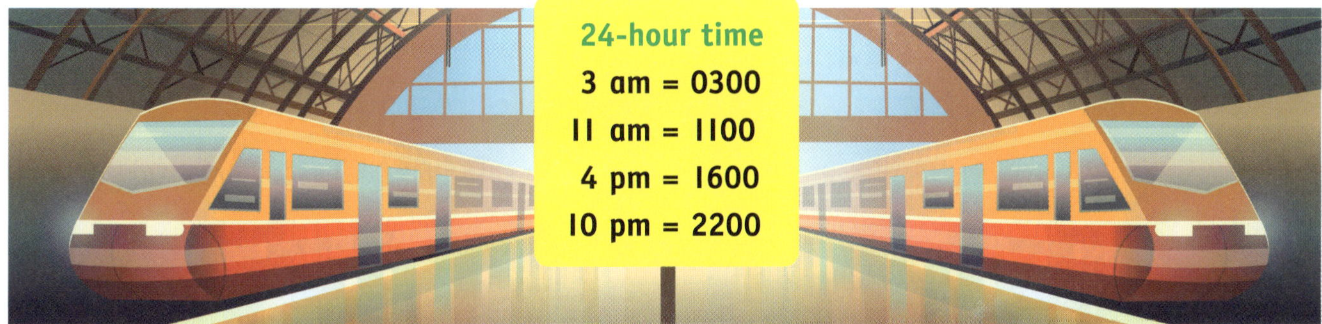

Terminal 1 to Central

Terminal 1	Jacksville	Daytown	Beltone	Central
1525	1533	1544	1556	1613
1540	1548	1559	1610	1628
1555	1603	1614	1625	1642
1610	1618	1629	1640	g
1625	1633	1644	h	i
1640	1648	1659	j	k

1 Complete the missing information on the timetable, keeping the same time lapses between stops.

2 a Josie's closest station is Central, and she wishes to meet her cousin on time at Terminal 1 at 3:30 pm. After meeting, the two will collect baggage, have a snack, then travel back to Central. Plan the travel for Josie and her cousin so that Josie is back at Central by 5:00 pm.

Leave Central ______________ Arrive Terminal 1 ______________

Collect baggage and have snack ______________

Leave Terminal 1 ______________ Arrive Central ______________

b When Josie arrives back at Central Station, how long will it have been since she left?

____

Unit 20 Using a timeline

This timeline shows the important events of Davina's life.

0	a	b	c	d	e	12 yrs
	Cut first tooth	Rode first bicycle	Moved to Albury	Holiday in Qld	Elected captain	

1 a Davina's timeline shows 12 years and is 18 cm long.
What scale has been used? ______ cm = ______ yr

b Accurately mark the other years of Davina's life.

2 How old was Davina when:

a she cut her first tooth? ____________
b she rode her first bicycle? ____________
c she moved to Albury? ____________
d she was elected school captain? ____________

3 Draw a timeline of your own life, placing 5 important events on this line.

Scale: 1 year = ____________

Write 3 questions for other students to answer about your timeline.

a ______________________________

b ______________________________

c ______________________________

4 a Draw a timeline for the next 5 years of your life. Add the events you hope will occur in that time.

Scale: 1 year = ____________

b Have a partner check your timeline for accuracy.

Unit 20 Timelines

1 Place these events in order of how a new game is developed, earliest (1) to latest (6).

November 2022 – Game idea created. ______

January 2023 – Code written. ______

May 2023 – Focus group feedback. ______

November 2023 – Animation completed. ______

April 2023 – Game testing. ______

February 2024 – Game goes on sale. ______

2 How many months from the earliest to the latest dates of the game's development? ________

3 If these events are on a timeline 15 cm long, what would be a suitable scale? ____________

4 Willgarong Public School was inaugurated in 2001. The following article in the Willgarong News relates the important events of its history on the occasion of its 22nd anniversary. Draw a line for WPS's timeline, using a scale of **1 cm = 2 yrs**.

Place the following events on the timeline.

SCHOOL **DAZE**

Ellie Snapshut: Willgarong. Hundreds of ex-pupils of Willgarong PS flocked to the 22nd Anniversary celebrations. Some ex-pupils even remembered a similar celebration 20 years ago. That was the year the library was completed and opened.

Current Headmaster, Mr Floggins, who arrived at WPS in 2013 spoke of his most vivid memory: that of the visit of the Prime Minister in 2016 to honour students who had gained high distinctions in the National Science/Mathematics Challenge the year before.

The oldest teacher present was Mr Rasem, Sport and PE, who wore the pin awarded to him by the P & C in 2006, when the school won the district athletics carnival. Mr Rasem retired in 2017 and still lives in Willgarong.

The latest addition to the school, an arts centre, opened in 2021, was open for inspection. It was voted "the most dazzling addition to the school" by all who saw it.

Timeline

Mastery Checklist I can:

- ☐ convert between 12-hour and 24-hour time
- ☐ interpret timelines
- ☐ draw timelines.

Unit 21 Map reading

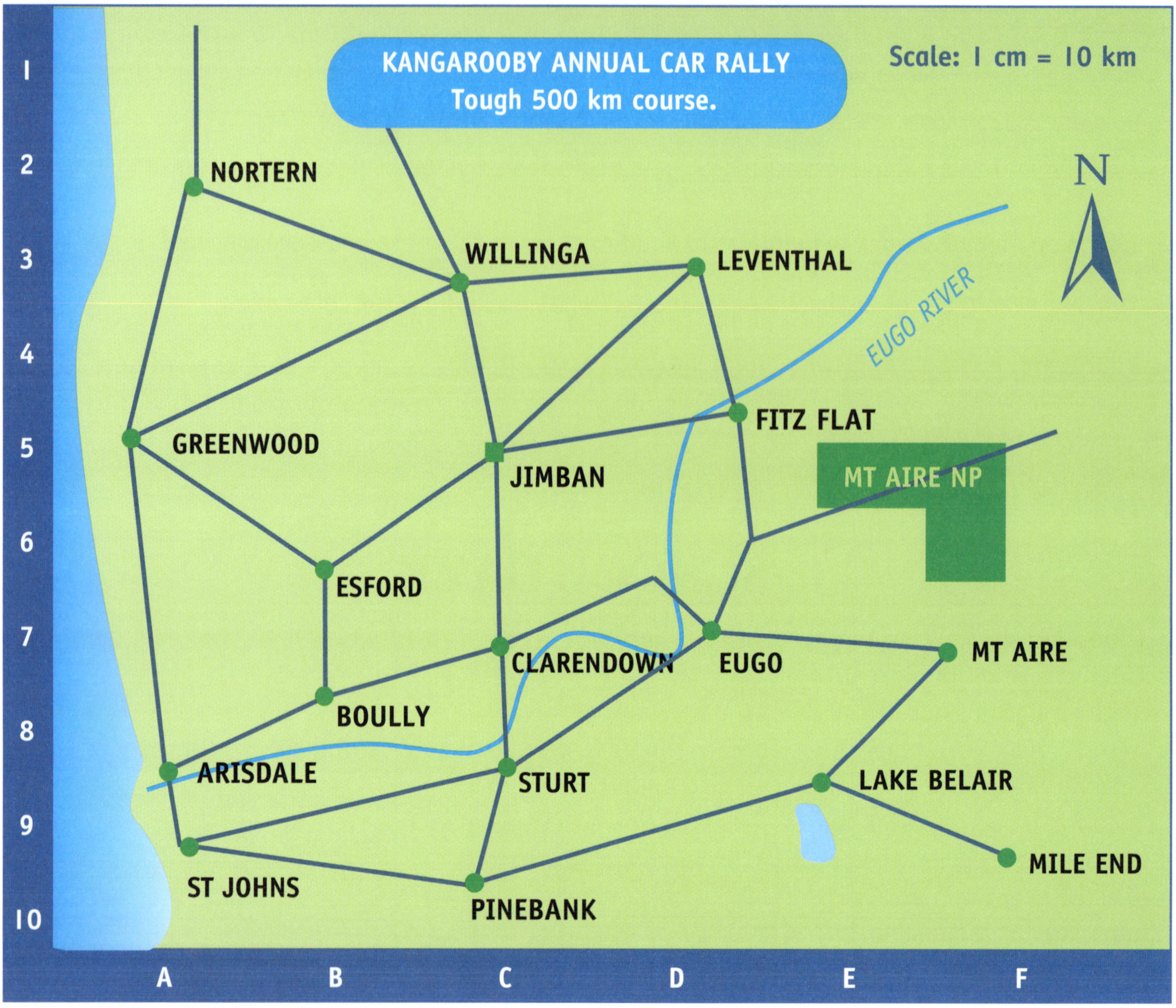

Position 

KANGAROOBY ANNUAL CAR RALLY
Tough 500 km course.

Scale: 1 cm = 10 km

N

NORTERN
WILLINGA
LEVENTHAL
EUGO RIVER
GREENWOOD
FITZ FLAT
JIMBAN
MT AIRE NP
ESFORD
CLARENDOWN
EUGO
MT AIRE
BOULLY
ARISDALE
STURT
LAKE BELAIR
ST JOHNS
PINEBANK
MILE END

1 2 3 4 5 6 7 8 9 10

A B C D E F

1 Calculate the distance between Arisdale and Clarendown. ______________

2 You find Nortern at the coordinate A2. What are the coordinates for:

a Jimban? ______________ b Lake Belair? ______________

Scale can be expressed as ratio. This scale would be 1:1 000 000 as a ratio.

3 1 cm on the map is equal to ____________________ cm on the land.

4 The directions to drive from home in Leventhal to Arisdale are: **leaving Leventhal, drive west to Willinga, south to Jimban, south-west to Esford, south to Boully, and south-west to Arisdale.**

Write the directions to get home again. ______________________________

____

____

5 What is the shortest route from Mt Aire to Greenwood? ______________________________

____

AC9M6N01 Number **AC9M6SP02** Space **MA3-GM-01** Geometric measure A • Position: Explore the Cartesian coordinate system • Geometric measure B • Length: Solve problems involving the comparison of lengths using appropriate units

Unit 21 Scale and ratio

Scale 1 cm = 5 km means 1 cm on paper equals 5 km on land.
Scale = 1:10 means the drawing is $\frac{1}{10}$ the real size.
Multiply to find the real measurements from the scale drawing.

1 Label the dimensions of these polygons.

Scale 1 cm = 5 m or 1:500

a

b

c

d

e

f

2 If the scale of the above shapes is 1:10, what are the dimensions?

	a	b	c	d	e	f
Length of sides						

3 Refer to the map on page 96. Use the scale to calculate distances.

a To the nearest 10 km, how long is the coastline on this map? ____________

b How far from Eugo is Mt Aire? ____________

c Which is further from Jimban, Sturt or Nortern? ____________

d The rally is not exactly 500 km but very close. Leaving Arisdale, it travels to Nortern, Leventhal, Jimban, Eugo, Lake Belaire and finishes in Arisdale.
Find another course that is close to 500 km. ____________

____

4 The land covered on the map is 170 km wide by 145 km long and the map is 17 cm × 14·5 cm. If the scale was changed to 1 cm = 20 km, would the rectangle be larger or smaller?

____

5 How many square kilometres is Mt Aire National Park? ____________

Challenge!

Which scale would be on the smallest map representing Mt Aire National Park?
1:250, 1 cm = 10 000 m, 1:100 000, 5:5000, 1 cm = 500 000 cm, 2 cm = 10 000 cm

Unit 21 Using a street directory

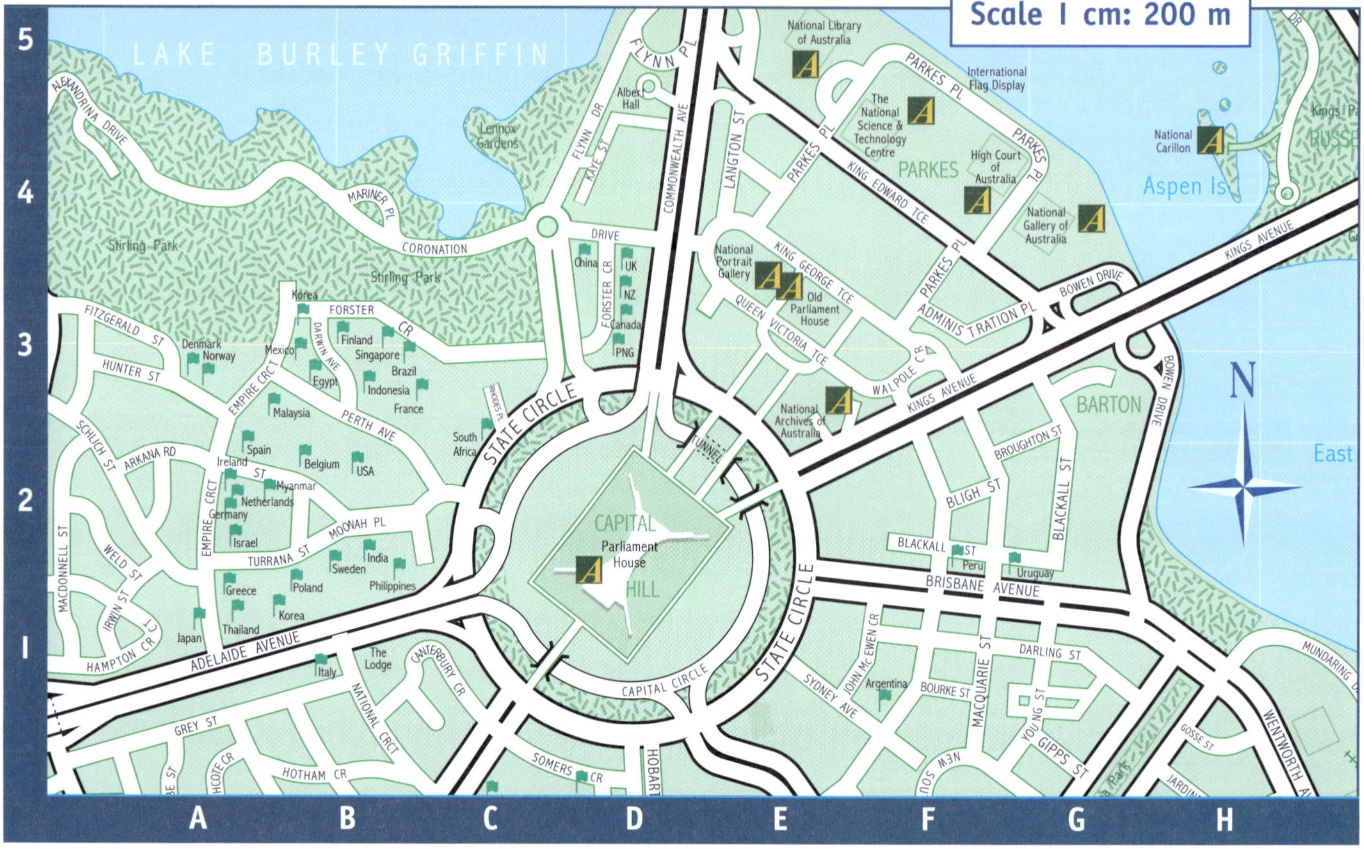

Position

Scale 1 cm: 200 m

1 What can be found at the following coordinates?

a C4 ______ b E5 ______ c E4 ______ d D2 ______

e D5 ______ f A3 ______ g C3 ______ h A5 ______

2 What are the coordinates for:

a National Carillon? ______ b the Lodge? ______ c the US Embassy? ______

3 To walk from Kings Avenue Bridge to Old Parliament House, the following directions were given. Walk south-west along Kings Avenue, turn right onto King Edward Terrace, and north on Parkes Place to King George Terrace. Where did they go wrong? ______

4 Give the directions correctly. ______

______

______

______

5 Give two references for the following places:

a Commonwealth Avenue ______ b Flynn Drive ______

c Stirling Park ______ d Parliament House ______

6 Note the scale on the map. What is the:

a distance across State Circle? ______ b length of King Edward Terrace? ______

c distance from the National Gallery to the High Court of Australia? ______

Problem solving

Scale on maps

1 Study this map.

Draw and label a grid on it to assist in finding places listed on the key.

Hint: Use 2 cm spaces.

It is 10 km from Skubbo to Coren. Calculate the scale and write it on the key.

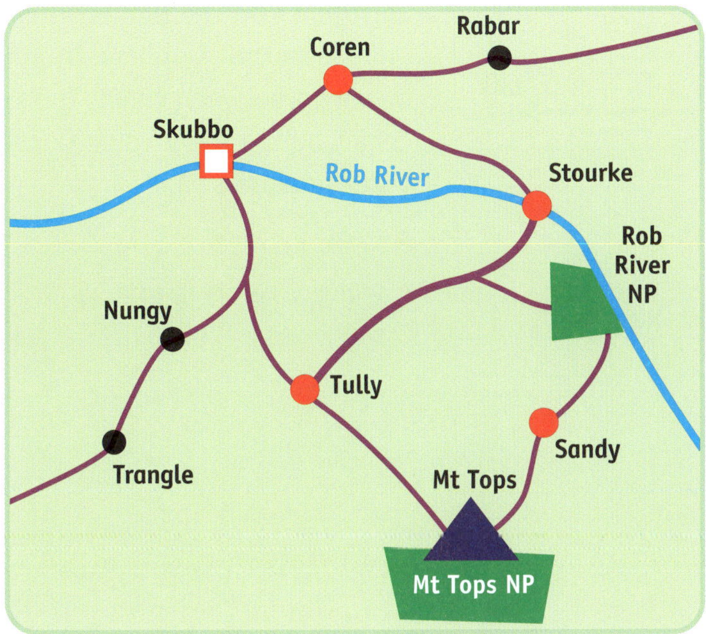

KEY

Scale: ______

Coren	C 5
Mt Tops NP	D 1
Mt Tops	D 1
Nungy	B 3
Rabar	D 5
Rob River NP	E 3
Sandy	D 2
Skubbo	B 4
Stourke	D 3
Trangle	A 2
Tully	C 2

2 This map is of the same area as in Question 1. What is the scale of this new map?

______

3 a On map 1, what direction is Coren from Tully?

______

b On map 2, what direction is Coren from Tully?

______

4 Complete:

Different scale makes ______ difference to direction.

5 a What direction is Mt Tops from Tully? ______

b What town is East of Coren? ______

c What direction is the Rob River flowing as it leaves Stourke and flows past the Rob River National Park? ______

d Symbols show different things on maps. What does each of these mean? ☐ ______

I can solve problems by:

☐ undertanding scale on maps ☐ using visual thinking.

Unit 21 The Cartesian Plane

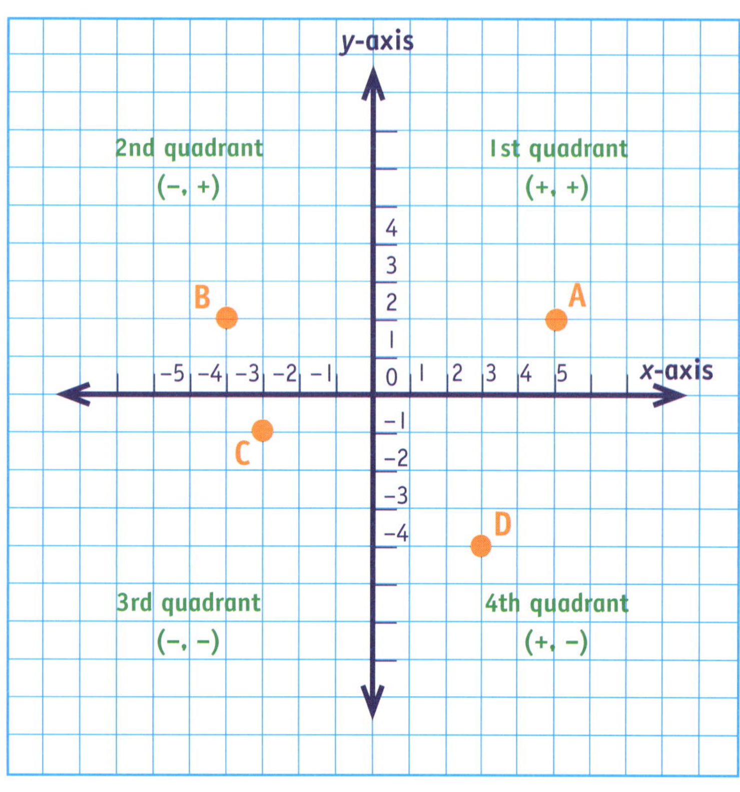

The plane has 4 quadrants and two axes.

The axes intersect at right angles at the point of origin (0, 0).

Axes can go on forever, so they have arrows at each end.

Each point on the plane is named by an ordered pair of numbers, in brackets with a comma between them. The *x* value always comes before the *y* value (x comes before y in the alphabet).

A is (5, 2), **B** is (–4, 2),

C is (–3, –1), **D** is (3, –4)

On this Cartesian Plane mark and name:

1 the axes.

2 the origin.

3 the scale (one number per square).

4 these points **G** (2, 2), **R** (4, –3), **E** (–1, 4), **A** (3, 1), **T** (–2, –4).

5 Write the ordered pair for:

M ___________

N ___________

P ___________

Q ___________

6 Add three of your own points to the plane. Write the ordered pairs.

____

____

____

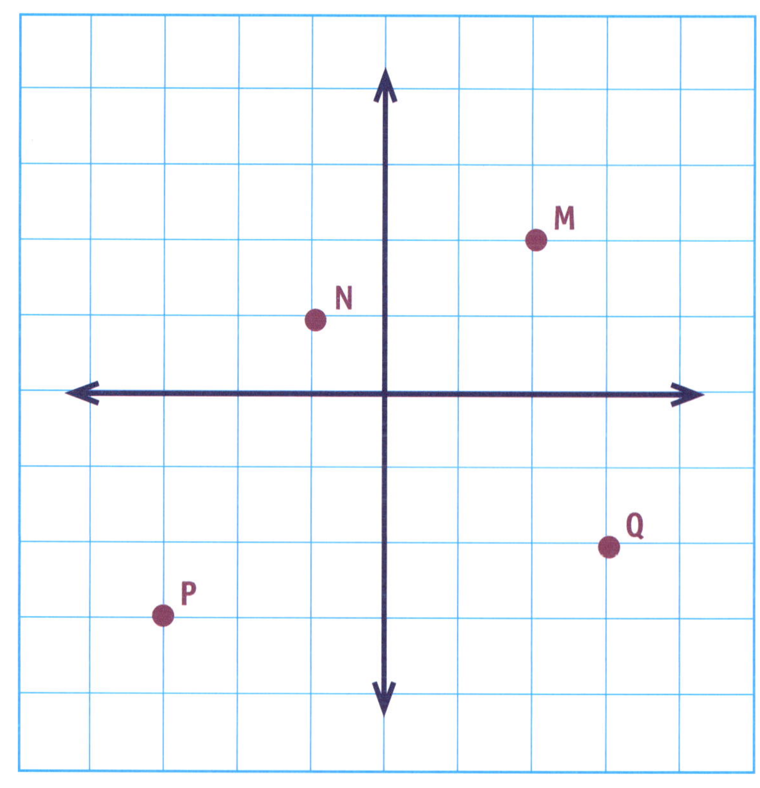

Unit 21 Plotting points

Position

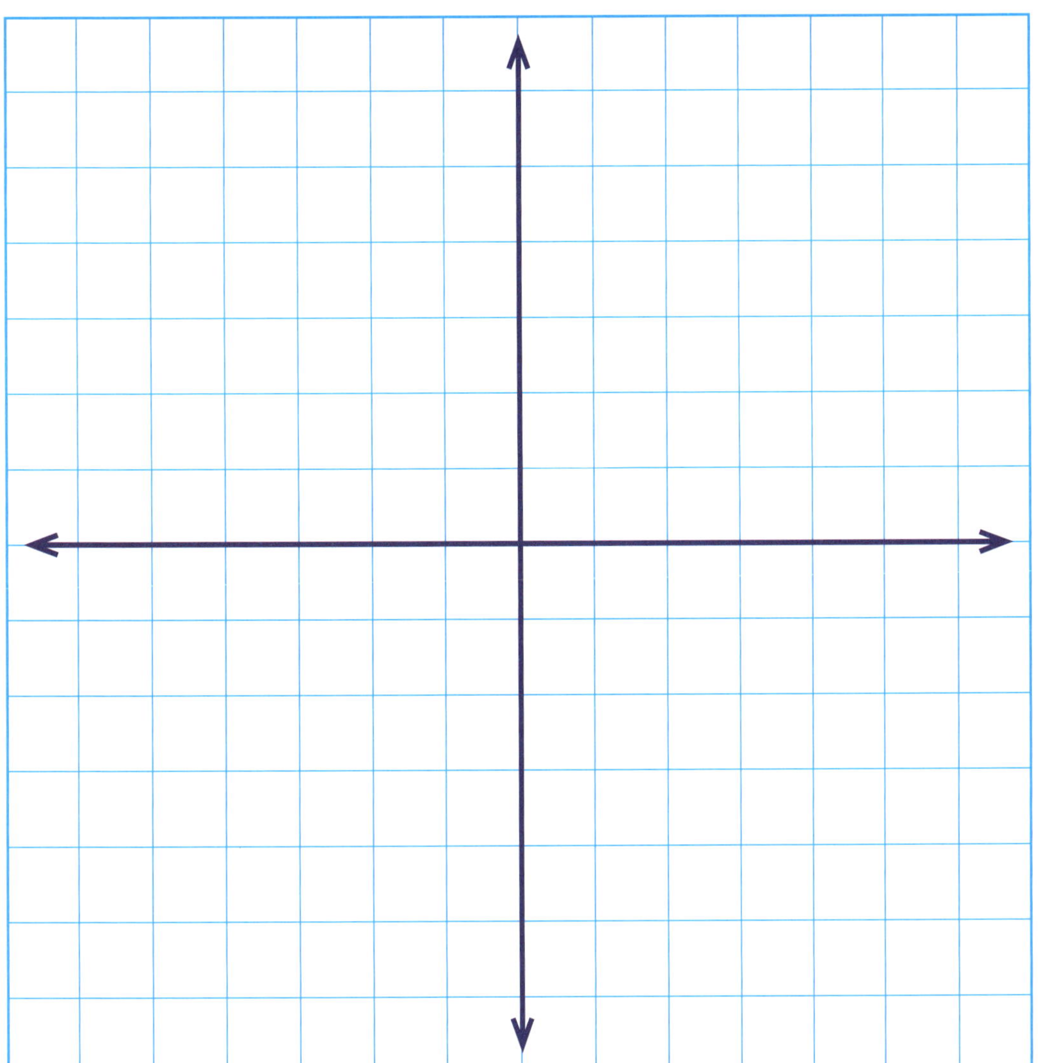

1 Mark:

a the axes. b the origin. c the scale on each axis.

2 Mark in these points:

A (0, 6), B (–5, –5), C (6, 2), D (–6, 2), E (5, –5)

3 In which quadrant does each point lie?

A ____________, B ____________, C ____________, D ____________, E ____________

4 Join A → B → C → D → E → A

5 What shape have you drawn? ______________________________

Mastery Checklist I can:
- ☐ use scale to solve length problems
- ☐ use a grid to identify locations
- ☐ identify features of the Cartesian number plane
- ☐ read point on the Cartesian number plane
- ☐ plot points on the Cartesian number plane.

Unit 22 Line graphs

Graphs 1 & 2

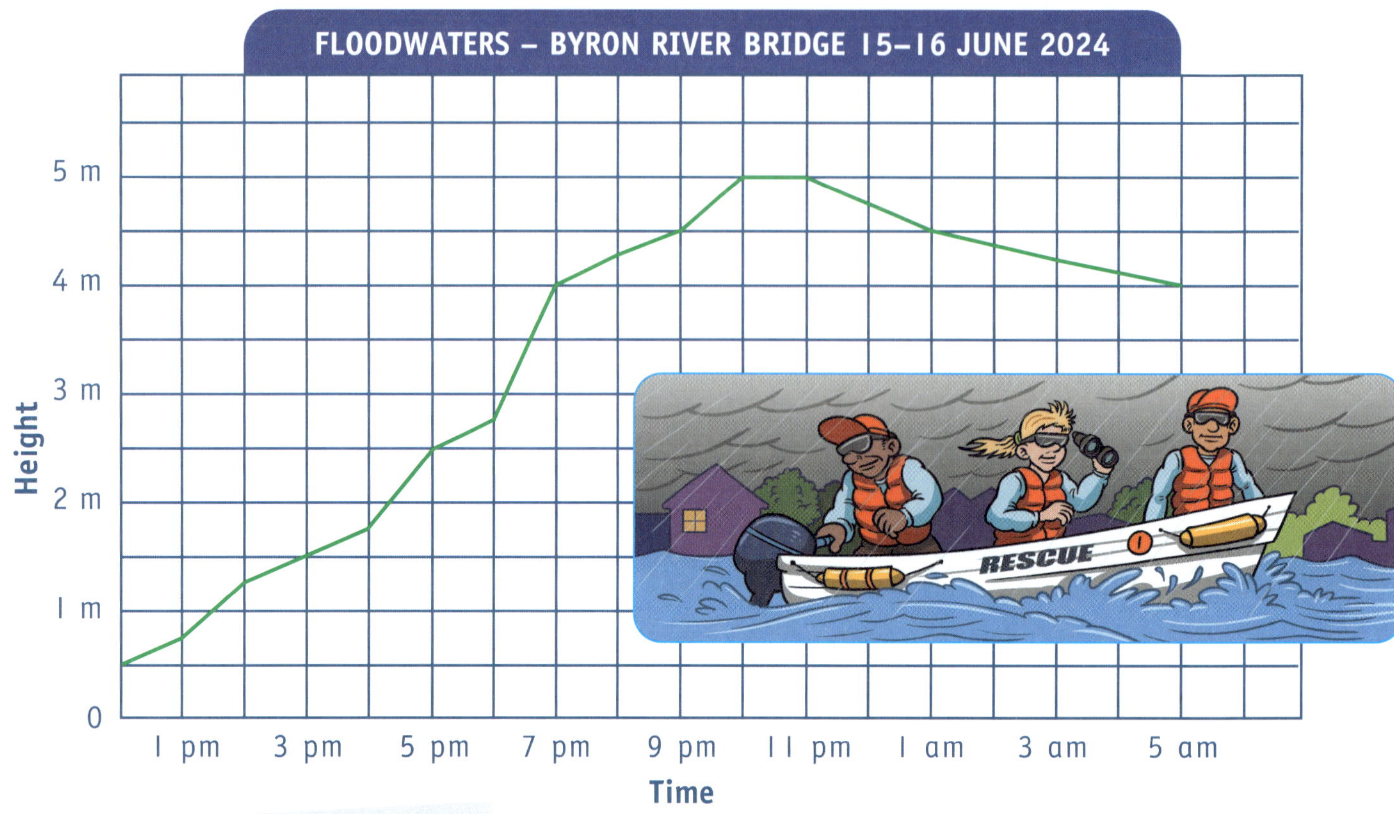

DISASTER NEAR

Byron floodwaters on the rise.

Floodwaters have risen alarmingly on the Byron River. The Byron Bridge on the road to town is under water. Measurements are regularly being taken to determine when rescues will need to be made. The Byron District Rescue Squad is on standby, ready to swing into action.

Colour the bubble beside the best answer.

1 What would have made the news report more useful?

- a the writer's name ◯
- b the river heights during the afternoon ◯
- c the height of the river that will cause evacuations ◯
- d the number of people in the District Rescue Squad ◯

2 What types of writing can be misleading in a news report?

- a Descriptive writing ◯
- b Factual writing ◯
- c Emotional writing ◯

3 Which sentence more accurately describes 'Floodwaters have risen alarmingly on the Byron River'?

- a Floodwaters have risen sharply on the Byron River. ◯
- b Floodwaters have risen by 4.5 metres on the Byron River. ◯
- c Floodwaters have risen in 10 hours on the Byron River. ◯
- d Floodwaters on the Byron River have risen all day. ◯

4 What information about rescues should be included in this news report?

- a the time the water will go down ◯
- b the number of houses in the danger area ◯
- c how rescues will be made ◯
- d the river height when evacuations will start ◯

Unit 22 Making comparisons

Graphs 1 & 2

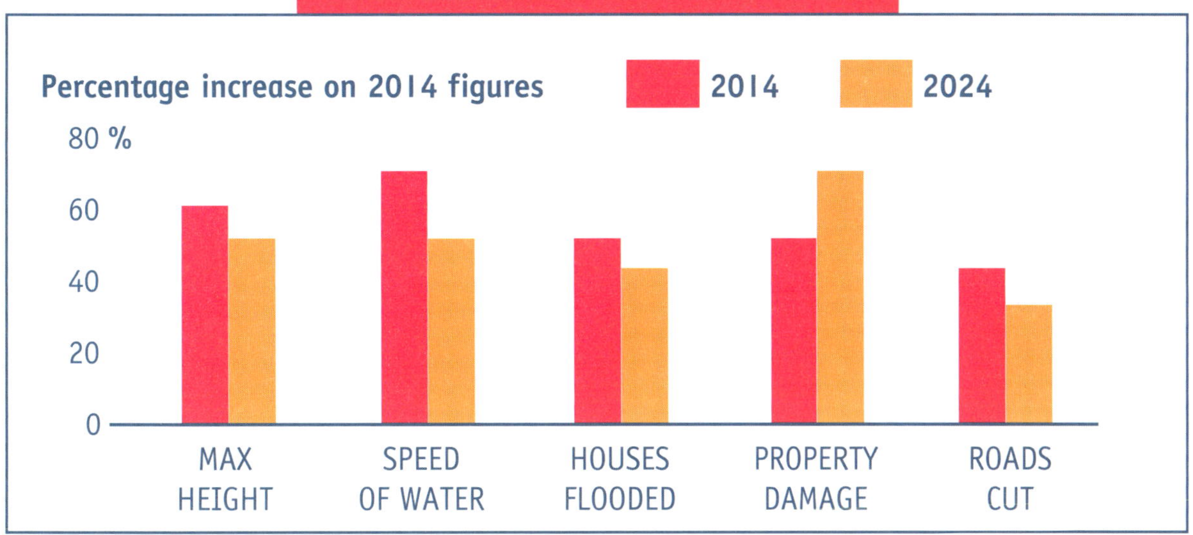

1 Which statements are true? Tick them.

The river heights, compared to those in 2014, were higher in 2014 than in 2024. ☐

More houses were inundated in 2024 than in 2014. ☐

The damage to property was greater in 2024 than in 2014. ☐

The flood of 2014 was worse than in 2024 in all categories. ☐

Property damage was greater in 2024 because more houses were flooded in that year. ☐

2 Why were fewer roads cut in 2024 than in 2014? Tick two reasons.

The water was not as high. ☐

It was harder for the water to cut a road in 2024. ☐

There were more roads cut in 2024. ☐

The water was not flowing so quickly. ☐

3 Study this side-by-side graph.

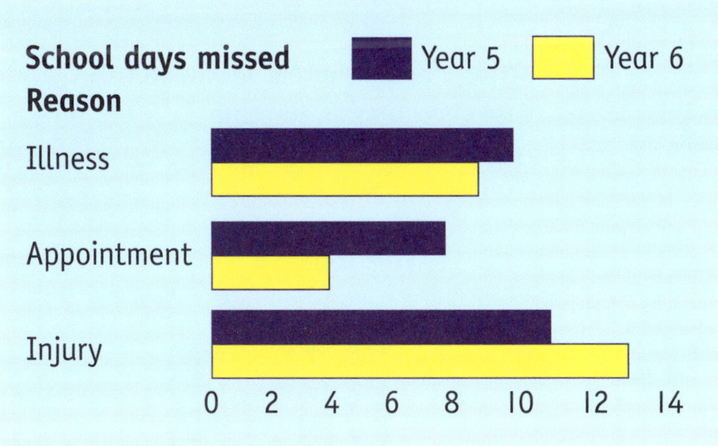

True or false?

a One grade has a better record than the other in all areas. ________

b This graph measures reasons for school days being missed. ________

c The Year 5 and Year 6 total days missed is the same. ________

Mastery Checklist I can:
- ☐ investigate how data is presented in media reports
- ☐ decide if statements about data are accurate.

Revision Term 2

1 Complete the series.

a prime numbers >10 and <30 p 58

11, ______

b composite numbers >18 and <30 p 59

20, ______

2 Fill in this number line from –5 to +5, including zero. p 60

3 Follow the correct order of operations. p 63

a $30 + 4^2 \times 3 - 16$ = ______

b $25 - 15 \div 3 + 6$ = ______

c $\frac{1}{2}$ of $54 - 6 \times 3$ = ______

d $(72 \div 8 - 7) \times 2$ = ______

4 p 67

a 708 × 25

b 902 × 53

5 Write equivalent fractions. p 69

a $\frac{1}{3}, \frac{\square}{6}, \frac{\square}{12}, \frac{\square}{15}, \frac{\square}{24}$

b $\frac{1}{4}, \frac{\square}{8}, \frac{\square}{12}, \frac{\square}{16}, \frac{\square}{24}, \frac{\square}{100}$

c $\frac{3}{4}, \frac{\square}{8}, \frac{\square}{12}, \frac{\square}{16}, \frac{\square}{100}$

d $\frac{1}{5}, \frac{\square}{10}, \frac{\square}{15}, \frac{\square}{20}, \frac{\square}{100}$

6 p 70

a $\frac{5}{8}$ of the children went by bus and $\frac{1}{8}$ drove in cars. What fraction travelled? ______

b $\frac{3}{4} - \frac{3}{8}$ = ______

c From 1 take $\frac{5}{12}$. ______

d $\frac{3}{16} + \frac{5}{16} + \frac{1}{16}$ = ______

e $\frac{3}{10}$ of the day was spent walking and $\frac{2}{10}$ was spent resting. What fraction of the day was left? ______

7 p 73

a $\frac{1}{5} \times 3$ = ______

b $\frac{3}{8} \times 2$ = ______

c $\frac{7}{100} \times 6$ = ______

d $\frac{3}{20} \times 5$ = ______

Write answers as mixed numerals. p 74

e $\frac{3}{4} \times 3$ = ______

f $6 \times \frac{2}{3}$ = ______

g $8 \times \frac{1}{5}$ = ______

h $\frac{5}{8} \times 4$ = ______

8 Calculate the new price in each case. p 77

a Discount 25%

b Discount 10%

c GST 10%

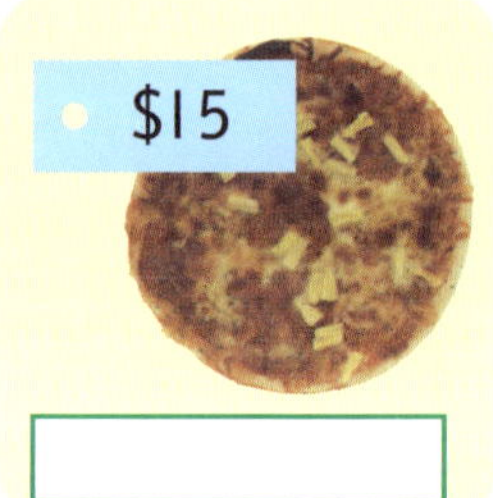

d GST 10%

9 Write the perimeters in kilometres and the areas in hectares. p 87

a

300 m

100 m

100 m

150 m

P = ______ A = ______

Revision Term 2

b

p 87

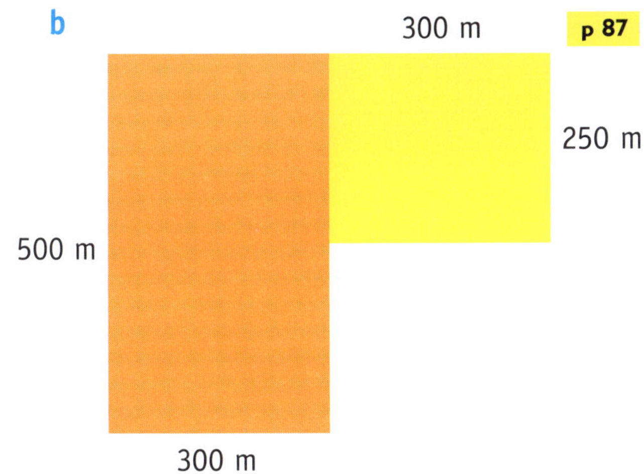

P = __________ A = __________

10

p 87

How many wooden blocks 3 cm × 2 cm × 2 cm will fit into a box 12 cm × 8 cm × 8 cm?

p 88

11 Draw an object with a volume of 10 cm^3.

12

p 89

a Volume of water before object is added:

____

b Volume of water and object: __________

c Volume of object: __________

13 What is the volume?

p 92

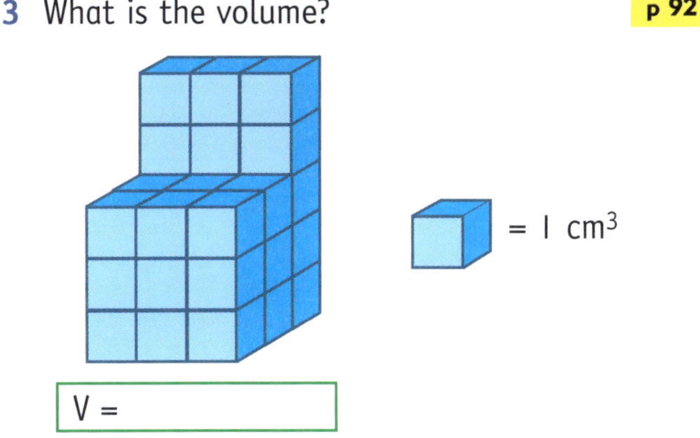

14 Name these points on the second quadrant of the Cartesian plane.

p 100

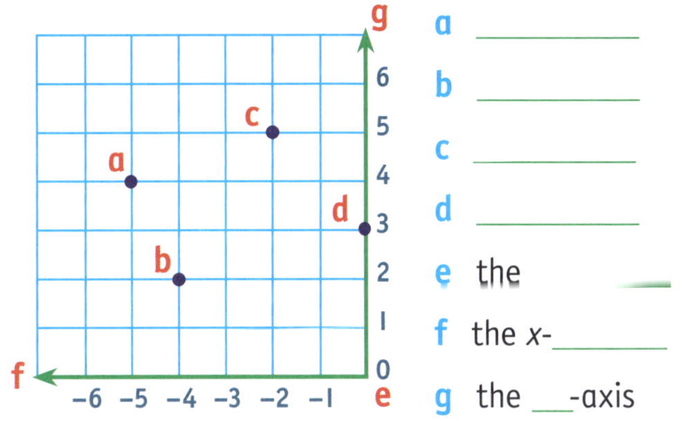

a __________

b __________

c __________

d __________

e the __________

f the *x*-__________

g the ___-axis

15

p 103

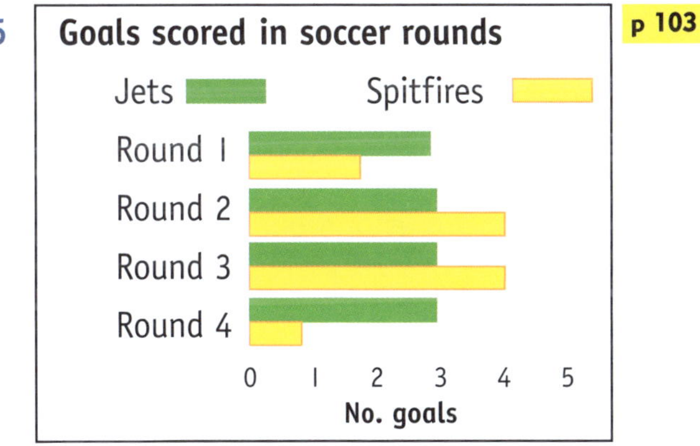

True or false?

a After 4 rounds, the teams had equal wins. __________

b The Jets scored an average of 3 goals per match. __________

c The Spitfires' results were unpredictable. __________

Unit 23 Operations with money

BANK ONE
City Place, WA

BANK STATEMENT

Mrs Kristine Jones
2/67 Walgett St
Trangle WA 6894
Account Number: 234-534-763489 00021

Statement period: 15/5/24-15/6/24

page 23

Date	Transaction description	Debit Withdrawals	Credit Deposits	Balance
2024				500·60
15 May	Eftpos, XBC	-127·00		373·60
17 May	Payment to HMF	-135·00		238·60
18 May	Pay/Salary		+3105·00	3343·60
19 May	Eftpos, Johnstone Bros	-38·25		3305·35
20 May	Account Fees	-8·50		
22 May	Bank One, ATM	-250·00		
26 May	Eftpos, Phyxme Chemist	-65·05		
28 May	Eftpos, Vegie Delight	-62·00		
30 May	Payment to Veester Gold	-204·00		
2 Jun	Pay/Salary		+3105·00	
4 Jun	Bank One, ATM	-250·00		
5 Jun	Interest		+1·25	

1 Complete the balance details.

2 Define the features of a bank statement.

a Withdrawal ______________________

b Deposit ______________________

c Transaction ______________________

d Salary ______________________

e Debit ______________________

f Credit ______________________

g Balance ______________________

h ATM ______________________

i Eftpos ______________________

j Interest as credit ______________________

Unit 23 Budget calculations

Use Mrs Jones' bank statement on page 106 to answer the following questions.
Estimate your answers first.

Problem	Working
1 Each fortnight, Mrs Jones earns $3105 and has to pay rent of $790. What does she have left for all other expenses each fortnight?	Estimate ________
2 Bank fees are a debit and Interest is a credit. What is the difference between them?	Estimate ________
3 From the ATM cash Mrs Jones took out on 22 May, she spent $27.35 on vegetables and fruit. How much did she have left?	Estimate ________
4 On the Veester Gold account, $75.10 was for clothing, $25.70 was for a gift, $22.95 was for a book and the balance was spent at restaurants. How much did Mrs Jones spend at restaurants?	Estimate ________
5 For the fortnight 18 May to 30 May inclusive, what was the total of Mrs Jones' expenditures?	Estimate ________
6 On 6 June, Mrs Jones pays $89.95 for shoes, $76.85 for groceries, as well as repays $950 to her mother. How much will she have left?	Estimate ________
7 How often is Mrs Jones' salary deposited into her account?	Estimate ________

Unit 23 Cost calculations

- Read each question carefully.
- Use estimation strategies to approximate the answer.
- Show your working, and record your answer.

Problem	Estimate	Working	Answer
1 Discount shopping You have a 15% discount on a $38 toy. Estimate the final price after the discount using rounding to the nearest dollar.			
2 Groceries estimate Estimate the total cost of these grocery shops: $18.75, $42.50 and $32.25. Round to the nearest $10.			
3 Percentage increase A shirt was priced at $30 and now it is $36. Estimate the percentage increase using rounding.			
4 Budgeting estimate You want 15% of your $120 allowance. Estimate the amount left over using rounding.			
5 Movie Ticket estimate A movie ticket costs $10.75. Estimate the cost of 4 tickets using rounding.			
6 Petrol cost estimate You estimate your car will need 32 L of petrol for a road trip. Petrol costs $2.38 per litre. Use rounding to estimate the total cost.			
7 Sale and regular price A pair of shoes is labelled 30% off. The discounted price is $42. Estimate the original price using rounding.			

Mastery Checklist I can:
- ☐ recognise features of a bank statement
- ☐ answer questions about a bank statement
- ☐ estimate answers to money problems.

Problem solving

Best buy

The Krumpit Kids are having a celebration for their win.

1 Find the best buys for the group of 3 Krumpit Kids and their 3 friends.

Pizza	large	12 slices	$22
	medium	8 slices	$15
	small	6 slices	$12

______________________ is best at __________ for 1 slice.

Drinks	3 L bottle	12 drinks	$4
	2 L bottle	8 drinks	$3.50

______________________ is best at __________ for one 200 mL drink.

Sweets	500 g bag	$4.80
	1 kg bag	$8.60

______________________ is best at __________ for 100 g.

Cupcakes	10 for $8
	20 for $12

______________________ is best at __________ each.

Working space

Challenge!

How many of each item is needed for the 6 friends if they have two of everything?

Pizza __________ Drink __________ Sweets __________ Cupcakes __________

I can solve problems by:

☐ adding, subtracting and multiplying decimals ☐ writing algorithms.

Unit 24 Factors and multiples

1 Circle the correct set of factors for the number given.

a **124** 1, 124, 4, 31, 8, 13
1, 124, 2, 62, 4, 31
1, 124, 2, 62, 6, 24

b **136** 1, 136, 2, 68, 4, 34, 8, 17
1, 136, 2, 68, 8, 17, 6, 14
1, 136, 2, 68, 4, 34, 12, 13

To reduce a fraction to its lowest terms, divide numerator and denominator by their highest common factor.

$\frac{12}{18}$ **HCF = 6**

$\frac{12 \div 6 = 2}{18 \div 6 = 3}$

2 Circle the numbers that are divisible by both three and five.

a 140 b 225 c 365 d 530

3 Which of these numbers are:

84 24 96 72 50 121 41 36 35 53

a multiples of 7? ____________ b multiples of 4? ____________
c divisible by 6? ____________ d divisible by 9? ____________
e multiples of 3 and 4? ____________ f square numbers? ____________
g prime numbers? ____________ h multiples of 2 and 5? ____________

4 Find the cloud to fit each space.

a 52 ____________ = 315 b 46 ____________ = 215 c 36 ____________ = 9
d 48 ____________ = 144 e 63 ____________ = 99 f 91 ____________ = 52

A × 2 ÷ 8
B ÷ 7 × 4
C × 6 + 3
D × 5 − 15
E ÷ 4 × 12
F ÷ 7 × 11

5 To reduce fractions like $\frac{25}{100}$ to their lowest terms, find the Highest Common Factor (HCF) of 25 and 100.

a 15 factors ____________ divide 15 ÷ ________ = ______
20 factors ____________ HCF = ________ 20 ÷ ________ = ______

b 18 factors ____________ divide 18 ÷ ________ = ______
24 factors ____________ HCF = ________ 24 ÷ ________ = ______

c 35 factors ____________ divide 35 ÷ ________ = ______
50 factors ____________ HCF = ________ 50 ÷ ________ = ______

Unit 24 Strategies for dividing by tens

36 ÷ 4 =9
36 tens ÷ 4 = 9 tens
360 ÷ 4 = 90
36 tens ÷ 4 tens = 9
360 ÷ 40 = 9

1 a 27 ÷ 3 = ______ 270 ÷ 30 = ______
b 54 ÷ 6 = ______ 540 ÷ 60 = ______
c 45 ÷ 9 = ______ 450 ÷ 90 = ______

2 a 280 ÷ 70 = ______ b 1200 ÷ 120 = ______
c 960 ÷ 80 = ______ d 770 ÷ 70 = ______

3 Write the missing numbers.
a 450 ÷ ______ = 5 b 720 ÷ ______ = 8 c 440 ÷ ______ = 40
d 350 ÷ ______ = 70 e ______ ÷ 70 = 5 f ______ ÷ 40 = 6 g ______ ÷ 80 = 50

4 Complete.
a 60) 360
b 80) 640
c 30) 240
d) 200 = 5
e 70) = 8

5 Sort the following numbers into their correct boxes.

270, 320, 450, 1000, 630, 180, 160, 810, 480

a **Divisible by 40**

b **Divisible by 50**

c **Divisible by 90**

6 How many 30 cm rulers equal the following lengths?
a 2·7 m (270 cm) ______ b 1·5 m ______
c 4·2 m ______ d 2·1 m ______
e 3 m ______ f 0·9 m ______

Challenge!

Use a calculator for repeated division. Note the pattern.

	÷ 10	÷ 10	÷ 10	÷ 10	÷ 10
a 36 796 300					
b 58 040 700					

c What happens to the decimal point? ______

Unit 24 Division by multiples of ten

3520
352 tens ÷ 1 ten = 352
352 tens ÷ 2 tens
= 352 ÷ 2
= 176

1 a 10)4680 b 10)2920 c 10)8320 d 10)7080

e 20)4680 f 40)2920 g 40)8320 h 30)7080

2 a 10)25 760 b 10)64 840 c 10)11 190 d 10)34 500

e 20)25 760 f 40)64 840 g 30)11 190 h 50)34 500

3 a 10)318 090 b 10)869 000 c 10)190 660 d 10)460 080

e 30)318 090 f 50)869 000 g 20)190 660 h 40)460 080

4 Twenty people share a winning lottery ticket with a prize of $4 500 000. How much did each receive?

Working

5 A house sells for $885K. The owner wishes to donate 10% to charity. How much will the charity receive?

Working

6 A woman's salary is $257 000 which is ten times what her son earns. How much does her son earn?

Working

Challenge!

Insect Model Scale 40:1

Length	Leg	Feeler	Abdomen	Head	Overall
Model	560 mm	360 mm	320 mm	160 mm	800 mm
Actual					

AC9M6N06 • AC9M6N09 Number MA3-MR-01 Multiplicative relations B • Multiply and divide decimals by powers of 10 • MA3-GM-02 Geometric measure B • Length: Connect decimal representations to the metric system

Unit 24 Multiply by 10, 100, 1000

1 Multiply by 10.

a 10 × 2 = ______ b 10 × 61 = ______

c 4 × 10 = ______ d 8 × 10 = ______

e 10 × 10 = ______ f 13 × 10 = ______

g 12 × 10 = ______ h 18 × 10 = ______

i 10 × 42 = ______ j 10 × 53 = ______

k 15 × 10 = ______ l 38 × 10 = ______

m 10 × 64 = ______ n 59 × 10 = ______

o 10 × 773 = ______ p 10 × 189 = ______

q 293 × 10 = ______ r 420 × 10 = ______

10 has 1 zero, so when you multiply by 10, add 1 zero.
eg 10 × 6 = 60

2 Multiply by 100.

a 7 × 100 = ______ b 100 × 56 = ______

c 863 × 100 = ______ d 24 × 100 = ______

e 100 × 34 = ______ f 97 × 100 = ______

g 100 × 33 = ______ h 100 × 20 = ______

i 4 × 100 = ______ j 349 × 100 = ______

k 100 × 62 = ______ l 81 × 100 = ______

m 100 × 78 = ______ n 69 × 100 = ______

o 100 × 42 = ______ p 9 × 100 = ______

q 124 × 100 = ______ r 100 × 176 = ______

100 has 2 zeros, so when you multiply by one hundred, add 2 zeros.
eg 100 × 6 = 600

3 Multiply by 1000.

a 1000 × 3 = ______ b 808 × 1000 = ______

c 1000 × 37 = ______ d 1000 × 80 = ______

e 382 × 1000 = ______ f 101 × 1000 = ______

g 1000 × 64 = ______ h 123 × 1000 = ______

i 1000 × 1000 = ______ j 1000 × 433 = ______

k 139 × 1000 = ______ l 1000 × 506 = ______

m 1000 × 103 = ______ n 1000 × 920 = ______

o 1000 × 684 = ______ p 1000 × 247 = ______

q 139 × 1000 = ______ r 251 × 1000 = ______

1000 has 3 zeros, so when you multiply by 1000, add 3 zeros.
eg 1000 × 6 = 6000

Unit 24 Divide by 10, 100, 1000

1 Divide by 10.

a $8{\cdot}27 \div 10 =$ ____________
b $47{\cdot}1 \div 10 =$ ____________
c $4{\cdot}09 \div 10 =$ ____________
d $334{\cdot}63 \div 10 =$ ____________
e $26{\cdot}83 \div 10 =$ ____________
f $201{\cdot}2 \div 10 =$ ____________
g $616{\cdot}2 \div 10 =$ ____________
h $9 \div 10 =$ ____________
i $24{\cdot}65 \div 10 =$ ____________
j $534 \div 10 =$ ____________
k $325{\cdot}14 \div 10 =$ ____________
l $0{\cdot}03 \div 10 =$ ____________
m $7{\cdot}9 \div 10 =$ ____________
n $1{\cdot}09 \div 10 =$ ____________

10 has 1 zero, so when you divide by 10, move the decimal point 1 place to the left.

eg $32 \div 10 = 3{\cdot}2$

2 Divide by 100.

a $72 \div 100 =$ ____________
b $36{\cdot}4 \div 100 =$ ____________
c $41{\cdot}3 \div 100 =$ ____________
d $0{\cdot}8 \div 100 =$ ____________
e $9 \div 100 =$ ____________
f $97{\cdot}43 \div 100 =$ ____________
g $23{\cdot}6 \div 100 =$ ____________
h $8{\cdot}24 \div 100 =$ ____________
i $1{\cdot}47 \div 100 =$ ____________
j $43{\cdot}6 \div 100 =$ ____________
k $0{\cdot}5 \div 100 =$ ____________
l $3 \div 100 =$ ____________
m $5{\cdot}27 \div 100 =$ ____________
n $5{\cdot}4 \div 100 =$ ____________

100 has 2 zeros, so when you divide by 100, move the decimal point 2 places to the left.

eg $32 \div 100 = 0{\cdot}32$

3 Divide by 1000.

a $7{\cdot}9 \div 1000 =$ ____________
b $0{\cdot}92 \div 1000 =$ ____________
c $4{\cdot}3 \div 1000 =$ ____________
d $440 \div 1000 =$ ____________
e $77 \div 1000 =$ ____________
f $2{\cdot}36 \div 1000 =$ ____________
g $630 \div 1000 =$ ____________
h $0{\cdot}7 \div 1000 =$ ____________
i $0{\cdot}59 \div 1000 =$ ____________
j $380 \div 1000 =$ ____________
k $970 \div 1000 =$ ____________
l $0{\cdot}401 \div 1000 =$ ____________
m $0{\cdot}37 \div 1000 =$ ____________
n $0{\cdot}03 \div 1000 =$ ____________

1000 has 3 zeros, so when you divide by 1000, move the decimal point 3 places to the left.

eg $32 \div 1000 = 0{\cdot}032$

Mastery Checklist

I can:
- ☐ identify factors and multiples
- ☐ find the highest common factor
- ☐ multiply by 10, 100 and 1000
- ☐ divide by 10, 100 and 1000.

Unit 25 Decimals in everyday life

	Bo	Thom	Serena	Chen	Pia	Leonie	Taj	Lew
Weight in kg	72 800 g	76 500 g	62 400 g	81 250 g	58 620 g	65 750 g	78 559 g	80 000 g
Height in m	178 cm	168 cm	172 cm	165 cm	159 cm	152 cm	195 cm	192 cm
Salary p/week in $	85 000c	84 800c	78 350c	82 000c	65 050c	79 450c	92 800c	86 250c

1 Complete the statistics chart above by writing the information in decimal notation.

2 a Who is the tallest? ______________________ b Who is the shortest? ______________________

c Who earns the least? ______________________ d Who earns the most? ______________________

e Who is the heaviest? ______________________ f Who is the lightest? ______________________

3 Write the names in order from shortest to tallest.

____

4 Write the names in order from heaviest to lightest.

____

Unit 25 Reading and writing decimals

Write as decimals.

1 a $\frac{19}{100}$ ______ b $\frac{32}{100}$ ______

c 7 and $\frac{64}{100}$ ______ d 3 and $\frac{45}{100}$ ______

e $\frac{1}{100}$ ______ f 2 and $\frac{6}{100}$ ______

g $\frac{459}{1000}$ ______ h $\frac{251}{1000}$ ______

i 2 and $\frac{679}{1000}$ ______ j 9 and $\frac{210}{1000}$ ______

k 16 and $\frac{67}{1000}$ ______ l 12 and $\frac{37}{1000}$ ______

m $\frac{1}{1000}$ ______ n 5 and $\frac{9}{1000}$ ______

1	$\frac{1}{10}$	$\frac{1}{100}$	$\frac{1}{1000}$
7 ·	6	8	3

$2\frac{13}{100} = 2{\cdot}13$

$4\frac{357}{1000} = 4{\cdot}357$

$1\frac{3}{100} = 1{\cdot}03$

$5\frac{78}{1000} = 5{\cdot}078$

$2\frac{6}{1000} = 2{\cdot}006$

Use page 115.

2 Show how they grew, centimetre by centimetre.

a Bo: 1·7 m								1·78 m
b Pia: 1·51 m								1·59 m
c Taj: 1·87 m								1·95 m

3 Show how they have lost weight, 100 g at a time.

a Serena: 63·3 kg								62·5 kg
b Lew: 80·8 kg								80 kg
c Chen: 82·05 kg								81·25 kg

4 Write a measurement between the heights of:

a Chen and Pia. ______ b Taj and Lew. ______

c Thomas and Bo. ______ d Leonie and Pia. ______

5 Circle the largest number.

a 58·468, 58·648, 58·864 b 66·606, 66·016, 66·066

c 84·074, 84·704, 84·077 d 90·01, 90·010, 91·001

6 Round and sort. **80·08, 80·808, 80·008, 80·18, 80·88, 80·018, 80·188, 80·811**

a **Smaller than 80.8**

b **Larger than 80.8**

Challenge! **RESEARCH:** DECI = TEN

Which other words contain this Greek root and what are their meanings?

AC9M6N04 Number **MA3-RN-02** Represents numbers A • Decimals and percentages: Recognise that the place value system can be extended beyond hundredths • **MA3-AR-01** Additive relations B • Apply known strategies to add and subtract decimals

Unit 25 Rounding decimals

1 Round the following decimals to the nearest whole number.

a 7·2 ________ b 9·8 ________ c 13·6 ________ d 72·1 ________

e 58·8 ________ f 135·3 ________ g 07·5 ________ h 3·28 ________

2 Round off the following decimals to one decimal place.

a 3·26 ________ b 4·65 ________ c 1·27 ________ d 15·92 ________

e 31·741 ________ f 19·286 ________ g 133·07 ________ h 150·926 ________

3 Round off the following decimals to two decimal places.

a 1·748 ________ b 3·056 ________ c 10·721 ________ d 16·059 ________

e 32·163 ________ f 54·835 ________ g 100·642 ________ h 98·173 ________

4 When multiplying decimals, do you round off before or after multiplying? ________

5 Why? ____

6 A baseball diamond has a perimeter of 109.8 m. A home run means running once around the perimeter. How many metres does a player run making:

a 1 home run in baseball? ____________

b 5 home runs? c 10 home runs? d 3 home runs?

____________ ____________ ____________

____________ ____________ ____________

7 A softball diamond has a perimeter of 73.2 m. How many metres does a player run making:

a 1 home run in softball? ____________

b 5 home runs c 10 home runs? d 3 home runs?

____________ ____________ ____________

____________ ____________ ____________

8 Multiply and round off your answers to the nearest whole number.

a 3·75 × 5 = ________ Rounded: ________

b 7·38 × 4 = ________ Rounded: ________

c 2·56 × 6 = ________ Rounded: ________

d 9·54 × 8 = ________ Rounded: ________

9 Eight scouts each paid $18.85 for their extra lesson. The teacher could only make a bank deposit in whole dollars.
How much did he bank? ____________

10 Magazines cost $5.65 to download.
If I download 4 for the year, how much credit do I need to have in my account?

____

Unit 25 Subtraction of decimals

Subtracting decimals

Align units under units, tenths under tenths, etc. Fill spaces with a zero. eg 2·4 – 1·046

$$\begin{array}{r} 2{\cdot}400 \\ -\ 1{\cdot}046 \\ \hline 1{\cdot}354 \end{array}$$

1 Work mentally.

a 1·0 – 0·5 = ________ b 2·0 – 1·6 = ________

c 1·5 – 0·5 = ________ d 0·95 – 0·40 = ________

e 1·13 – 0·12 = ________ f 2·45 – 0·32 = ________

g 5·7 – 2·4 = ________ h 7·5 – 6·54 = ________

2 a 4·60 – 2·27 = ________

b 3·5 – 1·35 = ________

c 7·8 – 3·52 = ________

d 6·8 – 1·04 = ________

e 5·473 – 2·318 = ________

f 2·061 – 0·534 = ________

g 10·51 – 7·01 = ________

h 7·468 – 3·171 = ________

i 5·39 – 1·184 = ________

j 4·2 – 3·947 = ________

3 Show your working.

a 2·6 – 1·865

b 7·5 – 2·568

c 5·99 – 3·501

d 5 – 1·64

4 At Bo's factory, 4·25 days a week are spent building Zippy Doos. If 1·5 days were lost because of a strike last week, how many days were spent building Zippy Doos?

____

Working

5 Serena bought 3 m of fabric for a dress. After she cut it out, 0·27 m was left. How many metres of fabric did she use?

____

Working

6 Change from $50 after buying:

a a paperback. ________

b a T-shirt. ________

c a vest. ________

Unit 25 Division of decimals

× & ÷ decimals

Decimal division

When dividing, the decimal point moves to the left.

Divide by 10 – move the decimal point 1 place.

Divide by 100 – move the decimal point 2 places.

Divide by 1000 – move the decimal point 3 places.

1 Use a calculator.

Number	÷ 10	÷ 100	÷ 1000
a 26 765·0			
b 19 045·0			
c 58 838·0			
d 10 028			
e 2900			

2 a 27·84 ÷ 10 = ________ b 0·56 ÷ 10 = ________ c 17·4 ÷ 10 = ________

d 614·5 ÷ 100 = ________ e 385·1 ÷ 100 = ________ f 8964 ÷ 1000 = ________

g 1723 ÷ 1000 = ________ h 4·2 ÷ 100 = ________ i 767 ÷ 1000 = ________

3 Work mentally.

a Mr Farmer has to pay a total of $476.20 to his 10 workers.

How much will they each receive? ________

b 378·5 m of rope arrives in a shipment. The store sells rope in 10 m lengths.

How many lengths will they be able to cut? ________

How many metres are left over? ________

c What is the average of 6, 8, 3, 9, 12, 15, 10, 8, 7 and 5? ________

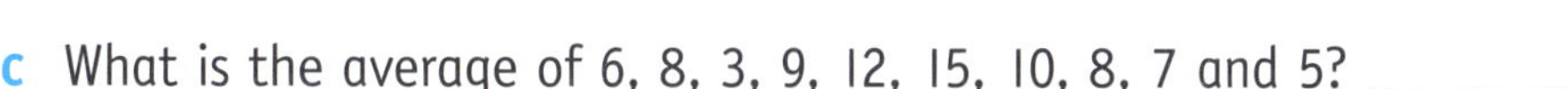

d $4 000 000 in a lottery win is shared between 100 people in an office.

How much will they each receive? ________

e 75 350 oranges are picked in 100 hours on Farm A.

How many oranges are picked in an hour? ________

f On Farm B, 7465 oranges were picked in 10 hours.

Which picking rate is better? ________

Challenge! A rare Chimpilla has been sighted in Goolarbie Rainforest. Using these dimensions and a scale of 1:10, draw it on paper.

Length – Head 35 cm, Body 68 cm, Tail 25 cm, Legs (four) 33 cm each, Ears 12 cm

Width – Head 18 cm, Body 36 cm

Mastery Checklist I can:

- ☐ compare and convert amounts in kilograms and grams, metres and centimetres, and dollars and cents
- ☐ write fractions as decimals
- ☐ subtract decimals to three places
- ☐ divide decimals to three places.

Problem solving

Use decimal measures

Read these sport reports and fill in appropriate measurements, scores and times to make these stories clear.

1 **Measurement bank: 157 km, 1 min 13·4 seconds, 238 km, 2·5 km, 2 min 14·5 seconds**

The disappointing effort by Raddel means that Fiddo leads by _______ after the 15th stage, a _______ ride over difficult territory. With just _______ to go he shot out to the lead. Raddel is still _________ behind with little hope of catching the leader. The 16th stage, a _______ ride in easier territory will see other challengers come up.

2 **Measurement bank: 4·44 m, 4·8 m, 10·2 m, 16·5 cm, 4·04 m, 5·1 m, 8·2 cm**

They lifted the bar to _______ for the 3rd jump. Lily strolled to the beginning of her ________ run up and waited. Gathering all her strength, she sailed over the bar, clearing it by ________. Again, they raised the bar, this time to ________ and Lily again strolled to her run-up spot. Again she sailed over, clearing it by at least ________. However, when the bar stood at _______ from the ground, Lily found it more difficult to clear and we wondered if she would make the record vault of _________ this time.

3 **Measurement bank: 6·2 metres, 52·3 metres, 58·5 metres, 7·5 metres**

Andy mentally measured the distance from the spot on the field to the posts – ____________ he thought. He knew his longest kick to date was ____________. That was about ____________ short. Should he try to make it this time, banking on his ability to improve with every kick? Or should he dribble ____________ further and get within a safe distance before taking the kick. He would never know, because Jack from the wing took over and dribbled, then scored a fantastic goal.

4 **Dive scores: 9·98 points, 0·25 points, 1·25 points, 0·8 points**

After two dives, the Australian, Grantham, was ____________ ahead of his nearest rival, Foster from New Zealand. Grantham dived his specialty with a double pike and made a mistake on entry into the water, so Foster drew to the lead by ____________ after he dived cleverly and well. The third dive required Grantham to score at least ____________ to take the lead again and he gathered himself to make the dive of his life. He heard the crowd cheer and as he surfaced, saw from the scoreboard that he had made it, and was now ____________ in the lead again. Relief!

I can solve problems by:

☐ understanding decimals ☐ understanding written information.

AC9M6N09 Number **AC9M6M01** Measurement **MAO-WM-01** Working mathematically • choosing and applying mathematical techniques to solve problems • communicating thinking and reasoning coherently and clearly

Unit 26 Percentages at work

PRODUCTION COSTS DOWN BY 15%

EXPENSES UP 10% THIS YEAR – PARTS COST MORE

WORKPLACE ACCIDENTS DOWN 50% IN 2024

25% CUT IN PROFITS

UNEMPLOYMENT DOWN TO 6% THIS QUARTER

1 Last year's expenses were \$460 000. What are this year's if they are 10% more? ______________

2 If 6% of the workforce is unemployed, what percentage of workers have a job? ______________

3 There were 50 workplace accidents in 2023. How many were there in 2024? ______________

4 Production costs were \$100 000 last year. What are they this year? ______________

5 If machinery parts used to cost \$5, now they probably cost ______________.

6 Profits this year have gone down by \$20 000. What were they last year? ______________

Unit 26 Equivalence

To find a percentage of a number:

10% of 120 = $\frac{1}{10}$ of 120
= 120 ÷ 10 = 12

12 is 10% of 120.

1 Complete the table of equivalent fractions, decimals and percentages.

Fraction	Equiv. Fraction	Decimal	Percent	of $1	of $10	of $100	of 1 m
a $\frac{1}{2}$	$\frac{\quad}{100}$			50c			50 cm
b $\frac{1}{4}$							
c $\frac{3}{4}$							
d $\frac{1}{5}$							
e $\frac{2}{5}$							
f $\frac{3}{5}$							
g $\frac{4}{5}$							
h $\frac{9}{10}$							

2 a 50% of $120 ______ b 10% of 2 km ______ c 50% of 300 ______

d 25% of 1 kg ______ e 10% of 180 ______ f 25% of 16 ______

g 300 m = 10% of ______ h $2.50 = 25% of ______ i 500 L = 5% of ______

12 fish = 10% of Miro's collection

How many altogether?

12 = $\frac{1}{10}$ of the collection

12 × 10 = 120 fish altogether

3 Production has decreased by $10 million. If this is 10% of the total production, what was the full value of the production?

____

4 The cost of wages for those who assemble parts has gone up $50 000 or 10% of total wages. What were the total wages paid in the parts division?

____

5 Accidents to workers in the Belt-Up factory are down by 50%. This means there were 6 accidents less this year. How many accidents occurred last year?

____

6 20% of all workers at Mack's Mechs take the bus. Label the pie chart at the right to show the section that represents those workers.

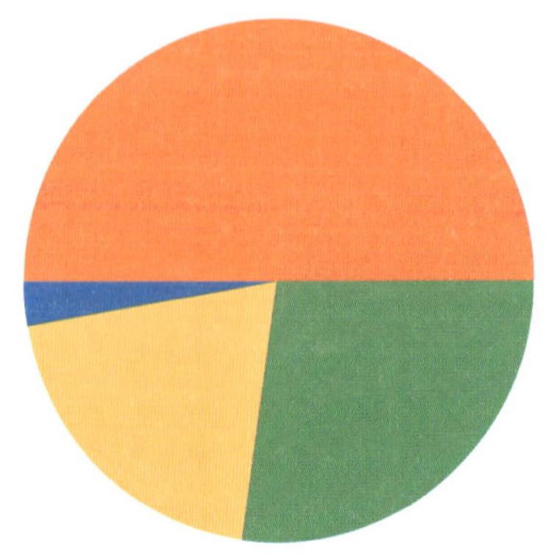

Unit 26 Finding percentages

1 Complete the following table.

100%	$\frac{1}{10}$ or 10%	$\frac{2}{10}$ or 20%	$\frac{1}{4}$ or 25%	$\frac{1}{2}$ or 50%	$\frac{3}{4}$ or 75%
a 60	6	12			
b 80					
c 120					
d	2				
e	5				
f 40					
g		50			

2 In the Ben Bee factory, 25% of the total profits came from appliances, 10% from machines and 50% from vehicles. Repairs made up the rest.

What % of profit came from repairs? Circle one.

a 25% b 15% c 5% d 85%

3 50% of expenses are wages, 25% cafeteria and the rest, parts and materials. If wages cost $50 000, how much is spent on cafeteria, parts and materials? Label the diagram.

$50 000

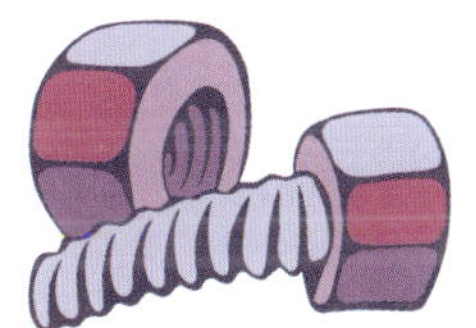

4 Use <, > or = to complete these.

a 50% of 20 ____ 25% of 50 b 10% of 60 ____ 50% of 20 c 25% of $1 ____ 10% of 10c

5 Mark the scale to show the likelihood that you will receive between 60% and 65% in your maths test this term. 0 = impossible and 1 = certain.

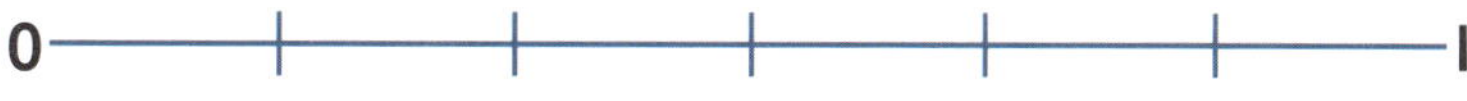

Challenge! In some countries, tipping at restaurants is common practice.
If 10% is the usual tip and I give $12, what is the total bill?

Unit 26 Discounts

Fill in the missing information.

Item	Fraction	Percentage discount	$ discount	Sale price
1 $30 20% off	$\frac{20}{100}$	20%	$6	$30 – $6 = $24
2 $120 15% off				
3 $40 30% off				
4 $210 50% off				
5 $60 25% off				
6 $200 60% off				
7 $60 10% off				
8 $20 75% off				

Unit 26 Percentages in everyday life

1 Change the following test marks to percentages.

a 50 out of 100 ______ b 75 out of 100 ______ c 95 out of 100 ______

d 10 out of 100 ______ e 25 out of 100 ______ f 20 out of 40 ______

g 10 out of 20 ______ h 10 out of 40 ______ i 25 out of 50 ______

j 15 out of 60 ______ k 2 out of 20 ______ l 60 out of 120 ______

2 a Zuri's spelling percentage was 100%, so she scored ______ out of 50.

b Song's percentage was 50%, so her score was ______ out of 50.

c Ari gained 90%, so his score was ______ out of 50.

d In Maths, Ronan scored 40 out of 80, so he gained ______%.

e Jamie's score was 20 out of ______, so he gained 25%.

3 The value of production in the Comdo Machines Factory in 2024–2025 was $48 000 000. 40% came from the heavy parts department, 30% from the fittings department, 20% from the finishing department and 10% from the paint department.

Add the value for each department's work to the diagram.

4 In the Super Skater Shop, 50% of skateboards sold are dark blue, 25% are red, 10% are black, and the rest are mixed colours. If 50 skateboards are dark blue, how many skateboards sold are:

a red? ______ b black? ______ c mixed? ______

Work backwards

In a test, Liam scored 10% less in Number than in Measurement, $\frac{1}{5}$ more in Measurement than in Statistics, 20% less in Space than in Mentals, 5% less in Statistics than in Space. He scored 100% in Mentals. What are his percentage scores in all tests?

Mentals:

Mastery Checklist I can:

- ☐ calculate percentages related to work
- ☐ calculate equivalent fractions, decimals and percentages
- ☐ use <, > and = to compare percentages of amounts
- ☐ work out discounts
- ☐ write real-world quantities as percentages.

Unit 27 Number sentences

> **Use your knowledge of inverse operations to solve equations.**
> **Change the side, change the sign.**
> eg $5 + x = 12$
> $x = 12 - 5$
> $x = 7$
> **Check your solution by substituting in the original equation.**

> **Remember!**
> $3^2 = 3 \times 3 = 9$

1 $d + d + d + d = 240$
$300 - d = 240$
$d - 10 = 50$
$d =$ ______

2 $b^2 = 40 - 4$
$2^2 + 1 = b - 1$
$b \div 2 = 3$
$b =$ ______

3 $m \div 10 = 5.6$
$m + 4 = 60$
$\frac{1}{2}m = 28$
$m =$ ______

4 ✧ + 15 = 22
✧ squared = 49
30 – ✧ = 23
✧ = ______

5 $k^2 = 121$
$k + 3 = 14$
$3^2 + 2 = k$
$k =$ ______

6 $\frac{1}{3}$ of $Y = 8$
$\frac{1}{2}$ of $Y = 12$
$Y + 6 = 30$
$Y =$ ______

7 600 – ★ = 580
4 × ★ = 100 – 20
★ + ★ = 40
★ = ______

8 $J - 75 = 2 \times 15$
$100 + J = 20.5 \times 10$
$J \div 5 = 7 \times 3$
$J =$ ______

9 $s + s + s = 42$
$28 - s = 7 \times 2$
$s + 6 = \frac{1}{3}$ of 60
$s =$ ______

10 $A^2 + 9 = 130$
$143 \div 13 = A$
$6 \times A = 57 + 9$
$A =$ ______

11 Study these diagrams. Then match each diagram with its equation.

a
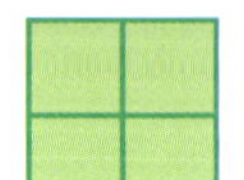

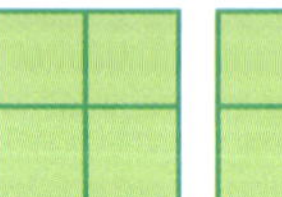

b
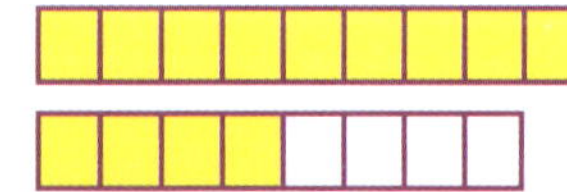

c
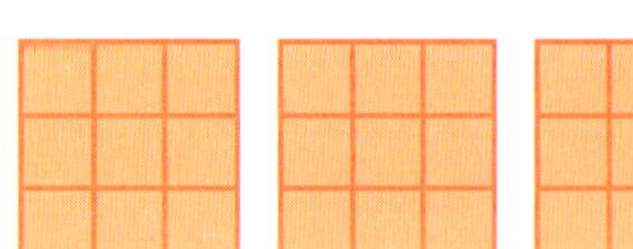

d
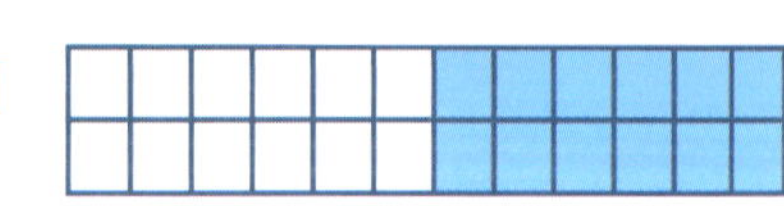

$3 \times 3^2 + 2^2 = 31$

$24 - 3 \times 4 = 12$

$\frac{3}{4} \times 16 + \frac{1}{2}$ of $8 - 16$

$2{\cdot}5 \times 4 = 10$

Work backwards

I think of a number and add 10 before I multiply by 3. I then divide by 4, subtract 2 and multiply by 9, and arrive at 63. What was my first number? ______

Unit 27 In the right order

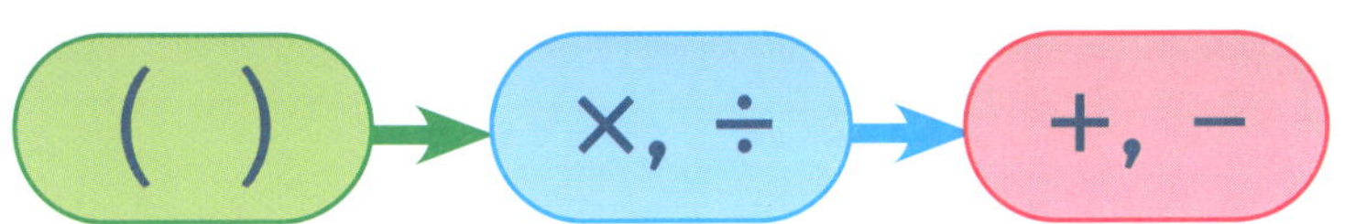

Remember!
Order of Operations
First - Brackets
Next - Multiply or divide in the order in which they appear.
Last - Add and subtract in the order in which they appear.

1 Explain these equations.
eg $14 \times 5 + 17 = 87$
Fourteen is multiplied by five before seventeen is added, for a total of 87.

a $11 \times 5 + 3^2 - 6 =$ ______________________

b $42 - 16 + 13 \times 2 =$ ______________________

c $1{\cdot}5 \times (5{\cdot}75 + 1{\cdot}25) =$ ______________________

d $48 \div (3 \times 4) + 6 =$ ______________________

Use the memory function on the calculator to check your work.

2 Write the number sentence and solve it.

a To 5·5, I add 3 before taking 1·5 away. ____________ = ______
b Add 12 to six multiplied by 14 and divide by 3. ____________ = ______
c Divide thirty-five by 5 then add the product of six and four. ____________ = ______
d Square 7 and multiply by the product of 15 and zero. ____________ = ______

3 Complete the table.

	☼	2·3	1·6	3·5	4·1	5	7·05
a	▲	1·6		1·8		4·9	1·5
b	☼ – ▲		0·65		2·9		
c	☼ + ▲						

Challenge!

Complete the table to show the number of matches needed to make this pattern of hexagons.

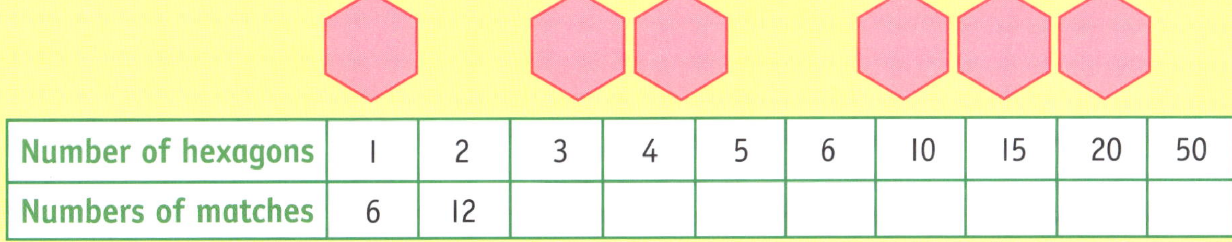

Number of hexagons	1	2	3	4	5	6	10	15	20	50
Numbers of matches	6	12								

Problem solving

On the plane

1 Mark the axes, the origin and the scale on each axis. Hint: See page 100.

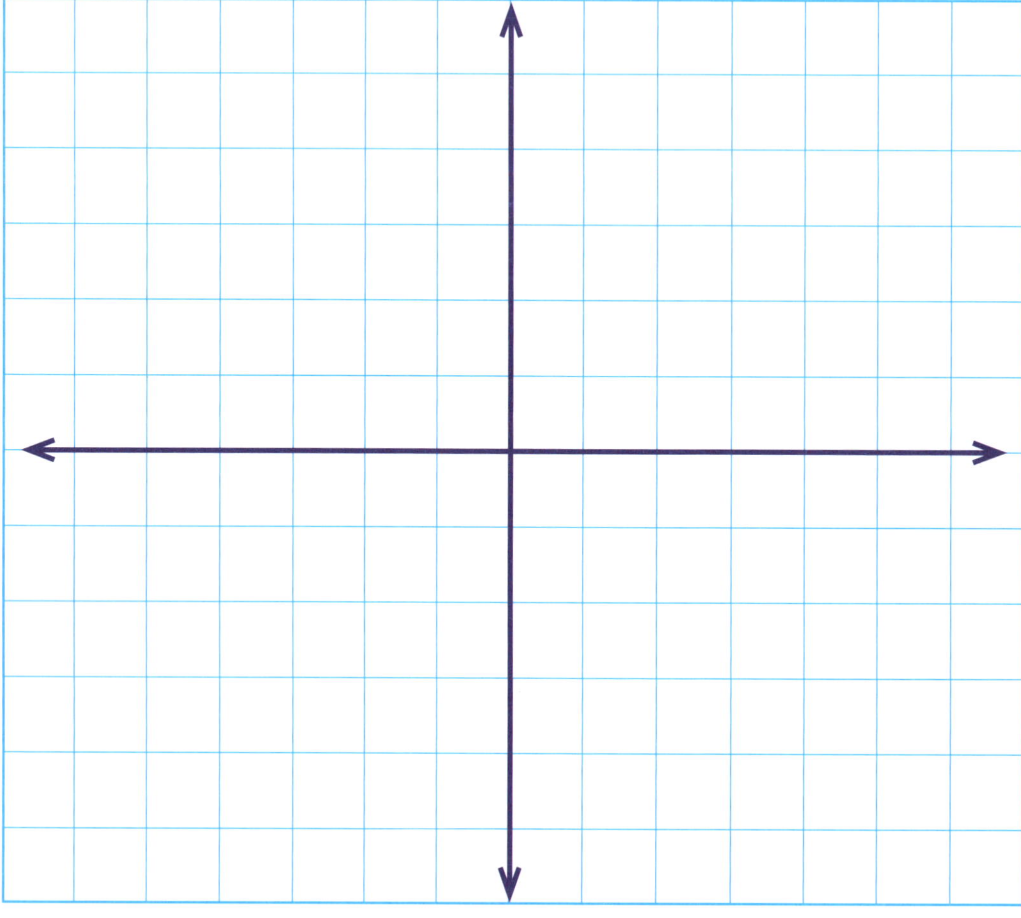

2 Iluka thinks that these coordinates make a rectangle: (–2, 2) (–2, –2) (1, –1) (1, 2). Plot them in red on the Cartesian plane. Is Iluka correct? Explain your answer.

____

____

3 Medika was told these points make a square: (–3, 4) (–3, 0) (1, 0) (1, 3). Plot them in blue on the Cartesian plane. Do they make a square? Explain.

____

____

4 Jedda is plotting the coordinates of a triangle with a vertical line of symmetry. Two of the coordinates are (–4, –1) and (–1, 2). Plot these in green on the Cartesian plane and add in the missing coordinate.

Write the missing coordinate here: ___

5 Design a symmetrical shape that has at least 4 points.

Write the coordinates here: _______________

Plot the coordinates in orange on the Cartesian plane. Draw the line(s) of symmetry.

I can solve problems by:

☐ plotting points on a Cartesian plane ☐ applying geometric knowledge.

Unit 27 Coordinates

	A	B	C	D	E	F	G	H	I	J	K
10										P	G
9			I		O		Y				
8		B						T			
7				J						E	
6	N					A		G			
5									U		
4		S		W							
3			H							D	
2	X					K		P			
1	R			F			L				
0					M						Y

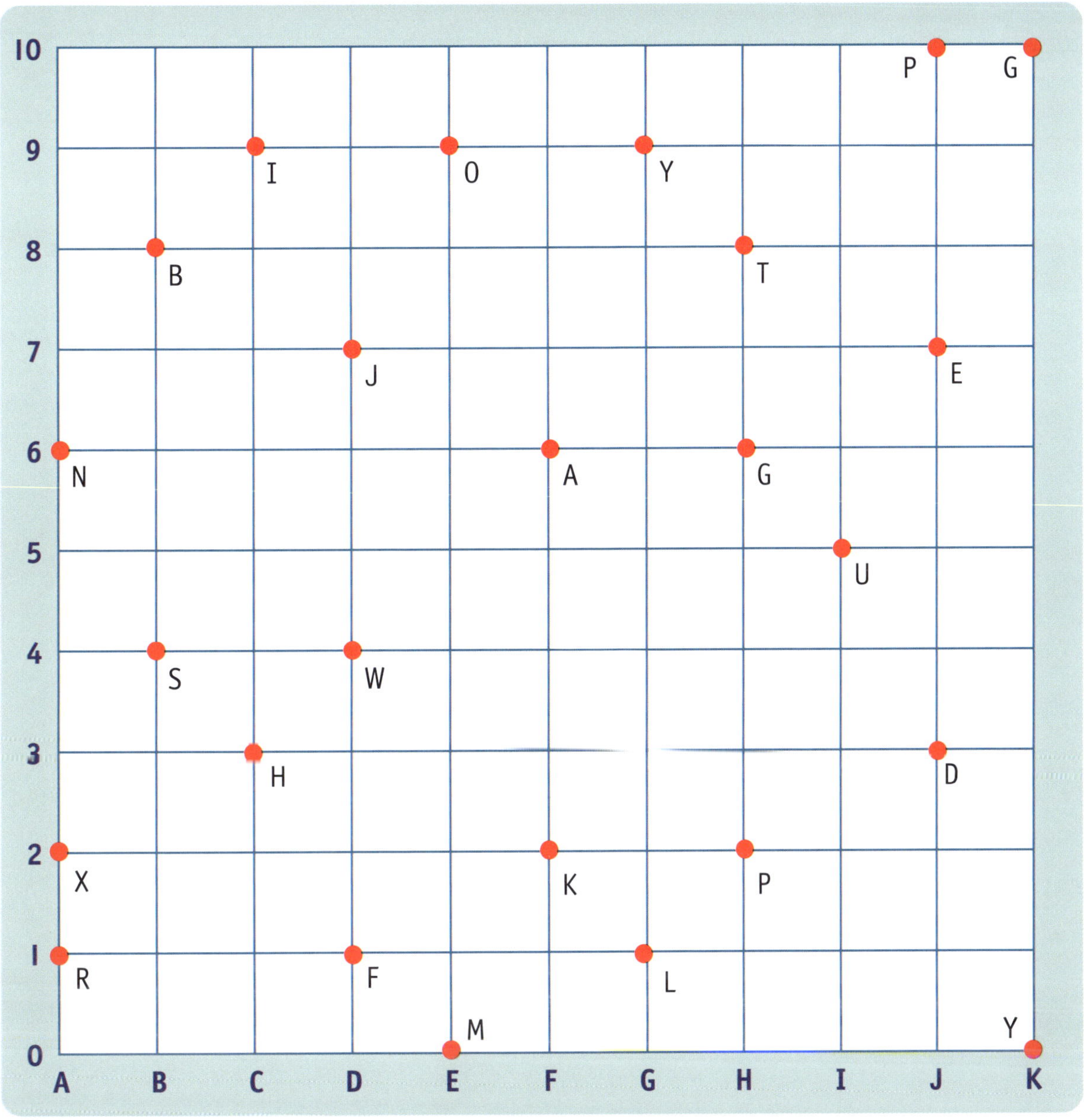

1 Write the letters of the points at each set of coordinates to find the hidden message.

___ ___ ___ ___   ___ ___ ___ ___ ___

(J, 3) (E, 9) (A, 6) (H, 8)   (D, 4) (E, 9) (A, 1) (A, 1) (K, 0)

___ ___

(B, 8) (J, 7)

___ ___ ___ ___ ___

(C, 3) (F, 6) (H, 2) (J, 10) (K, 0)

2 Using the grid above, write the coordinates for your own hidden message for a friend to solve.

Mastery Checklist I can:

- ☐ use inverse operations to solve equations
- ☐ use the order or operations to solve problems
- ☐ read points on the Cartesian number plane.

Calendar maths

Investigation 3

1 Cut out any month from a calendar. Paste it here.

Many interesting patterns can be found on the calendar. Try and find the most interesting patterns, eg try adding Mondays' and Fridays' numbers over the weeks, then try a Thursday number and a Saturday number.

Try vertical patterns and diagonal patterns.

Write a list of your findings here. Explain each pattern and its rule.

 AC9M6A03 Algebra **MAO-WM-01** Working mathematically • choosing and applying mathematical techniques to solve problems • communicating thinking and reasoning coherently and clearly • **MA3-AR-01** Additive relations A • Apply efficient mental and written strategies to solve addition and subtraction problems

Calendar maths

Investigation 3

2 a Look at the two blocks of 4 numbers. What patterns do you see?
Does it work with every block of numbers on a calendar?
What do you notice about the numbers on the diagonals of this block?

____

____

____

b Try other blocks of 4 or 9 numbers.

____

____

____

____

c What other patterns can you find on a calendar month?

____

____

____

____

To complete this task, I needed to:

- ☐ look for patterns in everyday items in the environment
- ☐ explain patterns in clear mathematical language
- ☐ experiment with patterns.

I enjoyed this task!

Revision

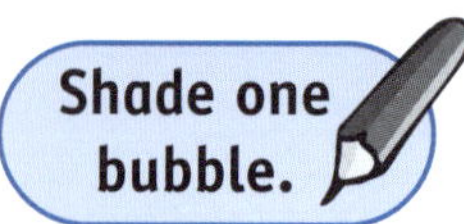

1 A pack of 4 lettuces costs \$2.50. A pack of 6 lettuces costs \$3.60.

Leo needs 28 lettuces.

What is the least amount he can pay?

\$16.90 ◯ \$17.50 ◯ \$18.00 ◯ \$18.30 ◯

---

2 Which one matches?

4·725

$\frac{5}{1000} + \frac{2}{100} + 4 + \frac{7}{10}$ ◯

$4 + \frac{725}{100}$ ◯

$4 + \frac{7}{1000} + \frac{2}{100} + \frac{5}{10}$ ◯

$\frac{47}{10} + \frac{25}{10}$ ◯

---

3 When a box of biscuits was shared equally between 6 people, they each received 12 biscuits and there were no biscuits left over.

If the biscuits had been shared equally by 8 people how many biscuits would each have received?

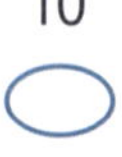

10 ◯ 16 ◯ 9 ◯ 8 ◯

4

PRODUCTION COSTS HAVE INCREASED BY 10%.

This means:

goods will cost more ◯

workers will earn more ◯

goods will be cheaper ◯

wages have halved ◯

Revision

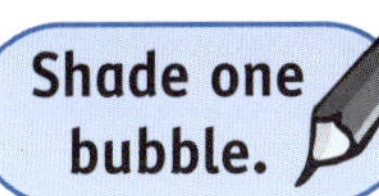

5 Larry scored 50% for his spelling test. His mark was 20.

How many marks did he lose?

20 ◯ 16 ◯ 9 ◯ 4 ◯

---

6 Callum bought his lunch 4 days last week.

He spent: Monday \$3.15, Tuesday \$2.95, Thursday \$3.65, Friday \$3.05.

What was the average cost of a lunch?

\$12  \$3.25 ◯ \$4   \$3.20 ◯

7

$\frac{1}{3}$ **of X = 3**

3^2 = X

X + 4 = 13

X = ?

6 ◯ 7 ◯ 8 ◯ 9 ◯

8

42 783·0 ÷ 100 = ?

42 783·0 ◯ 4278·3 ◯ 427·83 ◯ 42·783 ◯

9

8·5 – 6·43 = ?

2·03  2·13 ◯ 2·07 ◯ 2·17 ◯

Unit 28 Triangles

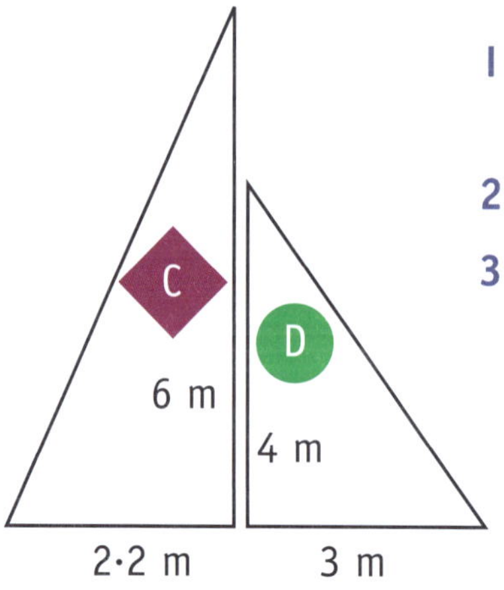

Think about using the measurements of a rectangle!

How can I work out how much fabric I'll need for these sails?

perpendicular height

base

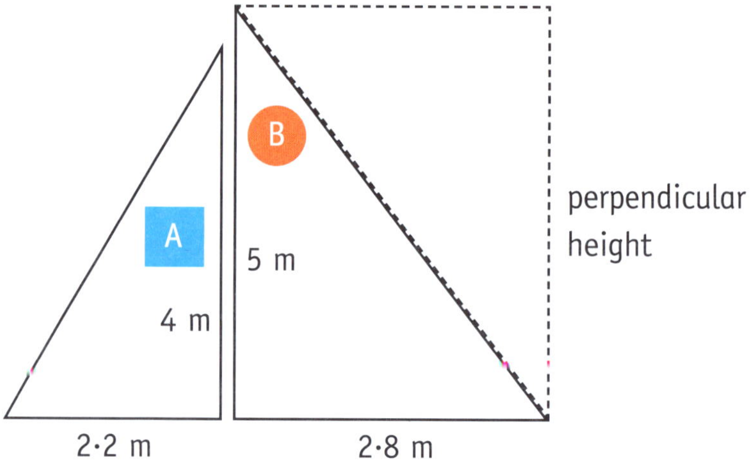

A 4 m 2·2 m

B 5 m 2·8 m

perpendicular height

C 6 m 2·2 m

D 4 m 3 m

1 Make a rectangle of each of the sailmaker's triangles.

2 Colour or shade the two halves differently.

3 Label base and perpendicular height of every triangle.

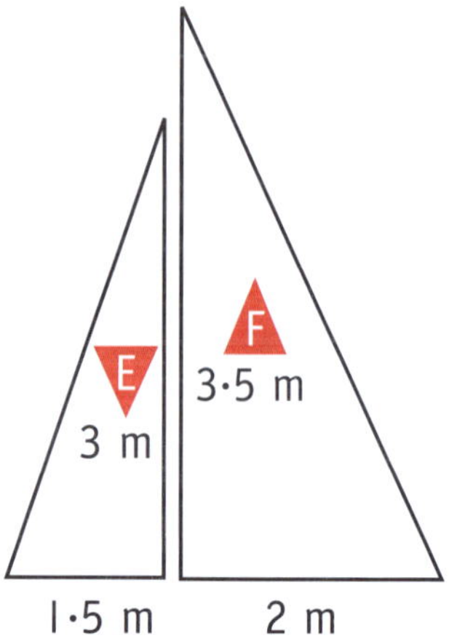

E 3 m 1·5 m

F 3·5 m 2 m

Unit 28 Areas of triangles

1 Complete the table by calculating the area of each rectangle on page 134. Halve it to make the area of each triangle.

	Area of rectangle (m^2)	Area of triangle (m^2)
Sail A base ______ height ______		
Sail B base ______ height ______		
Sail C base ______ height ______		
Sail D base ______ height ______		
Sail E base ______ height ______		
Sail F base ______ height ______		

Area of a rectangle = length × width (OR base × height)

height

base

Half the rectangle is a triangle.

Use the perpendicular height of each triangle to form a rectangle. Find the area of half of each rectangle.

2 Use the perpendicular height to calculate the area of each triangle.

a
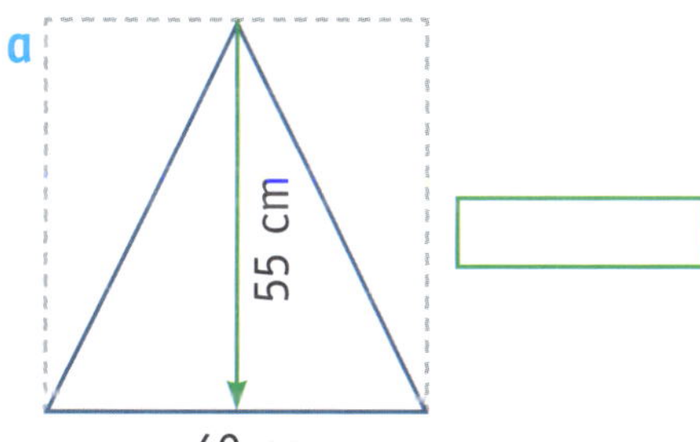

b
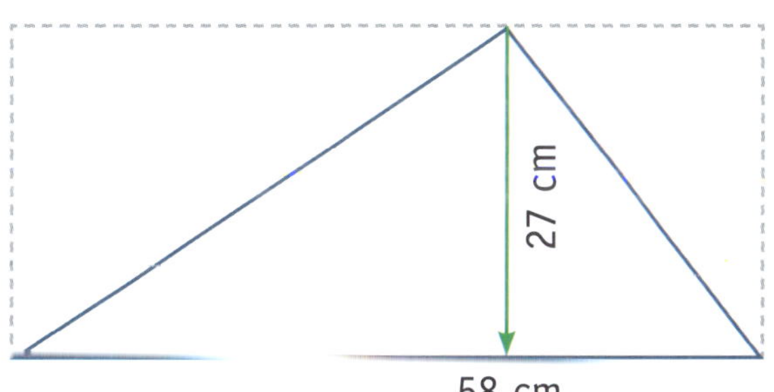

3 Write a rule to explain how to work out the area of each triangle.
Use the words height, base, multiply, half, square centimetres or metres (cm^2, m^2).

____

Challenge! What is the area of this trapezium?
Write how you worked it out.

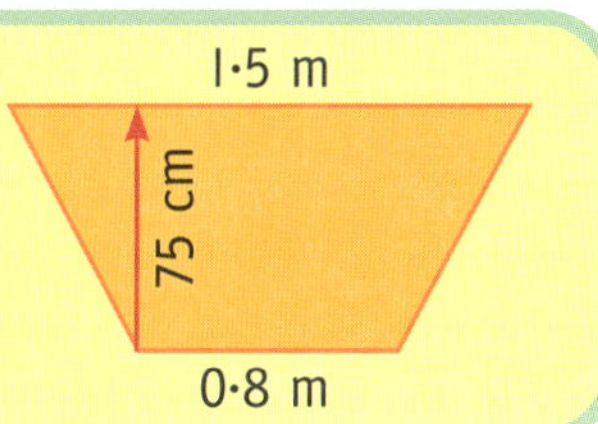

Mastery Checklist I can:
- ☐ find the perpendicular height of a triangle
- ☐ calculate the area of a triangle
- ☐ work out the rule for the area of a triangle.

Unit 29 Mass

Mass

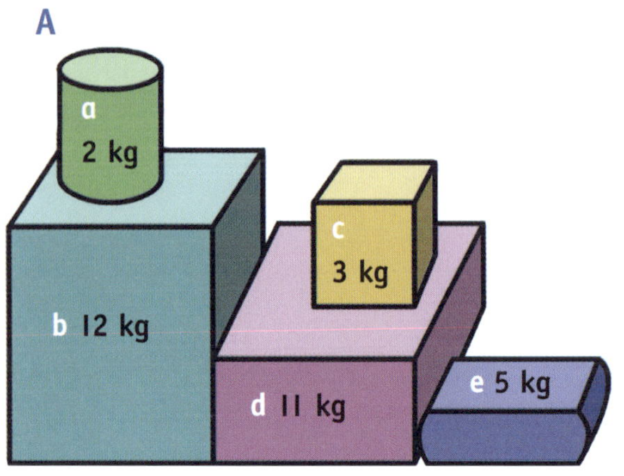

B
a
46 kg
b
10 kg
c 8 kg
d 16 kg
e 27 kg

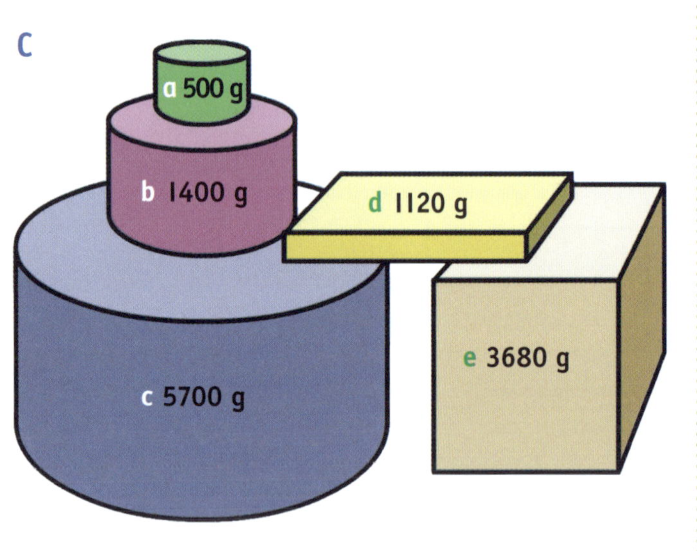

D
a
6·4 kg
b
5·3 kg
c
4·2 kg
d 3·7 kg
e
4·9 kg
f
2·5 kg

1 What is the total mass of each group of parcels?

A ______ B ______ C ______ D ______

2 For group A, write each weight in grams.

a ______ b ______ c ______ d ______ e ______

3 For group C, write each weight as a decimal.

a ______ b ______ c ______ d ______ e ______

4 For group D, change each weight to grams.

a ______ b ______ c ______ d ______ e ______ f ______

5 a Which is the lightest group of parcels? ______

b Which is the heaviest group of parcels? ______

AC9M6M01 Measurement **MA3-NSM-01** Non-spatial measure A • Mass: Connect decimal representations to the metric system • Non-spatial measure B • Mass: Convert between common metric units of mass

Unit 29 Grams and kilograms

Mass
gram – g
kilogram – kg
1000 g = 1 kg

Use the pictures on page 136.

1 Write the masses from lightest to heaviest.

A ______________________________

C ______________________________

2 Write the masses from heaviest to lightest.

B ______________________________

D ______________________________

3 Change to grams.

a 2 kg ________ b 9 kg ________ c 24 kg ________

d 17 kg ________ e 1 kg 250 g ________ f 3 kg 500 g ________

g 9 kg 750 g ________ h 31 kg 600 g ________ i 15 kg ________

4 Change to kilograms and write the answers as decimals.

a 13 000 g ________ b 64 000 g ________ c 19 000 g ________

d 38 000 g ________ e 8500 g ________ f 21 500 g ________

g 2250 g ________ h 10 750 g ________ i 9240 g ________

5 Write the mass to the nearest 100 g.

a 

b 815 g

c 

d 

e 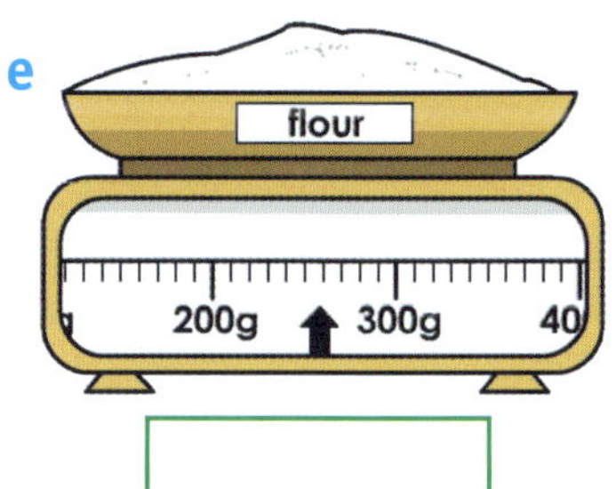

f 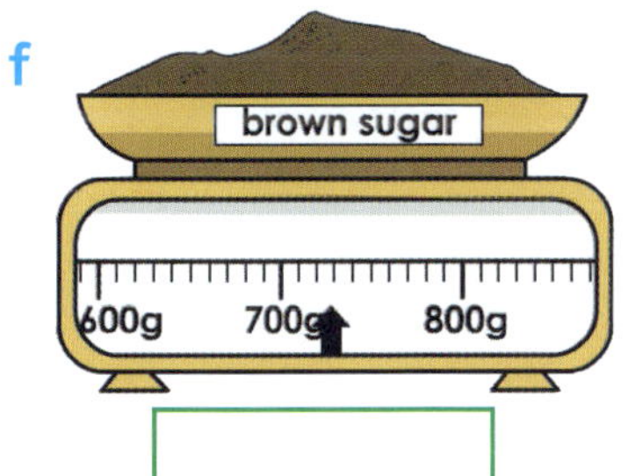

g 

Challenge! Search at home for packed foods which show their mass. Write the name and mass of 5 items which weigh less than 1 kg and 5 items which weigh more than 1 kg.

Unit 29 Estimating mass

1 Would you use grams or kilograms to find the mass?

2 Work with a partner.

a Find 6 objects in the room that have different masses and list them.

Item	Estimated mass	Actual mass

b Heft some standard masses: 1 kg, 500 g, 100 g, 50 g.

c Heft your objects. Write your estimate of their mass on the table.

d Weigh your objects. Write their actual mass on the table.

e Write your objects from lightest to heaviest. ______________________

____

f Use a calculator to find the total mass of your objects. __________

3 Write a list of 5 objects that each have a mass of:

a less than 100 g. ______________________

b about $\frac{1}{2}$ kg. ______________________

c about 1 kg. ______________________

d more than 10 kg. ______________________

Unit 29 Using measures for mass

1 Round to the nearest tonne.

a 1850 kg ______ b 5250 kg ______ c 950 kg ______ d 12 380 kg ______

e 5570 kg ______ f 15 600 kg ______ g 42 060 kg ______ h 13 290 kg ______

2 Estimate the mass by rounding, eg 4800 kg + 850 kg rounds to 5 t + 1 t = 6 t.

a 3 t − 850 kg = ______ t b 550 kg + 2·9 t = ______ t

c 10 t + 8880 kg = ______ t d 25 t − 15·2 t = ______ t

e 5 × 950 kg = ______ t f 31·95 t × 8 = ______ t

3 Which unit of measure is used to record the correct mass?

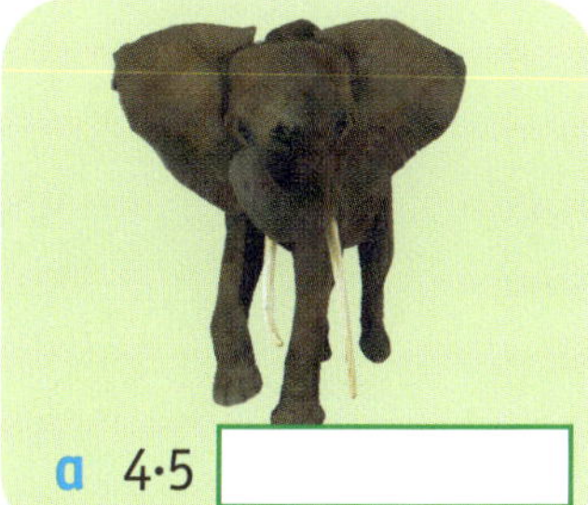
a 4·5 ______

b 6 ______

c 1·2 ______

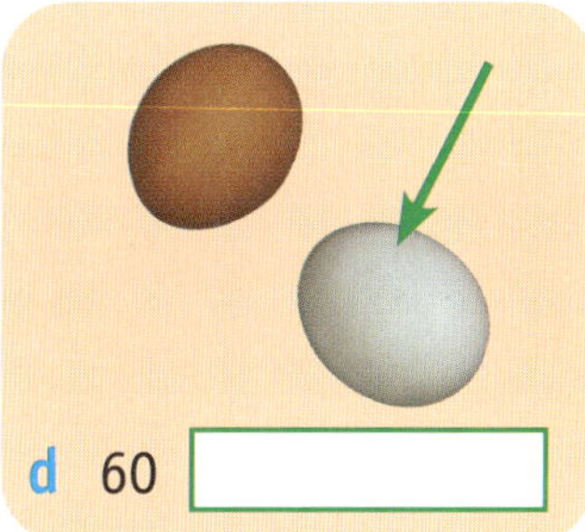
d 60 ______

e 80 ______

f 1·5 ______

g 150 ______

h 0·6 ______

4 Match the boxes with their mass to balance the scales exactly.

a wheat 0·8 t, oats 0·1 t, apples 0·5 t, oranges 0·4 t, tomatoes 0·7 t

b sand 0·2 t, gravel 0·3 t, mulch 0·8 t, rock 0·5 t, plants 500 kg

c sofa 300 kg, washing machine 250 kg, refrigerator 550 kg, bed 400 kg

A 2·3 t

B 1·5 t

C 2·5 t

Mastery Checklist

I can:
- ☐ compare and order masses in grams and kilograms
- ☐ read a scale in grams
- ☐ measure masses in grams and kilograms
- ☐ estimate masses in tonnes.

Unit 30 Diagonals and axes of symmetry

2D shapes

1 a Use a ruler to draw all the axes of symmetry in these shapes.

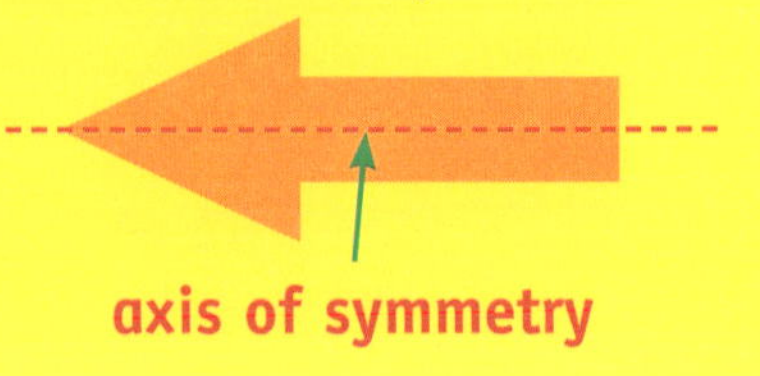

b Tick the axes of symmetry that are diagonals.

2 From question 1, which shapes have a diagonal which is also an axis of symmetry?

3 What is special about the number of sides in these shapes?

4 Draw two quadrilaterals that have diagonals that are equal in length. Mark them as equal.

5 Draw and label another polygon with diagonals equal in length.

Unit 30 Transformations

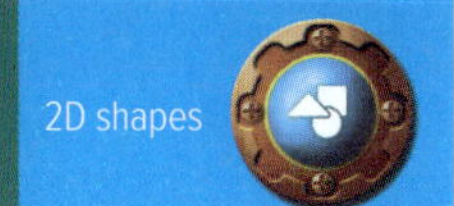

You are going to design a new logo or coat of arms for:

1 your family.
2 your school.
3 your favourite food.
4 something of your choice.

You can use more than one shape.

1 Use reflection.

2 Use translation.

3 Use rotation.

4 Your choice of transformation.

Unit 30 Changing patterns

1 Paper has been folded twice, cut or punched, then unfolded.
Circle the correct version of the unfolded paper.

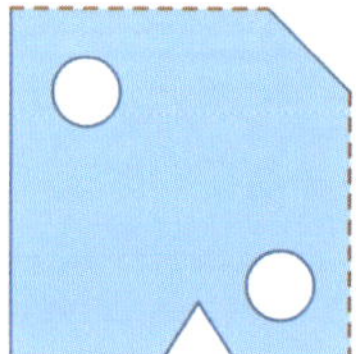

a 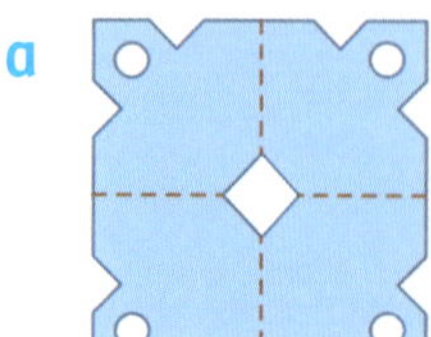

b 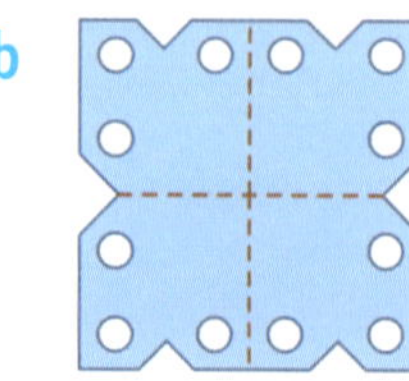

c 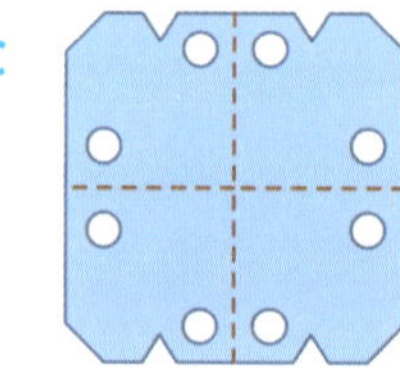

d 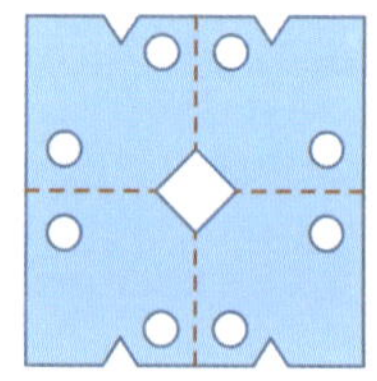

2 Study the first design. Label each following design **T** for translated, **R** for reflected or **Ro** for rotated. Complete the pattern.

3 Builders of a new museum received a brief for the decoration of the front of the museum.
They had to use a repeated motif to form a cohesive design.
The design had to fit on a wall 10 m long and 5 m wide.

Design a motif, then translate, reflect and rotate it to form your design in two rows.

Draw your original motif here.

Challenge! Use a computer program which has drawing tools.
Select and draw a shape from the drawing toolbar.
Use the turning tool to rotate the shape.
Place rotated shapes together to make a design.

Unit 30 Triangle tessellation

This equilateral triangle was used to make this tessellating pattern with translations (slides).

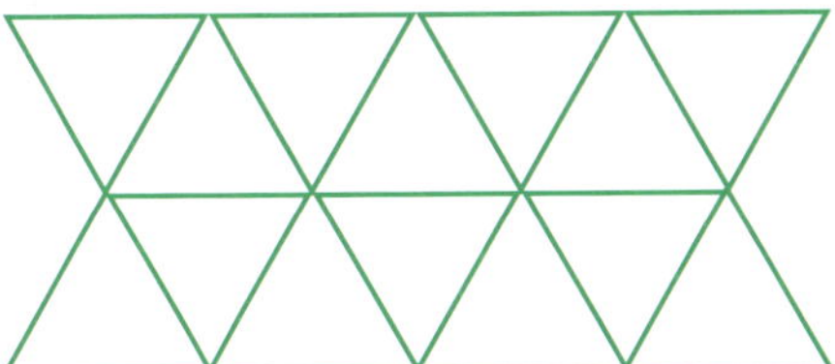

And this tessellating pattern, with rotations (turns).

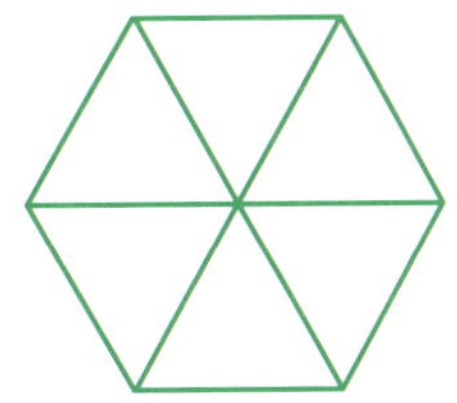

An equilateral triangle has sides of equal lengths and angles of equal sizes.

A tessellation is a pattern of repeated shapes that fit together without gaps and without overlapping.

Isosceles triangle

Two equal sides, two equal angles

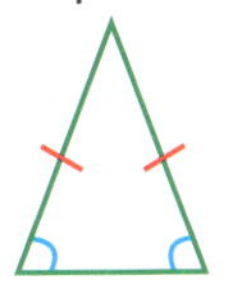

Right-angled triangle

One right angle

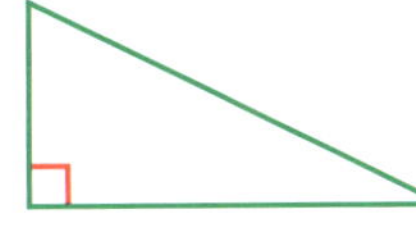

Scalene triangle

All sides different lengths, all angles different sizes

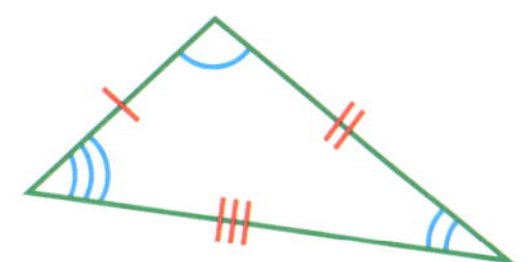

Do all triangles tessellate? Experiment here to find out.

Type of triangle
Isosceles triangle **Tessellate?** _____
Right-angled triangle **Tessellate?** _____
Scalene triangle **Tessellate?** _____

Mastery Checklist I can:

- ☐ identify lines of symmetry
- ☐ translate, reflect and rotate shapes
- ☐ identify transformations in patterns
- ☐ use transformations to design my own pattern
- ☐ explore tessellations with triangles.

Unit 31 Angles

1 Complementary angles add up to 90°. Fill in the missing angles.

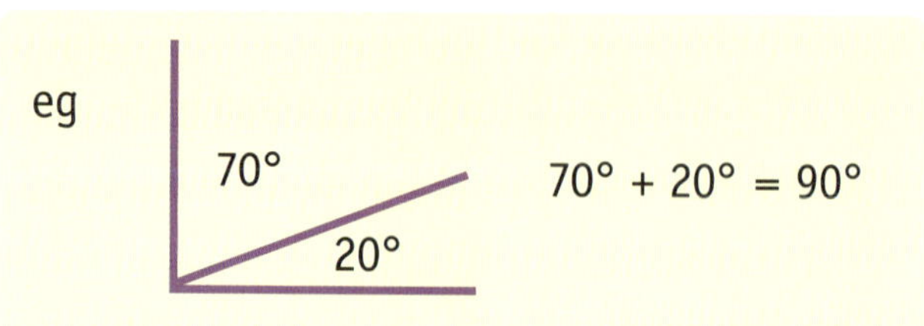

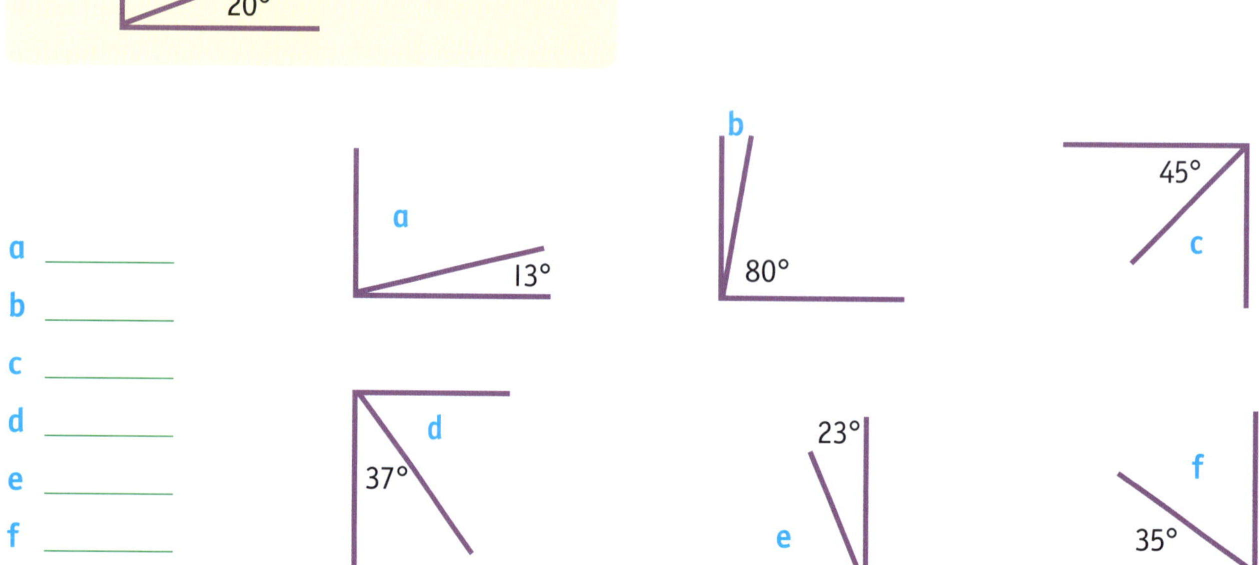

a ______

b ______

c ______

d ______

e ______

f ______

2 Supplementary angles add up to 180°. Fill in the missing angles.

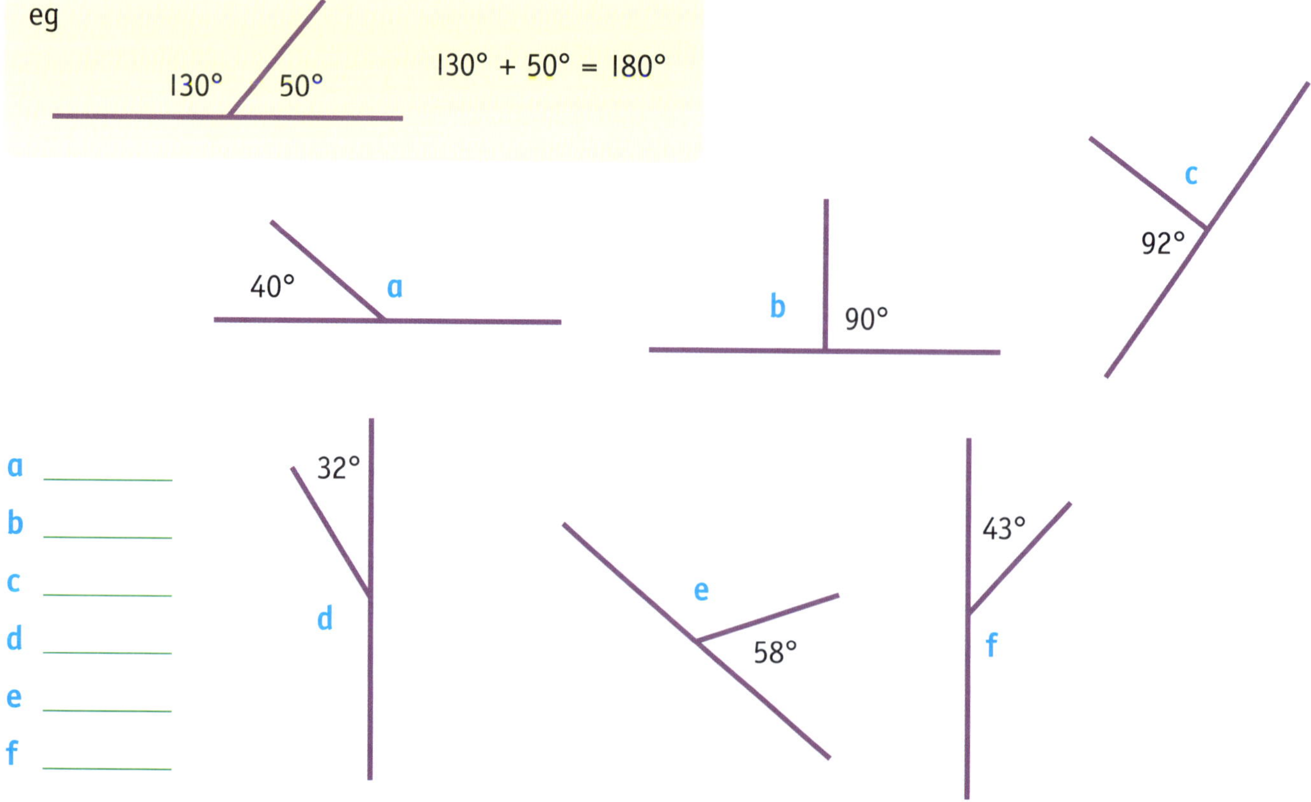

a ______

b ______

c ______

d ______

e ______

f ______

AC9M6M04 Measurement MA3-GM-03 Geometric measure A • Angles: Estimate, measure and compare angles using degrees • Geometric measure B • Angles: Investigate angles on a straight line and angles at a point

Unit 31 More angles

1 Revolutions add up to 360°. Write the missing angles.

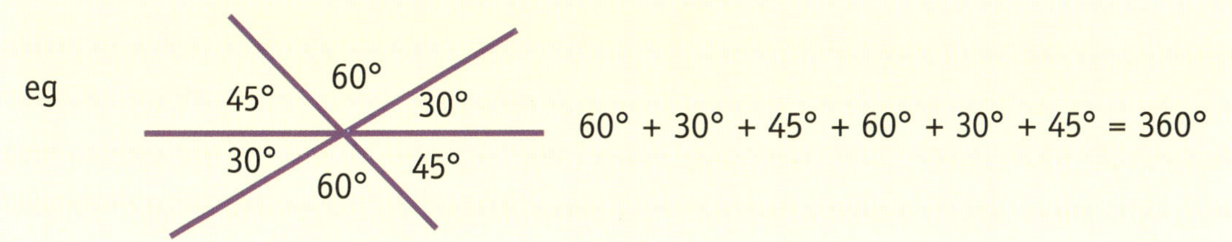

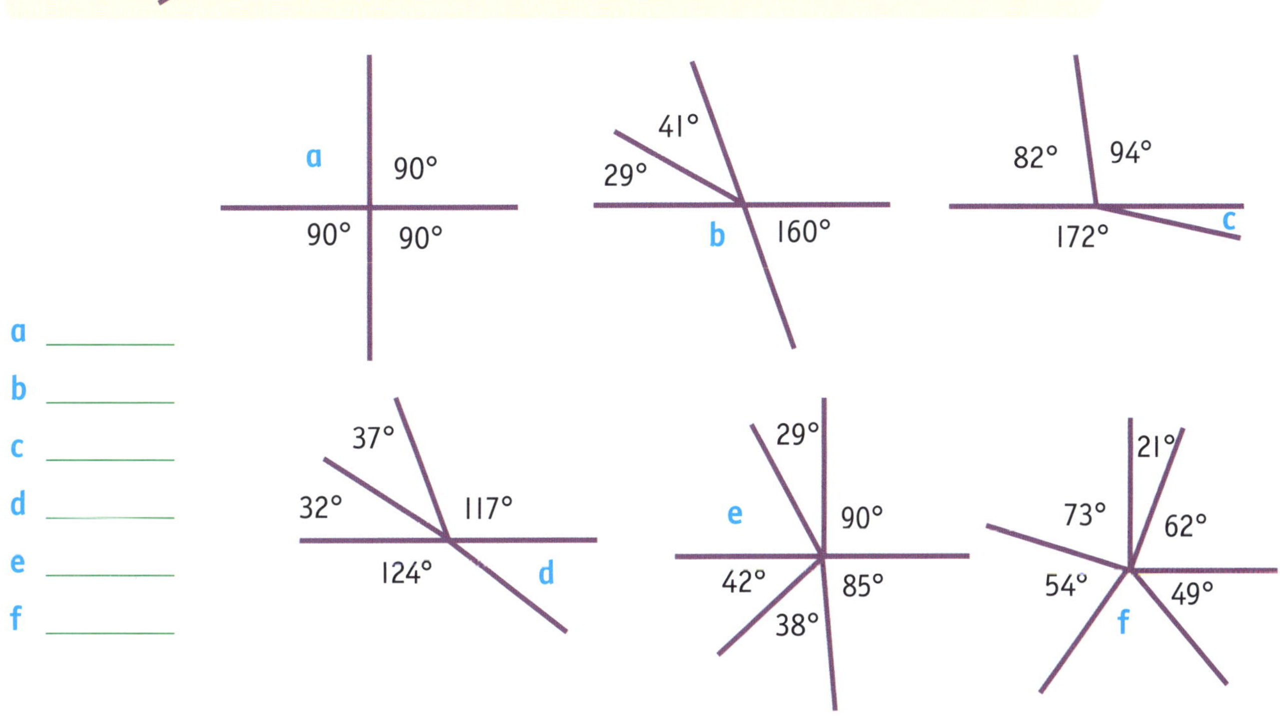

a ______

b ______

c ______

d ______

e ______

f ______

2 Vertically opposite angles are equal. Write the missing angles.

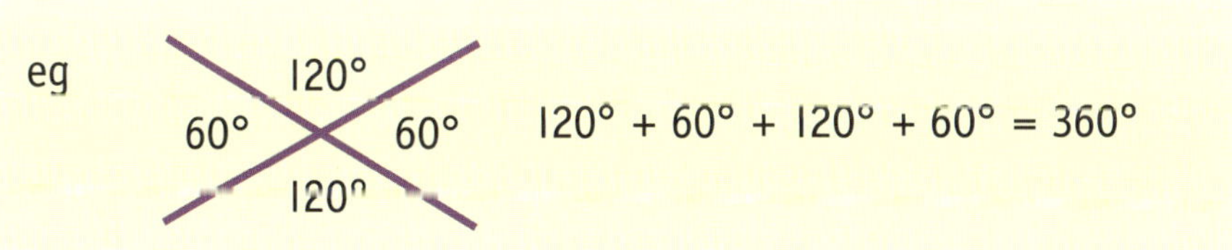

a ______

b ______

c ______

d ______

e ______

f ______

g ______

h ______

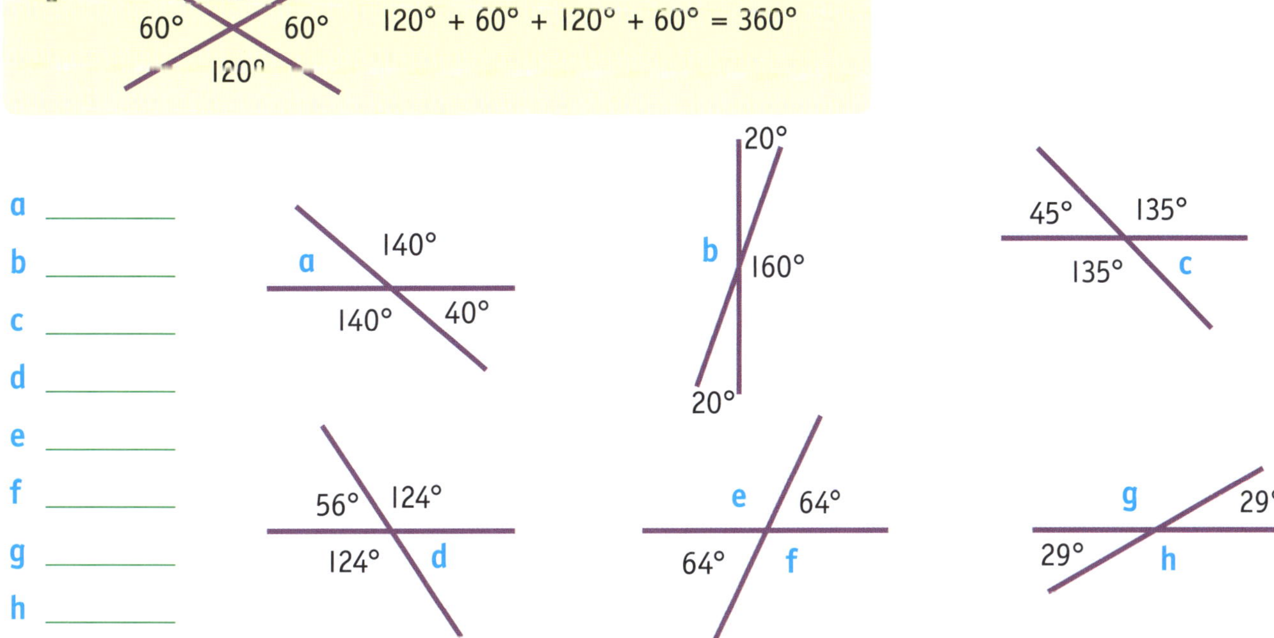

Unit 31 Missing angles

Angles in polygons

The angles of a triangle total 180 degrees.

The angles in a quadrilateral total 360 degrees.

1 a Write the size of each marked angle.
  b Write the reason for your answer.

A

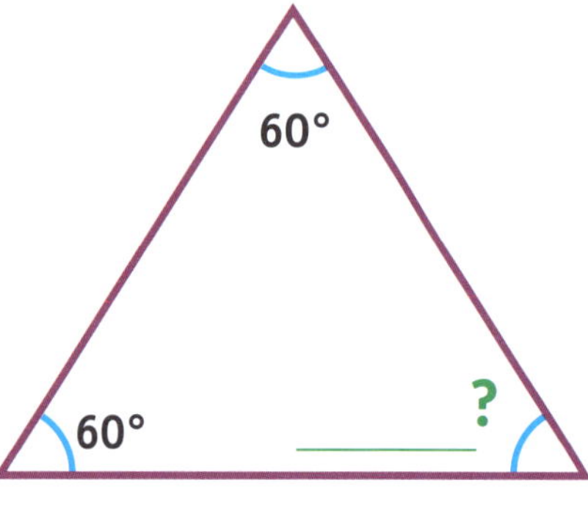

B

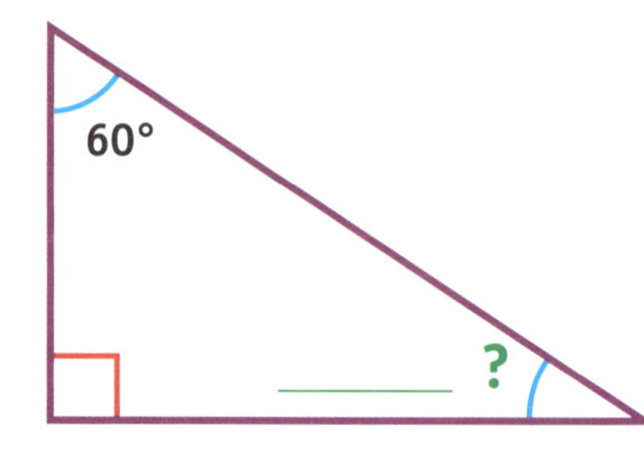

C

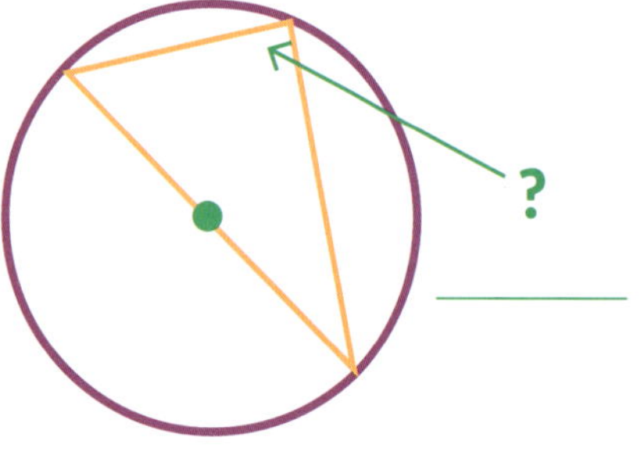

D

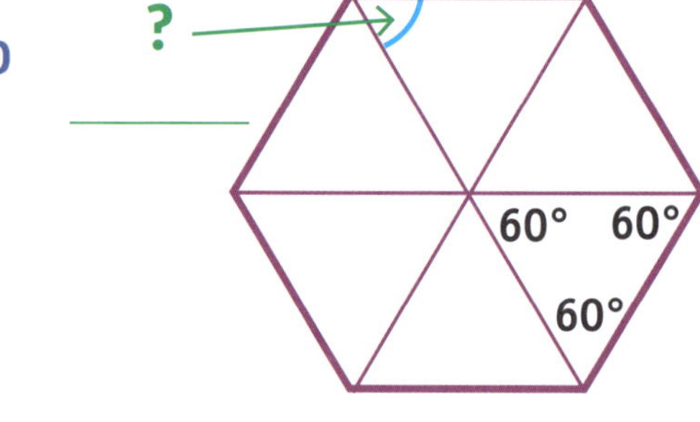

2 a Write the size of the marked angles.
  b Give reasons for your answers.

A

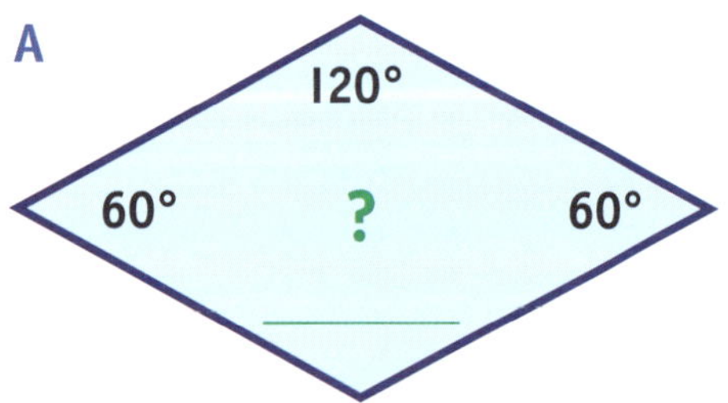

B

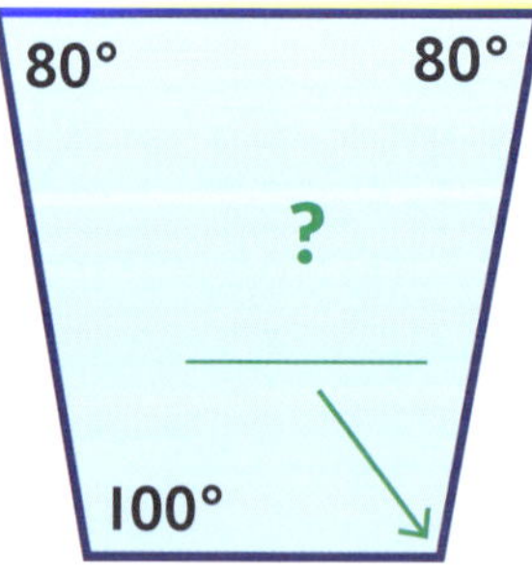

C

Mastery Checklist

I can:
- ☐ recognise complementary angles
- ☐ recognise supplementary angles
- ☐ recognise vertically opposite angles
- ☐ calculate angles in revolutions
- ☐ calculate angles in polygons.

Problem solving

Angles in polygons

1 **Find the size of the missing angles in this quadrilateral, without a protractor.**

Prove that the sum of the angles of a quadrilateral is 360°.

Write an explanation of your findings.

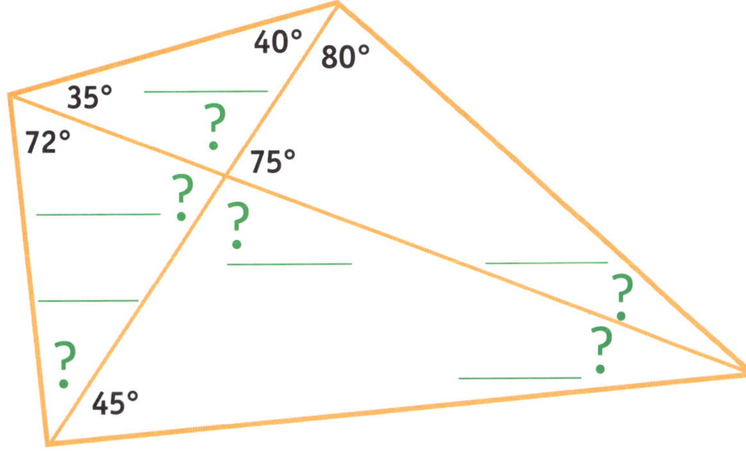

2 **Find the size of the missing angles in this pentagon, without a protractor.**

Prove that the sum of angles in a pentagon is 540°.

Write an explanation of your findings.

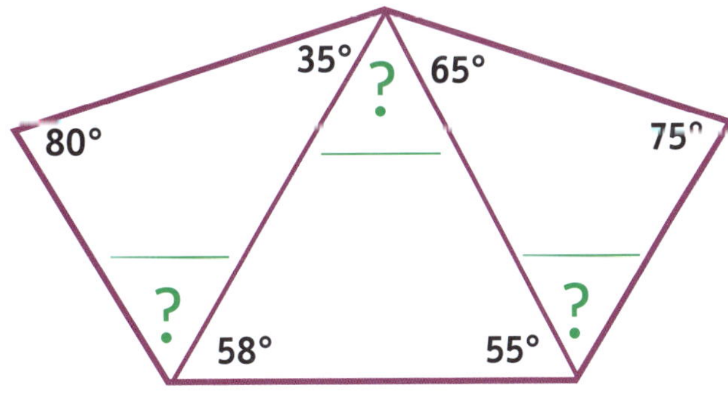

I can solve problems by:

☐ understanding angles ☐ writing algorithms.

Unit 32 Traffic report

MALLEY'S INTERSECTION

These are the results of a 1 hour survey taken at Malley's Intersection in Huddle.

a

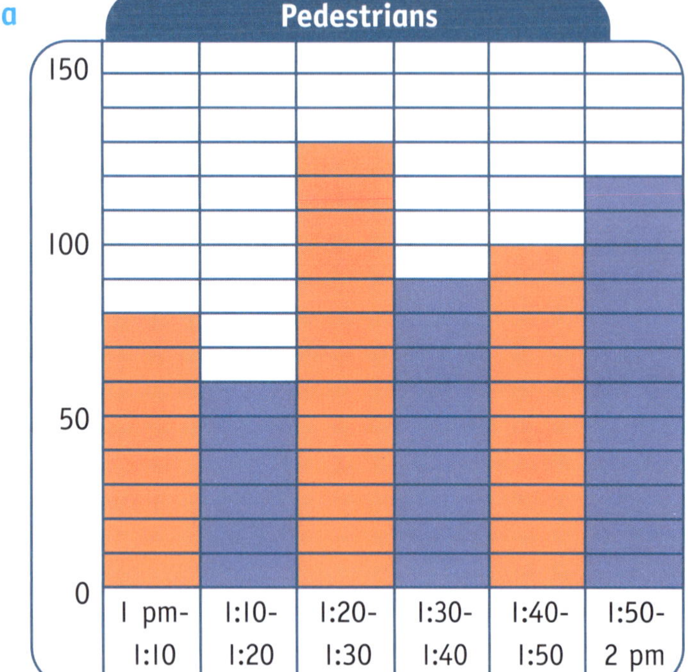

b

Vehicles on the road = 240

Buses	25%
Cars	45%
Trucks	20%
Bicycles	10%

c

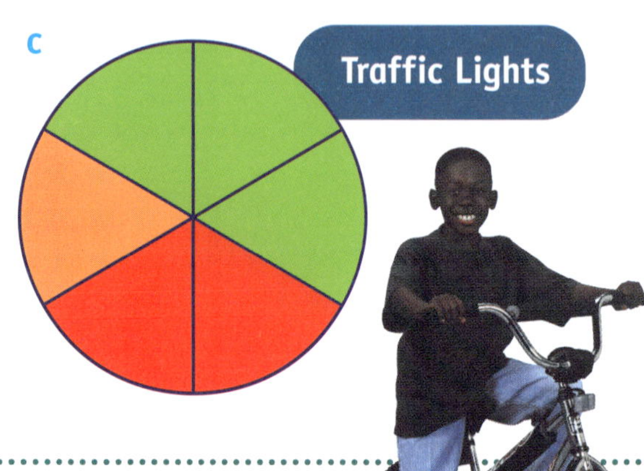

1 Traffic Lights

a Green lights show for $\frac{1}{2}$ the hour of the survey. True/False

b Red lights show for twice the time orange lights show. True/False

c Orange lights show for __________ minutes.

d What percentage of the whole time is taken up by red and orange lights? __________

2 Vehicles

a What fraction of the vehicles were cars? __________

b What percentage of the vehicles were not trucks? __________

c How many buses passed the intersection? __________

d How many trucks and bicycles together passed the intersection? __________

3 Pedestrians

a Between what times did most pedestrians cross the road? __________

b How many pedestrians used the intersection in the last 10 mins? __________

c What is the total number of pedestrians? __________

d During which half-hour did most pedestrians use the crossing? __________

Unit 32 Choosing graphs

Refer to page 148.

1 What data was shown:

a on the column graph? ______________________

b on table b? ______________________

c on diagram c? ______________________

2 Give reasons why this was a good choice for the data.

a column graph (a) ______________________

____

b table (b) ______________________

____

3 Could the pedestrian data be shown on a diagram? __________

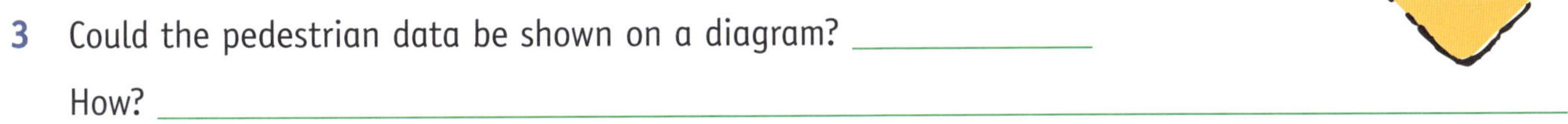

How? ______________________

____

4 A and B are representations of the same data.

A Test mark groups			
51–60	||||	61–70	𝍸 |
71–80	𝍸 𝍸 ||||	81–90	𝍸 |
91–100	||		

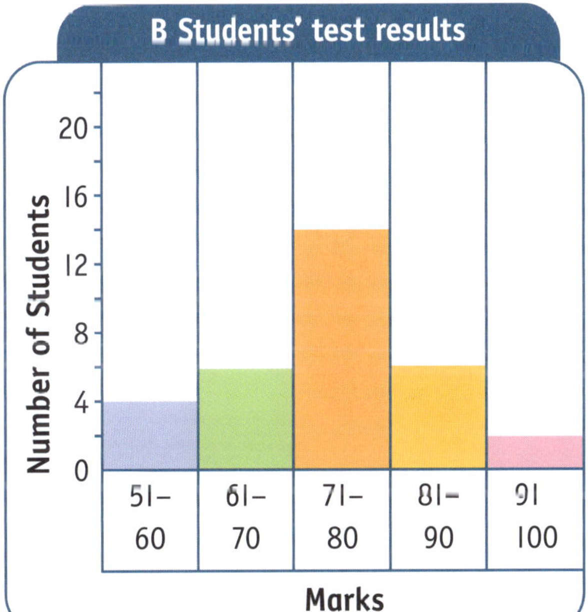

a How many students did the test? __________

b A is a ______________________.

B is a ______________________.

c Which one shows numbers more accurately?

____

d Which one shows highest and lowest groups easily? __________

e Which one shows clearly that the 71–80 scores are a larger group than any two other groups together? __________

Challenge!

Show the following information on either a column or a line graph.

Remember: Name and label the axes. Name the graph.

Time	2 pm	3 pm	4 pm	5 pm	6 pm	7 pm
Temperature °C	32	29	27	24	22	19

Unit 32 Graphs reporting the news

Graphs 1 and 2

1 Study the line graph below.

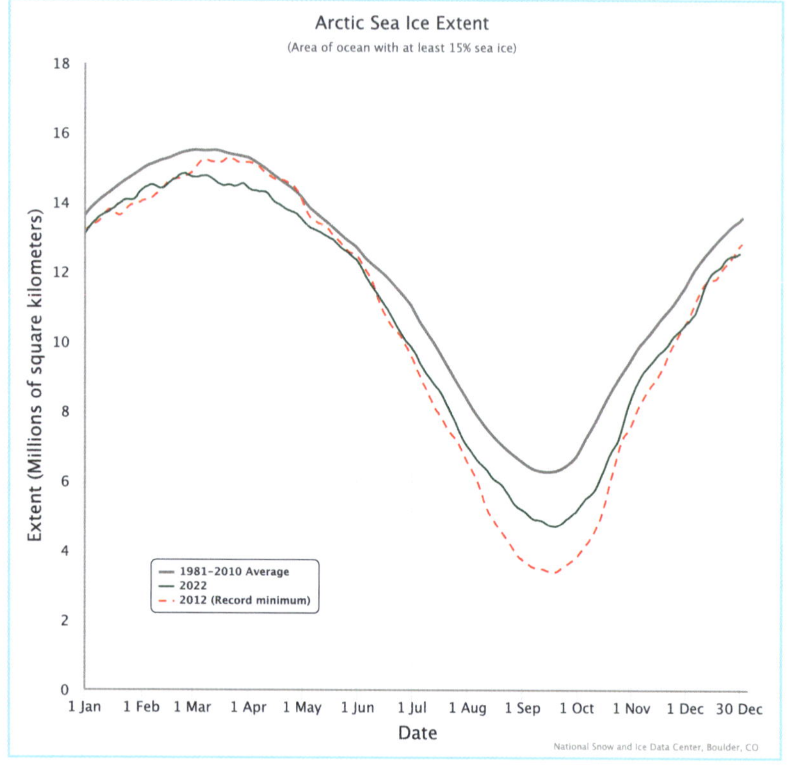

Credit: National Snow and Ice Data Center

a Why is the lowest extent of sea ice in September?

b Why is the highest extent of sea ice in March?

c Why is a line graph the best graph for this data?

2 Study this graph in comparison to the one above. Write **fact** or **opinion** for each statement.

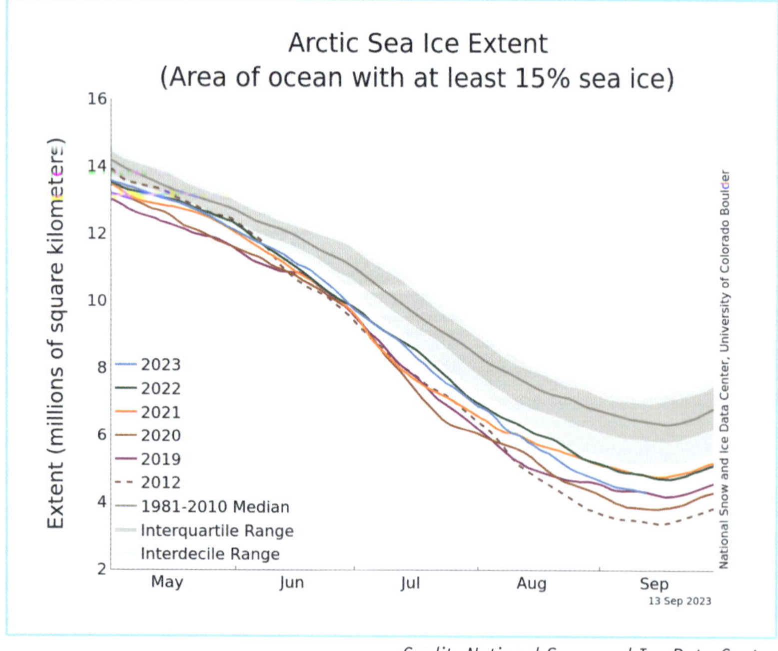

Credit: National Snow and Ice Data Center

a The extent of sea ice in 2022 was less than in 1981–2010.

b The extent of sea ice in 2022 has moved above the 2020 figures.

c The fall in the extent of sea ice in August to September is because more people are visiting the area.

d These graphs are made by scientists to see if the area is safe.

3 Write your own report on the extent of sea ice in the Arctic from the information in these graphs.

Unit 32 Sea ice

The **Save the Sea Ice Fund** publicity officer drew this graph to illustrate a report on the destruction of sea ice in the Arctic in 2012.

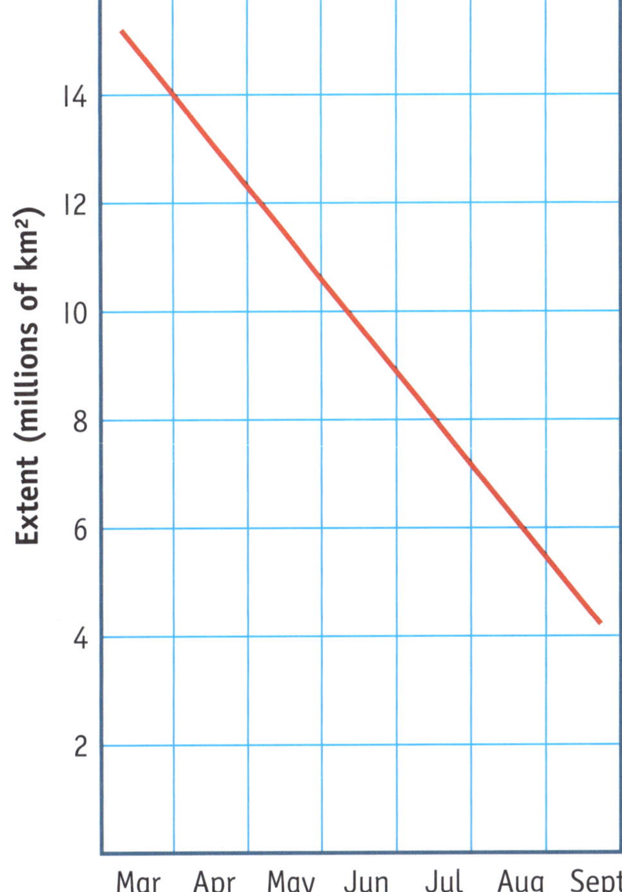

1 Compare this graph to the one in question 1 on page 150.

Information: ______________________

____

Scale of vertical axis: ______________________

____

Horizontal axis: ______________________

____

Bias of writer: ______________________

____

2 How would you describe this graph? Circle one.

factual non-factual emotive

biased unbiased misleading

3 What message is the writer trying to convey?

____

____

4 Explain how each of these graphs is misleading.

a

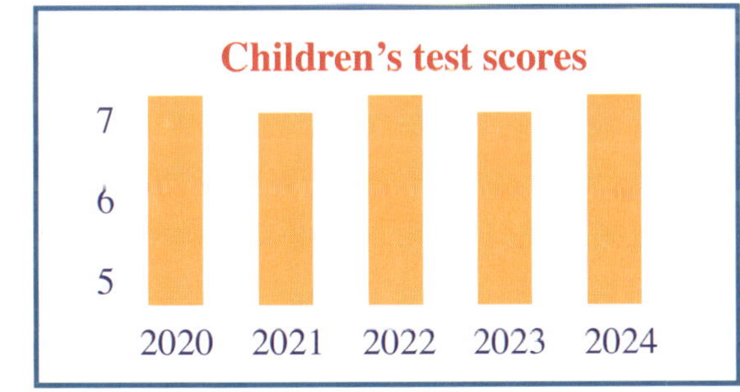

____

____

____

____

b

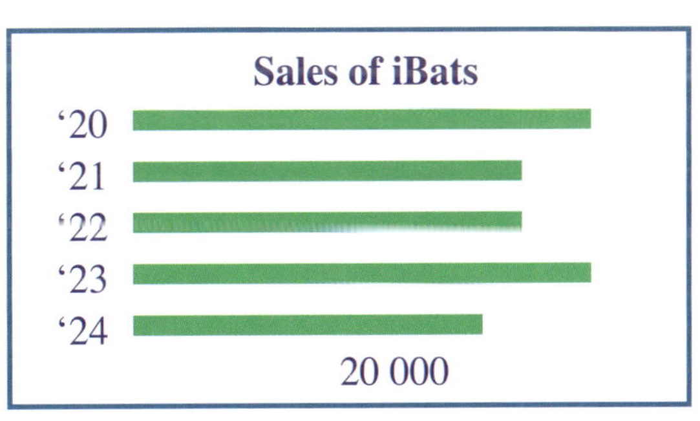

____

____

____

____

Mastery Checklist I can:

- ☐ interpret different types of graphs and tables
- ☐ choose the best way to present data
- ☐ tell facts from opinions
- ☐ identify bias in data.

Revision Term 3

1 Complete the Balance column. p 106

		Balance
Julia's Bank Balance		$4500
a Salary	$950	______
b Eftpos	$65	______
c Pay credit card	$210	______
d Deposit	$158	______
e Pay rent	$495	______
f Eftpos	$82	______

2 Mia bought 5 kg oranges for $12 and Minny spent $10 to buy 4 kg oranges. p 109

Who had the best buy?

______

3 p 110

256 762 121 5048 71 96 53 984

Which of these numbers are:

a multiples of 8? ______

b square numbers? ______

c divisible by 2 and 3? ______

d prime numbers? ______

4 Use HCF to reduce these fractions to equivalents in their lowest terms. p 110

a $\frac{10}{12}$ 10 factors ______ ÷ ______ = ______
12 factors ______ ÷ ______ = ______

b $\frac{15}{20}$ 15 factors ______ ÷ ______ = ______
20 factors ______ ÷ ______ = ______

5 Divide. p 111

a 240 ÷ 40 = ______ b 750 ÷ 50 = ______

c 720 ÷ 60 = ______ d 1200 ÷ 30 = ______

6 p 112

a $60\overline{)4500}$ b $30\overline{)4740}$

c $90\overline{)33\ 480}$ d $70\overline{)38\ 290}$

7 Multiply. p 113

	× 10	× 100	× 1000
a 9			
b 25			
c 638			
d 9250			

8 Divide. p 114

	÷ 10	÷ 100	÷ 1000
a 4872			
b 601			
c 98			
d 3			

9 Write in decimal notation. p 117

a 2480 cm = ______ m

b 42 500 g = ______ kg

c 750 g = ______ kg

d 12 000 m² = ______ ha

10 Round to two decimal places. p 117

a 12·462 ______ b 65·317 ______

11 Round to the nearest whole number. p 117

a 7·469 ______ b 324·099 ______

12 Show your working. p 118

a 10 − 3·45	b 2·75 + 3·08 + 0·6 + 12·54

Revision Term 3

13 a 162·54 ÷ 10 = ______________ **p 119**

b 600·9 ÷ 100 = ______________

c 1276 ÷ 100 = ______________

d 1276 ÷ 1000 = ______________

14 Complete: **p 122**

	10%	25%	50%	100%
a 240				
b 60				
c 1800				

15 Use <, > or = to complete. **p 123**

a 10% of 750 ________ 50% of 300

b 25% of 600 ________ 10% of 170

c $\frac{1}{4}$ of 16 ________ 20% of 20

d 1000 − 330 ________ 100% of 3·3

e 7·45 + 2·5 ________ 10

16 a 7 + 12 + 13 × 3 = 40 + ☐ **p 126**

b ☐ × 3 = 32 + 45 − 62

17 Write the number sentence. **p 127**
Use ( ) when necessary.

Divide the sum of 15 and 6 by 3.

____

18 Find the area.

a

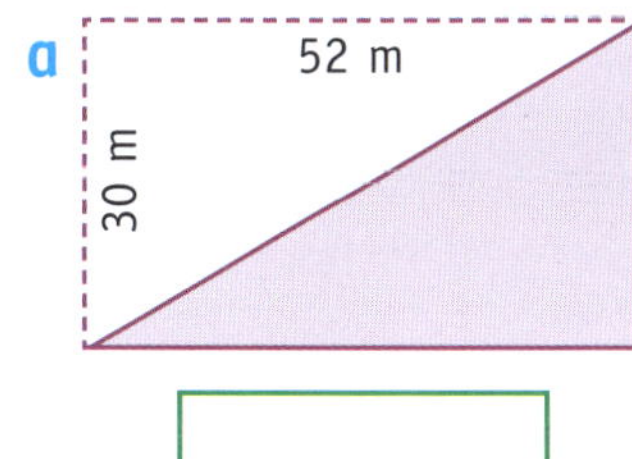

☐

b

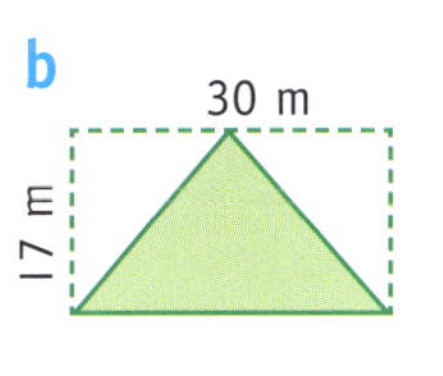

☐

19 Complete the table. **p 139**

Total	No. loads	Each load
3·2 t	4	a
b	5	1·2 t
2·5 t	c	0·5 t

20 Find the size of the missing angles. **p 144**

a

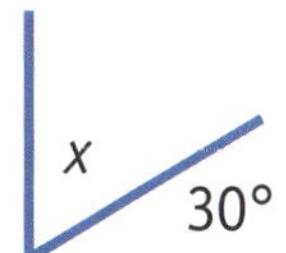

b

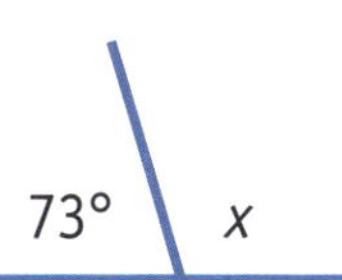

21 Find the size of the missing angles. **p 145**

a x = ______°

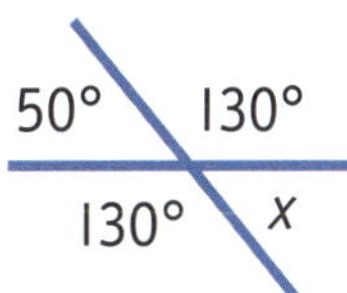

b x = ______°

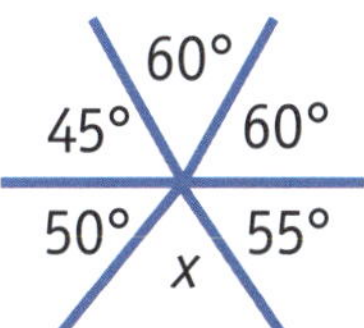

22 Find the size of the missing angles.

a

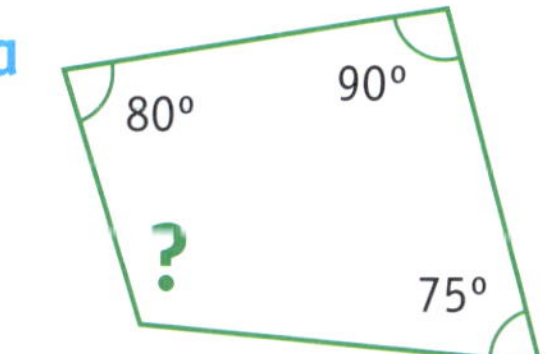

____

b

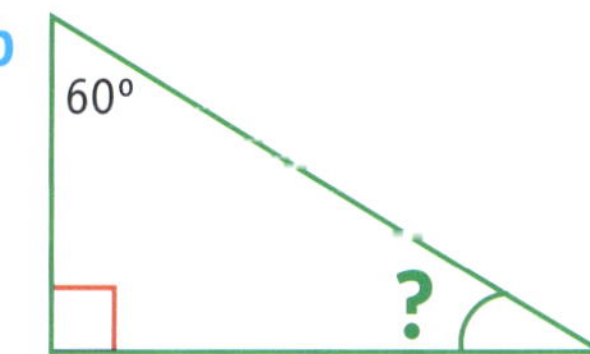

____

23 Prices for Tog Tops rose slowly for three years before slumping to an all-time low last March. **p 151**

Circle the graph that illustrates this information most accurately.

a

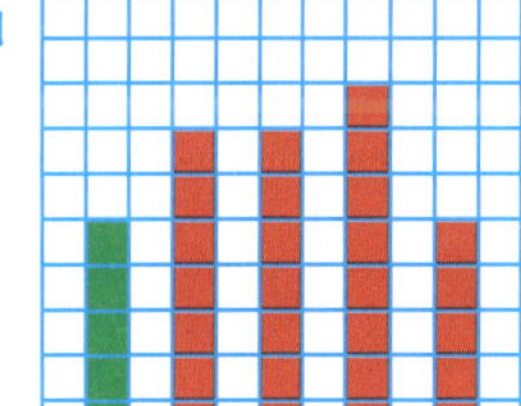

b

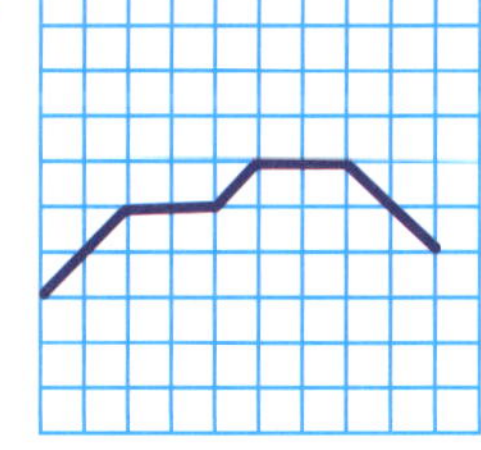

c

d

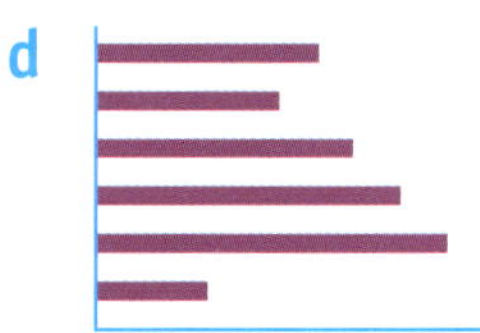

e Give reasons for your choice.

____

____

Unit 33 Multiply large numbers

Work out very large totals by multiplying small sections at a time.

A person who has lived 60 years has lived for 31 557 600 minutes.

1 Make up totals that will extend into tens of millions or beyond.

a Heart beats in 50 years ____________ b Hours ____________

c Steps ____________ d Meals ____________

e Words ____________ f Kilometres ____________

2 Breaths taken in the first ten years of my life.

a Calculate how many minutes in ten years.
(Don't forget leap years – say 2.) ____________

b Count breaths in one minute. ____________

c Multiply breaths per minute by minutes in ten years. ____________

d How many breaths in 100 years? ____________

3 Grandfather found it easy to explain how to work out how many minutes in ten years.

He said, **'Multiply 365 days by 10 and add 2 for leap years. Multiply those days by 24 to get hours. Multiply those hours by 60 to get minutes.'**

Is he right? ____________

4 He explains that using brackets, this would be written **{(365 × 10) + 2} × 24 × 60**.

Is he right? ____________ How many minutes in ten years? ____________

AC9M6N09 Number AC9M6A02 Algebra MA3-MR-01 • MA3-MR-02 Multiplicative relations B • Select and apply strategies to solve problems involving multiplication and division with whole numbers • Multiplicative relations B • Explore the use of brackets and the order of operations to write number sentences

Unit 33 Mixed operations

1 Solve the mystery message to find out who is leaving these footprints.

a 257×38 = ____ E

b 706×85 = ____ O

c 660×74 = ____ H

d 205×91 = ____ N

e 572×62 = ____ A

f 906×39 = ____ S

g 372×18 = ____ I

h $982 + 13\,976 + 435 + 4032$ = ____ T

i $397 + 2635 + 28 + 2805$ = ____ L

j 870×47 = ____ G

k 255×53 = ____ D

l 404×22 = ____ R

m $738 + 3686 + 32\,197 + 31$ = ____ B

n $7493 + 13\,957 + 9534 + 252$ = ____ F

19 425	48 840	9766		5865	60 010	35 334	19 425

19 425	8888	6696	36 652	9766		60 010	31 236

60 010	60 010	13 515	18 655	35 464	40 890	35 464	5865	35 464	8888

36 652	6696	9766

2 Show the working for the number sentences in the correct order.

eg $5 \times 4 + 17 \times 3 + 6 \times 16$
20 + 51 + 96 = 167

a $50 + $6.50 × 3 ____

b 16 + 8 × 22 ____

c 20 + 15 × 11 − 9 ____

d 18 × 5 × 2 + 75 × 3 ____

e 500 + 6 × 60 + 45 ____

f 30 × 8 + 12 × 15 ____

Unit 33 Multiplication and addition

1 Are brackets always necessary? Cross the number sentence where the brackets are not necessary.

a $8 \times 4 + (16 \times 2) - 6$

b $15 \times 8 - 4 \times (2 \times 3) - 10$

c $(72 - 10) \times 22$

d $32 \div 4 + \{(3 \times 18) - 2\} + 6 \times 11$

e Why aren't they necessary? ______________________________

____

2 Work the inner brackets first. Show your working.

a $\{(18 - 11) \times (7 + 4)\} =$

= ______________________

= __________

b $[(21 + 7) \times (5 - 3)] =$

= ______________________

= __________

c $15 + [(6 - 3) \times 2 \times 90]$

= ______________________

= __________

d $100 + [260 \times 2 \times (6 + 7)]$

= ______________________

= __________

The Jefferson Jets needed new equipment for their teams. They went to Tay's Team Togs for all their needs.

3 Help Tay with the invoice. Estimate answers by rounding to tens of dollars.

Item	Cost	Number	Estimated Total	Actual Total
A Boots	\$87.50	28 pairs		
B Socks	\$12	28 pairs		
C Shirts	\$38.70	28		
D Shorts	\$24.35	28		
E Trainers	\$158	36		
F Footballs	\$39.80	8		
		Total		

Challenge!

1 What will the Jefferson Jets pay? [ ]

2 Ted makes 10% profit on orders over \$5000.

What is his profit for this order? [ ]

25% discount for large orders!

AC9M6N08 Number AC9M6A02 Algebra MA3-AR-01 Additive relations A • Apply efficient mental and written strategies to solve addition and subtraction problems • MA3-MR-01 • MA3-MR-02 Multiplicative relations B • Select and apply strategies to solve problems involving multiplication and division with whole numbers • Multiplicative relations B • Explore the use of brackets and the order of operations to write number sentences

Unit 33 Using number sentences

Solve the equations and give values to the letters to read the message.

1

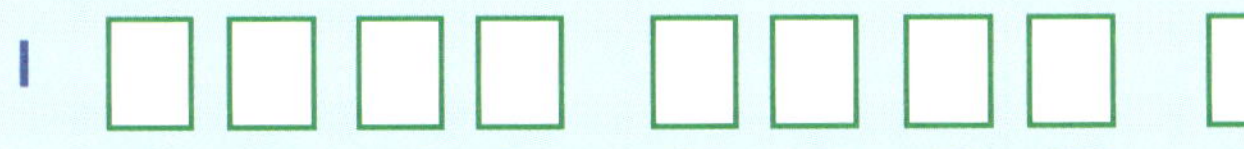

☐	☐	☐	☐	☐	☐	☐	☐	☐	☐	☐
7	15	40	32	8	15	40	32	4	15	10

a $C = 35 \div (3 + 2)$

b $E = 5^2 + 3^2 - 1^2 - 1$

c $\frac{1}{5} \times 45 - 1^2 = H$

d $M = 3 \times 17 - (6 + 5)$

e $0.8 \times 5 = N$

f $W = (6 \times 10) \div (3 \times 2)$

g $O = 8 + 49 \div 7$

2

☐	☐	☐	☐	☐	☐	☐	☐	☐	☐	☐	☐	☐	☐	☐	☐
6	5	3	9	8	1	2	5	6	8	7	2	4	10	5	6

a $56 \div A = 8$

A = ______

b $E + 24 = 30 - 1$

E = ______

c $45 - 5^2 = 2 \times I$

I = ______

d $M = 64 \div 2^3$

M = ______

Use inverse operations
$20 + Y = 17 + 6$
$Y = 17 + 6 - 20$
$Y = 3$

e $81 \div N = 27$

N = ______

f $42 \div (6 \times 7) = O$

O = ______

g $21 - 3 \times 4 = D$

D = ______

h $121 \div 11^2 + 1 = R$

R = ______

i $144 \div (S \times 2) = 12$

S = ______

j $T \times (5 + 4) = 36$

T = ______

Work backwards

I am thinking of a number.

Work backwards – use inverse operations.

a When I multiply the number by 6, add 12 and take away the product of 2 and 5, I have $\frac{1}{2}$ of one hundred.

What is the number? ☐

b I take a number, divide it by the sum of 6 and 2, add 15 and 6 and end up at 1 less than 37.

What number did I take? ☐

Unit 33 Number sentences

1 Write number sentences to solve the word problems.

a Davey had 14 hamsters but 3 died. Overnight 2 mother hamsters had 4 babies each. How many hamsters were now in Davey's cage?

Hamsters = ________________ = ______

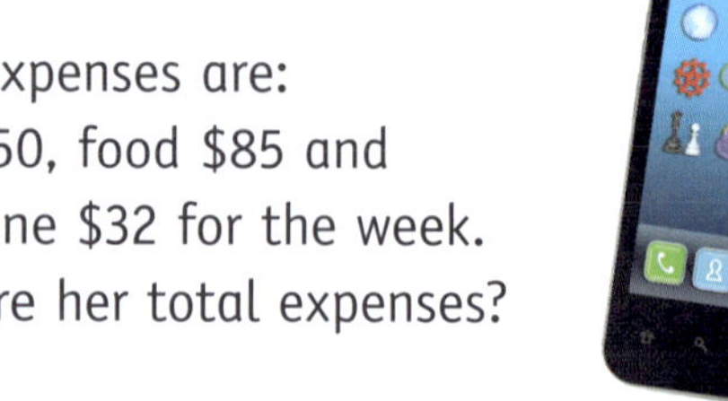

b Lina's expenses are: rent $150, food $85 and telephone $32 for the week. What are her total expenses?

Expenses = ________________ = ______

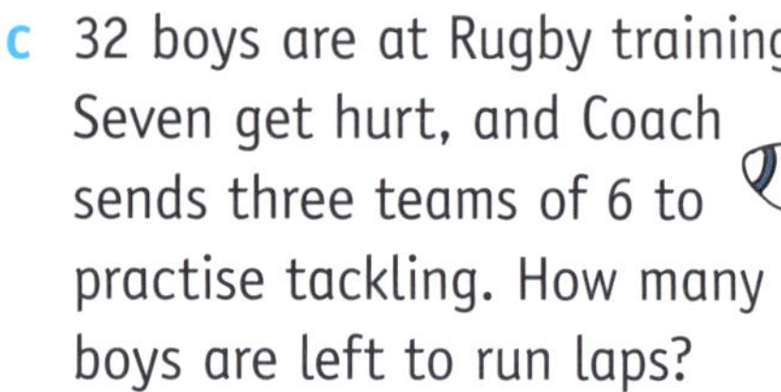

c 32 boys are at Rugby training. Seven get hurt, and Coach sends three teams of 6 to practise tackling. How many boys are left to run laps?

Boys = ________________ = ______

d Grandma plants 12 rows of lettuces, each containing 8 plants. Grandpa plants 4 more rows of 6 lettuces, but 12 are eaten by caterpillars. How many lettuces remain to grow?

Lettuces = ________________ = ______

e On the way to the train station, Nell rode 8 km before realising she had no money, so she rode back to get it. After getting some money, she rode 7 km towards the station before she found she had left her phone at home, so she rode back to get it. She then rode all the way to the station, a trip of 12 km, before boarding the train in a great hurry. How far did she ride altogether?

Kilometres = ________________ = ______

f In the cattery, 5 cats had 4 kittens each, and 3 cats had 5 kittens each. There is room for 30 kittens. How many kittens must have homes found immediately?

Kittens = ________________ = ______

g How many cats and kittens are in the cattery after homes are found for the first 10 kittens?

Cats and kittens = ________________ = ______

Challenge!

Choose the number sentence you would use to solve this:

Mum and Dad took 10-yr-old twins, Mai and Anh, to the movies with Grandma and Grandpa, who are pensioners.

Special Rates
Holiday Weekend
Adults $9.50
Pensioners $6
Children under 12
$5.80

a $9.50 = $6 + $5.80

b $9.50 + $9.50 + $5.80 + $6 × 2

c $19 + $10.80 + $12

d 2 × $9.50 + $5.80 × 2 + 2 × $6

Mastery Checklist

I can:
- ☐ use the order of operations
- ☐ use brackets correctly
- ☐ round to estimate answers
- ☐ work backwards to solve problems
- ☐ use inverse operations to solve equations
- ☐ write number sentences to solve word problems.

Unit 34 Division

Word problems

Many ways to be divided!

1 a Let's make teams!
175 players to make teams of 5.
How many teams?

b Share with me!
A $500 win to share with my 3 friends.
How much will we each receive?

c I'll do this job in 5 days.
4350 bricks to lay.
How many bricks to lay each day?

d Six for $8.40.
How much for one?

e 560 km in an eight-hour drive.
How fast am I travelling?

f Volume, 45 cm^3. Height, 3 cm.
Width, 3 cm.
How long is the box?

2 Write the number sentence you used for each problem in question 1.

a ______ b ______ c ______

d ______ e ______ f ______

3 Tell a story for each number problem.

a $119 \div 5 = 23\frac{4}{5}$

b $76 \div 20 = 3{\cdot}8$

c 225 eggs ÷ 6 per carton = 37 full cartons

d 26 people ÷ 4 per car = 7 cars

Unit 34 Remainders

1 Write the remainders as decimals.

a $5\overline{)238}$ b $4\overline{)146}$ c $8\overline{)306}$

When left with a remainder, add a decimal point and two zeros and keep dividing. eg 37 ÷ 4

$$4\overline{)37{\cdot}00} = 9{\cdot}25$$

	Working
2 a What is the average temperature of 35°, 28°, 32° and 30°?	
b How many kilometres per day will I need to ride to cover 118 km in 5 days?	
c Average of 36 runs, 29 runs, 16 runs, 56 runs and 22 runs.	
d If I put 7 apples in each box, how many boxes will I fill with 406 apples?	
e How many boxes of springs will I fill, putting 432 springs into boxes with 8 to a box?	
f Share 154 magazines with 7 classes. How many will each class receive?	

3 a How many carriages will be needed to transport the whole school of 362 students if 50 can fit in one carriage?

b Car trailers can fit 8 cars on one load. How many loads are required to transport 124 cars?

c How many containers of 30 marbles will be required to sort 1431 marbles?

Challenge! Divide and compare.

How much cheaper per issue is it to buy 6 months subscription to Scooby Doo Magazine at $45.30 plus 60c delivery each, than it is to buy 8 months of My Five at $65.60 delivered free?

AC9M6N09 Number **MA3-MR-01** Multiplicative relations A • Represent and solve division problems with whole number remainders

Unit 34 Subtraction

Add to check subtraction.
300 – 65 = 235
235 + 65 = 300

1 Subtract each number from 300.

a 167 ________ b 75 ________ c 287 ________

d 125 ________ e 206 ________ f 12 ________

2 What is the difference between:

a 65 and 49? ______ b 70 and 57? ______ c 120 and 58? ______ d 89 and 14? ______

e 100 and 38? ______ f 16 and 61? ______ g 27 and 72? ______ h 48 and 51? ______

3 a

	48
–6	
–3	
–9	
–10	
–16	

b

	112
–15	
–20	
–7	
–12	
–32	

c

	253
–42	
–36	
–19	
–107	
–28	

d

	309
–7	
–51	
–19	
–198	
–10	

The sum of the angles of a triangle is 180°. What is the size of the missing angles?

180° – ___° = ___°

4 a

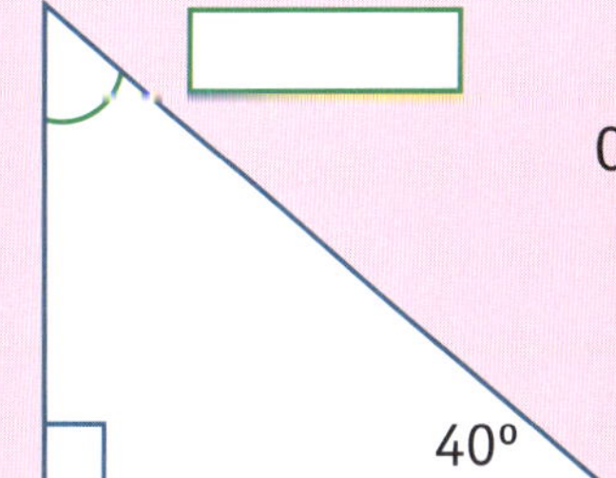

Check answers by adding to make 180°.

b

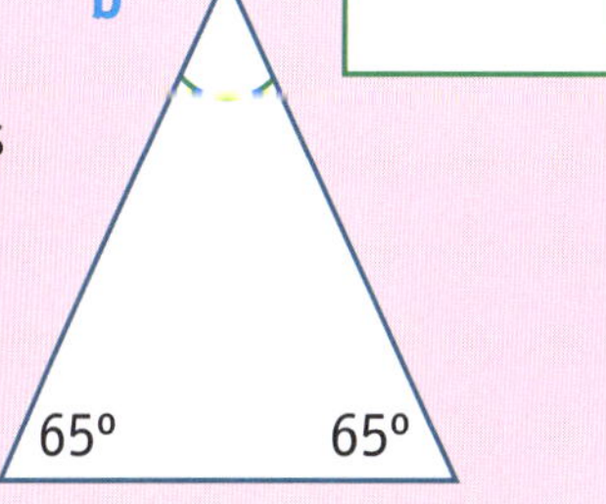

5 Do I make a profit (P) or loss (L)? By how much?

a **Bought** $4500 **Sold** $6250

b **Bought** $3275 **Sold** $4390

c **Bought** $10 850 **Sold** $8345

Challenge! Look for the pattern in each equation.

a 57 – 13 = 97 – ☐ b 85 – 19 = 75 – ☐

c 30 – ☐ = 40 – 16 d 68 – ☐ = 98 – 42

e 110 – 47 = 80 – ☐ f 26 – 11 = 46 – ☐

Pattern ____________

Mastery Checklist I can:

- ☐ solve real-world division problems
- ☐ write stories for number problems
- ☐ write remainders as decimals
- ☐ think about remainders in the real world
- ☐ solve subtraction problems.

Unit 35 Order fractions on a number line

1 Write smaller and larger fractions.

a 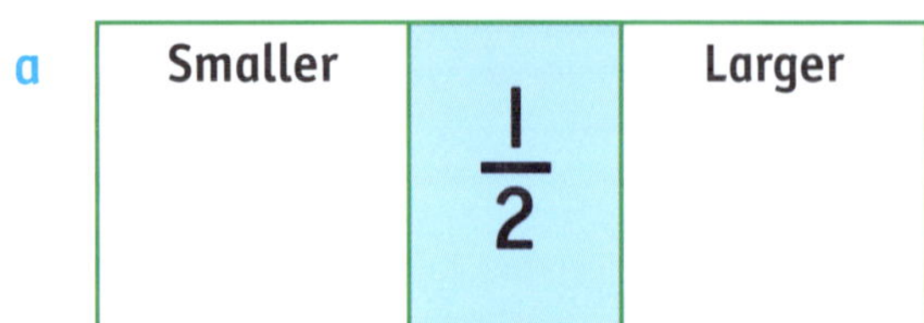

b 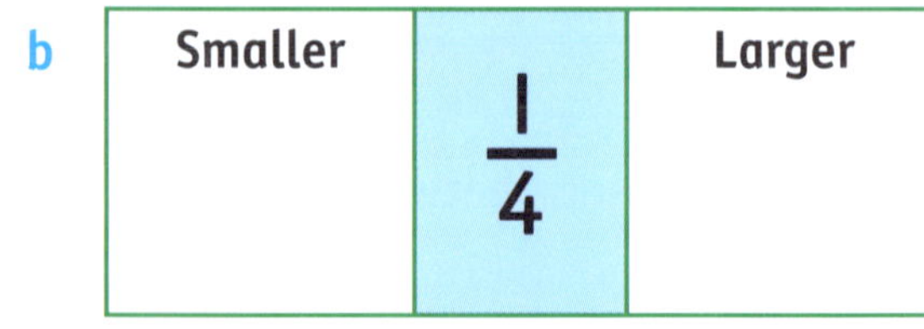

c 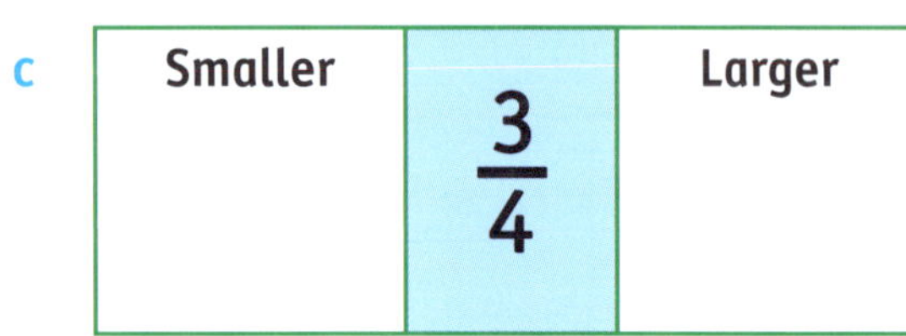

d 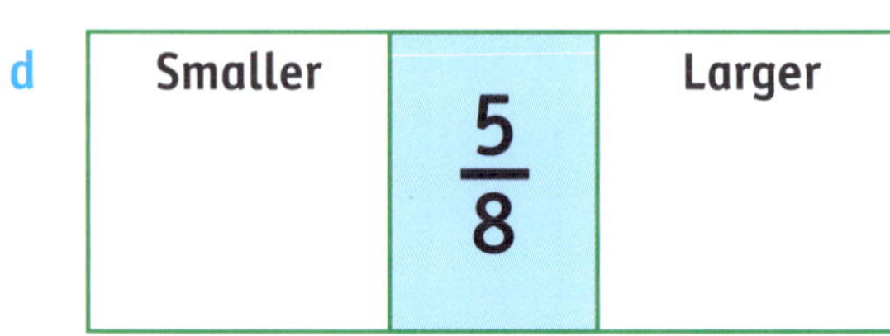

e 

f 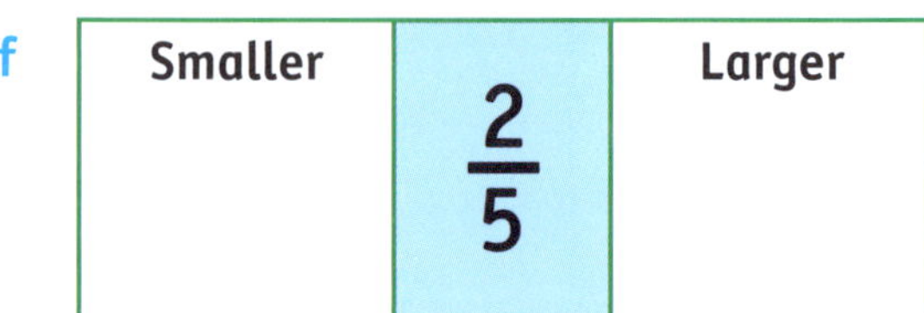

2 Write the missing fractions on the number lines.

a 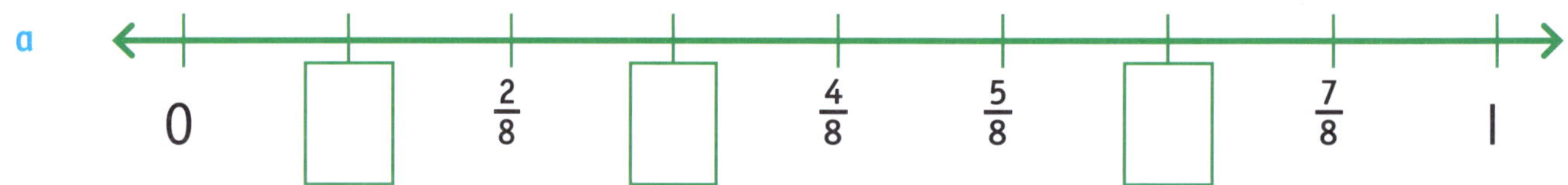

b 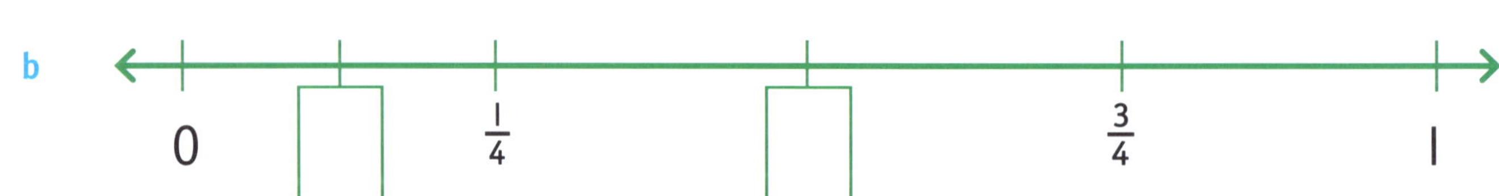

3 Draw lines to connect the fractions to the correct marks on the number line.

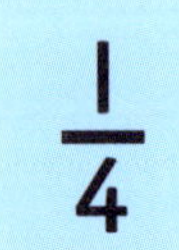

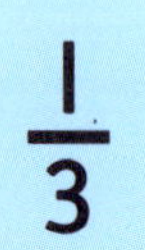

$\frac{2}{5}$ $\frac{3}{4}$ $\frac{1}{2}$ $\frac{5}{8}$

Unit 35 Recognise fractions as ÷

numerator → 2
denominator → 3

$\frac{2}{3} \rightarrow 2 \div 3$

$\frac{2}{3}$ represents dividing something into 3 equal parts and having 2 of those parts.

1 Draw lines to match the fractions to the correct division expressions.

a $\frac{1}{3}$	$3 \div 4$
b $\frac{4}{5}$	$1 \div 3$
c $\frac{7}{8}$	$4 \div 5$
d $\frac{3}{4}$	$6 \div 10$
e $\frac{2}{5}$	$7 \div 8$
f $\frac{6}{10}$	$2 \div 5$

2 Write the division expression for each fraction.

a $\frac{1}{3}$ $1 \div 3$ b $\frac{2}{10}$ ____________

c $\frac{3}{5}$ ____________   d $\frac{3}{8}$ ____________

e $\frac{7}{8}$ ____________   f $\frac{1}{5}$ ____________

g $\frac{7}{10}$ ____________   h $\frac{1}{2}$ ____________

3 Complete the table.

Fraction	Division	Out of
a $\frac{1}{4}$	$1 \div 4$	1 out of 4
b		5 out of 8
c	$9 \div 10$	
d $\frac{2}{4}$		
e	$4 \div 8$	
f		3 out of 10

Unit 35 Equivalent fractions

Equivalent fractions are different fractions that represent the same amount.

$\frac{1}{2}$ 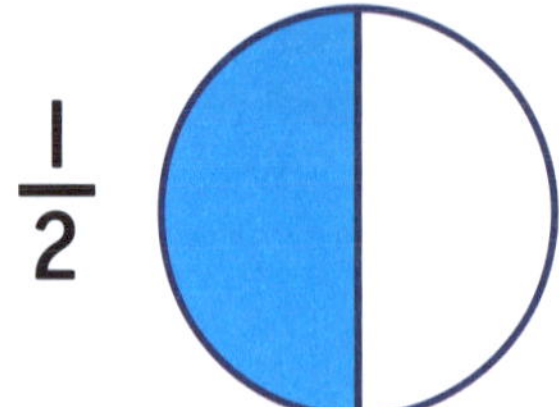 $\frac{4}{8}$ 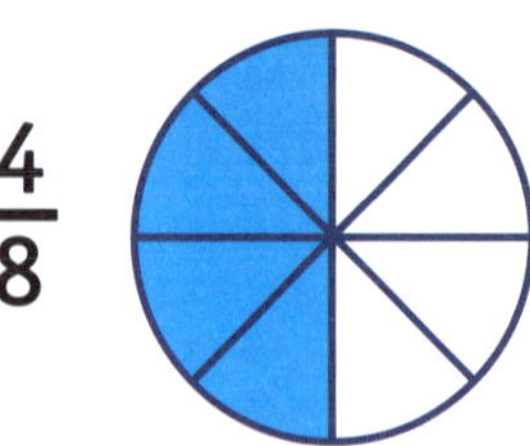

$\frac{1}{2}$ and $\frac{4}{8}$ are equivalent because they both represent one half of one whole.

1 Complete the equivalent fractions.

eg $\frac{1}{2} \overset{\times 4}{=} \frac{4}{8}$ (×4)

a $\frac{2}{5} = \frac{\square}{10}$ b $\frac{1}{4} = \frac{\square}{8}$ c $\frac{3}{4} = \frac{\square}{8}$ d $\frac{1}{2} = \frac{\square}{8}$

e $\frac{4}{5} = \frac{\square}{10}$ f $\frac{1}{2} = \frac{\square}{10}$ g $\frac{3}{3} = \frac{\square}{8}$ h $\frac{3}{5} = \frac{\square}{10}$ i $\frac{4}{4} = \frac{\square}{8}$

2 Make the denominators the same and then add or subtract.

a $\frac{3}{4} - \frac{2}{8} =$ $\frac{3}{4} - \frac{1}{4}$
$= \frac{2}{4}$

b $\frac{1}{5} + \frac{1}{4} =$ ________
$=$ ________

c $\frac{2}{5} + \frac{4}{10} =$ ________
$=$ ________

d $\frac{4}{5} + \frac{3}{10} =$ ________
$=$ ________

e $\frac{3}{5} + \frac{1}{10} =$ ________
$=$ ________

f $\frac{7}{8} - \frac{1}{4} =$ ________
$=$ ________

g $\frac{9}{10} + \frac{2}{5} =$ ________
$=$ ________

h $\frac{7}{10} - \frac{1}{5} =$ ________
$=$ ________

i $\frac{3}{5} + \frac{5}{10} =$ ________
$=$ ________

j $\frac{3}{4} - \frac{5}{8} =$ ________
$=$ ________

k $\frac{1}{5} + \frac{6}{10} =$ ________
$=$ ________

l $\frac{9}{10} + \frac{1}{2} =$ ________
$=$ ________

Mastery Checklist

I can:
- ☐ write fractions on a number line
- ☐ connect fractions with division
- ☐ identify and make equivalent fractions.

AC9M5N03 Number **MA3-RQF-01** Representing quantity fractions A • Compare and order common unit fractions • Representing quantity fractions B • Use equivalence to add and subtract fractional quantities

Unit 36 Operations using fractions

1 **Crunchy drops** (serves 4)

$\frac{1}{4}$ cup raisins $\frac{1}{2}$ cup coconut

$\frac{1}{3}$ cup peanuts $\frac{3}{4}$ cup butter

Double the contents and show the new level.

a raisins

b coconut

c peanuts

d butter

2 **Pikelets**

$\frac{1}{2}$ cup milk 2 tbsp sugar

$\frac{3}{4}$ cup flour 2 eggs

Show the new level.

a Add $\frac{1}{8}$ cup to the milk.

b Add $\frac{1}{8}$ cup to the flour.

c Add $\frac{1}{12}$ cup to the milk.

d Add $\frac{1}{12}$ to the flour.

Unit 36 Addition of fractions

Remember equivalent fractions.

$\frac{1}{4} = \frac{2}{8} = \frac{3}{12} = \frac{4}{16}$

Note the patterns of the numerators and denominators.

1 Change all Crunchy drops ingredients on page 165 to twelfths of a cup.

a raisins $\frac{1}{4}$ = ______ b coconut $\frac{1}{2}$ = ______

c peanuts $\frac{1}{3}$ = ______ d butter $\frac{3}{4}$ = ______

2 Use equivalent fractions and common denominators to add. Show working.

a $\frac{1}{4} + \frac{1}{3}$ = ______ = ______ b $\frac{1}{2} + \frac{1}{3}$ = ______ = ______ c $\frac{1}{4} + \frac{2}{3}$ = ______ = ______ d $\frac{3}{4} + \frac{1}{3}$ = ______ = ______

Change improper fractions to mixed numbers.

$\frac{5}{4} = 1\frac{1}{4}$

$\frac{8}{3} = 2\frac{2}{3}$

e $\frac{1}{2} + \frac{7}{8}$ = ______ = ______ f $\frac{3}{4} + \frac{5}{8}$ = ______ = ______ g $\frac{3}{8} + \frac{3}{4}$ = ______ = ______

h $\frac{1}{2} + \frac{5}{12}$ = ______ = ______ i $\frac{2}{3} + \frac{7}{12}$ = ______ = ______ j $\frac{1}{3} + \frac{11}{12}$ = ______ = ______

3 Study the Crunchy drops recipe on page 165. Then answer true or false.

a There is twice as much coconut as peanuts. ______

b Peanuts plus coconut equals butter. ______

c Raisins plus coconut equals butter. ______

d Order the ingredients from smallest amount to largest amount.

______

______

4 Circle the larger fraction in each pair.

a $\frac{3}{4}$ $\frac{2}{3}$ b $\frac{5}{6}$ $\frac{3}{4}$ c $\frac{3}{8}$ $\frac{7}{16}$ d $\frac{7}{10}$ $\frac{13}{20}$

5 Write each set of fractions in ascending order.

a $\frac{5}{6}, \frac{1}{2}, \frac{7}{12}$ ______ b $\frac{5}{8}, \frac{1}{4}, \frac{1}{2}$ ______ c $\frac{17}{20}, \frac{7}{10}, \frac{3}{4}$ ______ d $\frac{2}{5}, \frac{3}{10}, \frac{32}{100}$ ______

Challenge! Reduce these fractions to lowest terms using Highest Common Factors.

$\frac{6}{18}$ $\frac{16}{20}$ $\frac{15}{45}$ $\frac{10}{45}$ $\frac{12}{36}$ $\frac{20}{60}$ $\frac{14}{35}$ $\frac{25}{40}$ $\frac{65}{100}$

AC9M6N03 • AC9M6N05 Number MA3-RQF-01 Representing quantity fractions B • Use equivalence to add and subtract fractional quantities

Unit 36 Multiplication of fractions

1 Make the Crunchy drops recipe 3 times bigger.

a $\frac{1}{4}$ cup raisins × 3 = ______
= ______

b $\frac{1}{2}$ cup coconut × 3 = ______
= ______

c $\frac{3}{4}$ cup butter × 3 = ______
= ______

d $\frac{1}{3}$ cup peanuts × 3 = ______
= ______

$\frac{1}{4} \times 3 = \frac{1}{4} + \frac{1}{4} + \frac{1}{4} = \frac{3}{4}$

$\frac{3}{5} \times 3 = \frac{3}{5} + \frac{3}{5} + \frac{3}{5} = \frac{9}{5} = 1\frac{4}{5}$

Multiply fractions by using repeated addition. Change improper fractions to mixed numbers.

2 Multiply by 3 the Pikelets recipe on page 165. Write the new recipe here.

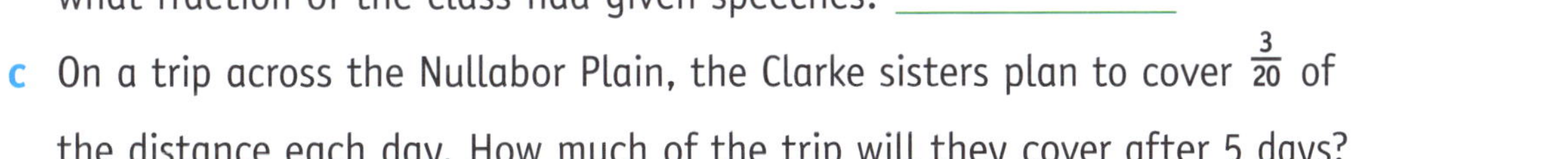

3 a $\frac{2}{3} \times 4 =$ ______ = ______ b $\frac{2}{5} \times 4 =$ ______ = ______ c $\frac{3}{8} \times 3 =$ ______ = ______ d $\frac{5}{12} \times 3 =$ ______ = ______

4 a $5 \times \frac{1}{4}$ hour = ______ = ______ b $4 \times \frac{1}{3}$ hour = ______ = ______ c $3 \times \frac{1}{5}$ hour = ______ = ______ d $10 \times \frac{1}{2}$ day = ______ = ______

5 a Twelve children were each offered a quarter of an apple. Write a number sentence.
How many apples were used? ______

b Each day, $\frac{1}{6}$ of the class gave speeches. After three days, what fraction of the class had given speeches? ______

c On a trip across the Nullabor Plain, the Clarke sisters plan to cover $\frac{3}{20}$ of the distance each day. How much of the trip will they cover after 5 days? ______

Draw a diagram

Sammy spent $\frac{1}{2}$ his money on magazines and another $\frac{1}{3}$ on downloads. He then had $10 left. How much did he spend on magazines? ☐

Mastery Checklist I can:
- ☐ double fractions
- ☐ add fractions
- ☐ use equivalent fractions and common denominators
- ☐ compare and order fractions with different denominators
- ☐ use repeated addition to multiply fractions.

Problem solving

Good food for good health

The corner shop sells freshly made foods. Explain how they can finish each ingredients list.

1 Muesli

$\frac{1}{2}$ oatmeal
$\frac{1}{4}$ bran
$\frac{1}{8}$ nuts

What fraction is left for sultanas? ______

2 Fruit salad

$\frac{1}{2}$ cup pineapple
$\frac{1}{3}$ cup peach
$\frac{1}{3}$ cup apricot
$\frac{1}{2}$ cup strawberries

What fraction of 2 cups is left for bananas? ______

3 Fruit bread

$\frac{3}{4}$ plain flour
$\frac{3}{4}$ wholemeal flour
$\frac{1}{5}$ sultanas
$\frac{1}{4}$ nuts

What fraction of 2 cups is left for coconut? ______

4 Green salad

$\frac{1}{2}$ bowl green lettuce
$\frac{1}{3}$ bowl purple lettuce
$\frac{1}{6}$ bowl avocado

What fraction of the bowl is left for celery? ______

5 Fruit punch

$\frac{3}{4}$ L lemonade
$\frac{2}{3}$ L pineapple juice
$\frac{1}{3}$ L orange juice
$\frac{1}{8}$ L cordial

How much of 2 L is still needed? ______

I can solve problems by:

☐ understanding and adding fractions ☐ writing algorithms.

AC9M6N05 Number MAO-WM-01 Working mathematically • choosing and applying mathematical techniques to solve problems • communicating thinking and reasoning coherently and clearly • MA3-RQF-01 Representing quantity fractions B • Use equivalence to add and subtract fractional quantities

Unit 37 Length conversions

We use different units to measure different things.

There are one hundred centimetres in one metre.

100 cm = 1 m

124 cm = 1·24 m

1 Complete the table.

Centimetres	m and cm	Decimal metres
a 324 centimetres	3 m 24 cm	3·24 m
b	6 m 15 cm	
c		8·10 m
d 1642 centimetres		
e	12 m 1 cm	
f		13·53 m
g	17 m 45 cm	
h 3894 centimetres		

There are ten millimetres in one centimetre.

10 mm = 1 cm

135 mm = 13·5 cm

2 Convert the measurements.

a 124 mm = ________ cm
b 8·9 cm = ________ mm
c 221 mm = ________ cm
d 9·1 cm = ________ mm
e 8430 mm = ________ cm
f 20·42 cm = ________ mm
g 3·5 cm = ________ mm
h 740 mm = ________ cm
i 6·4 cm = ________ mm
j 1240 mm = ________ cm
k 5030 mm = ________ cm
l 63·25 cm = ________ mm
m 250 mm = ________ cm
n 12·1 cm = ________ mm
o 8·7 cm = ________ mm
p 3560 mm = ________ cm
q 18·42 cm = ________ mm
r 4384 mm = ________ cm

Unit 37 Perimeter

Work out the perimeter. First, convert to the same units.

1

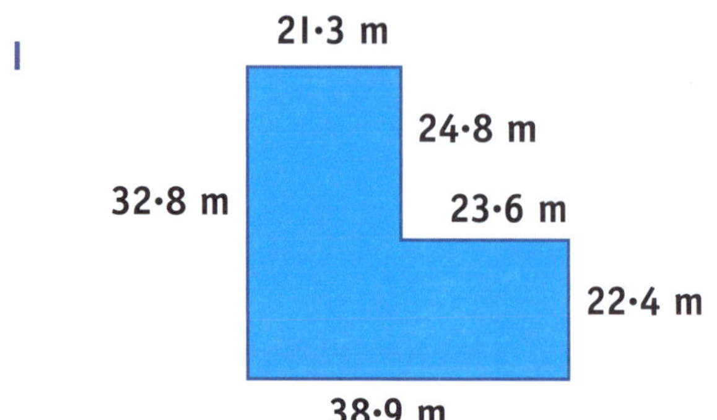

Perimeter = __________ m

2

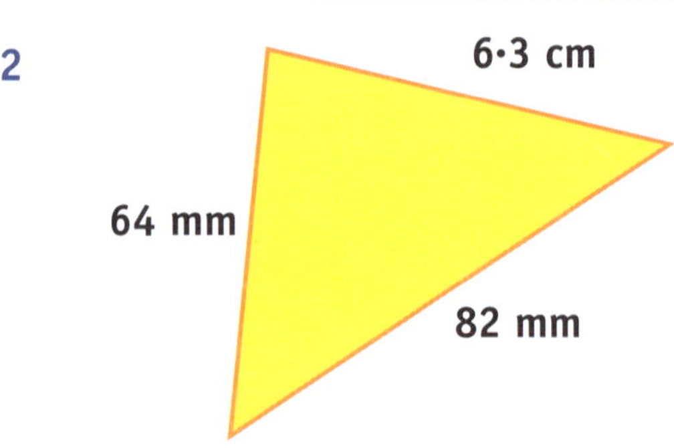

Perimeter = __________ cm

3

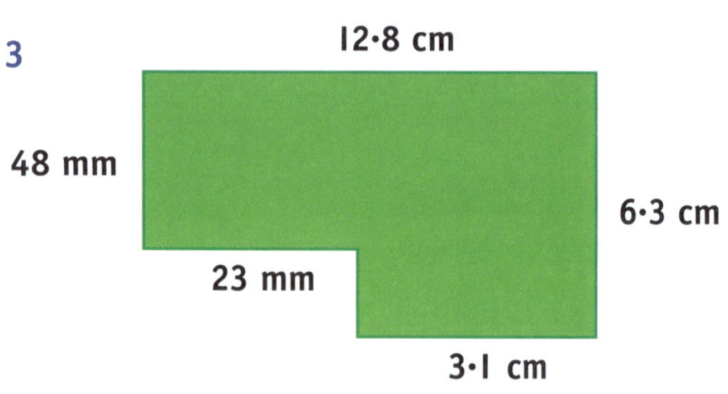

Perimeter = __________ cm

4

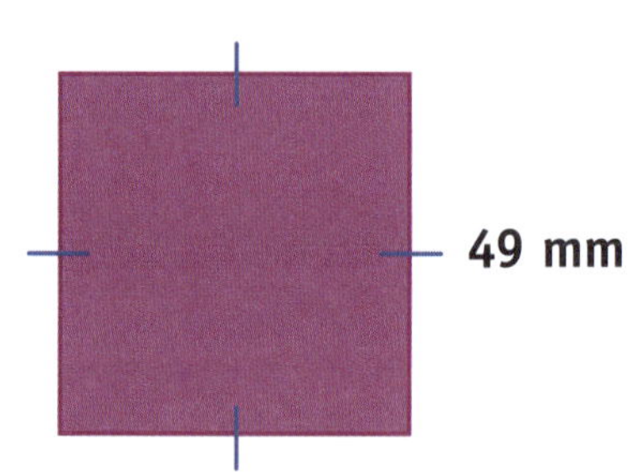

Perimeter = __________ mm

5

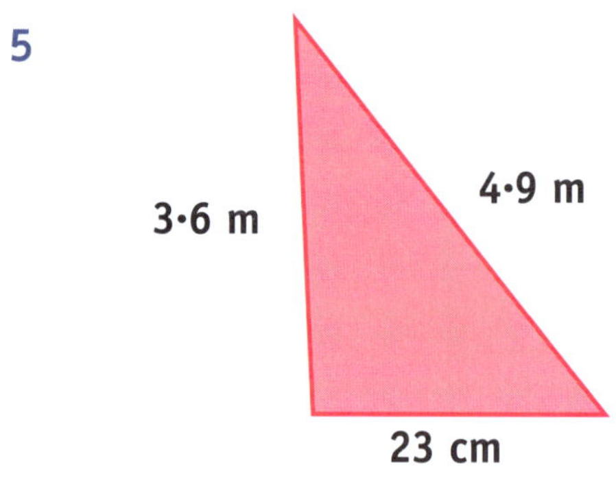

Perimeter = __________ m

6

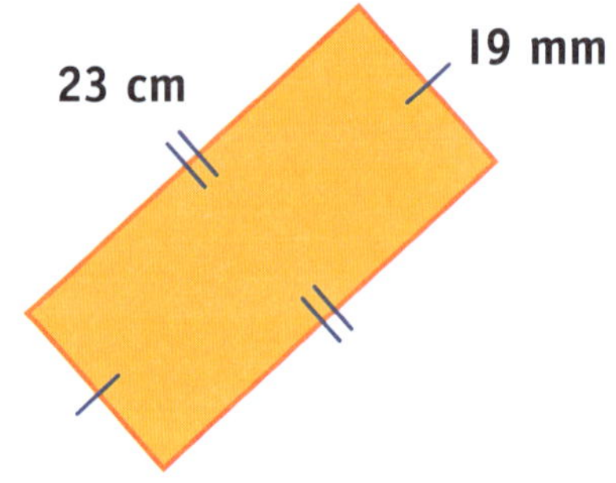

Perimeter = __________ cm

Unit 37 Area and perimeter

This is a plan for a new Community Play Centre at Collinsdene.

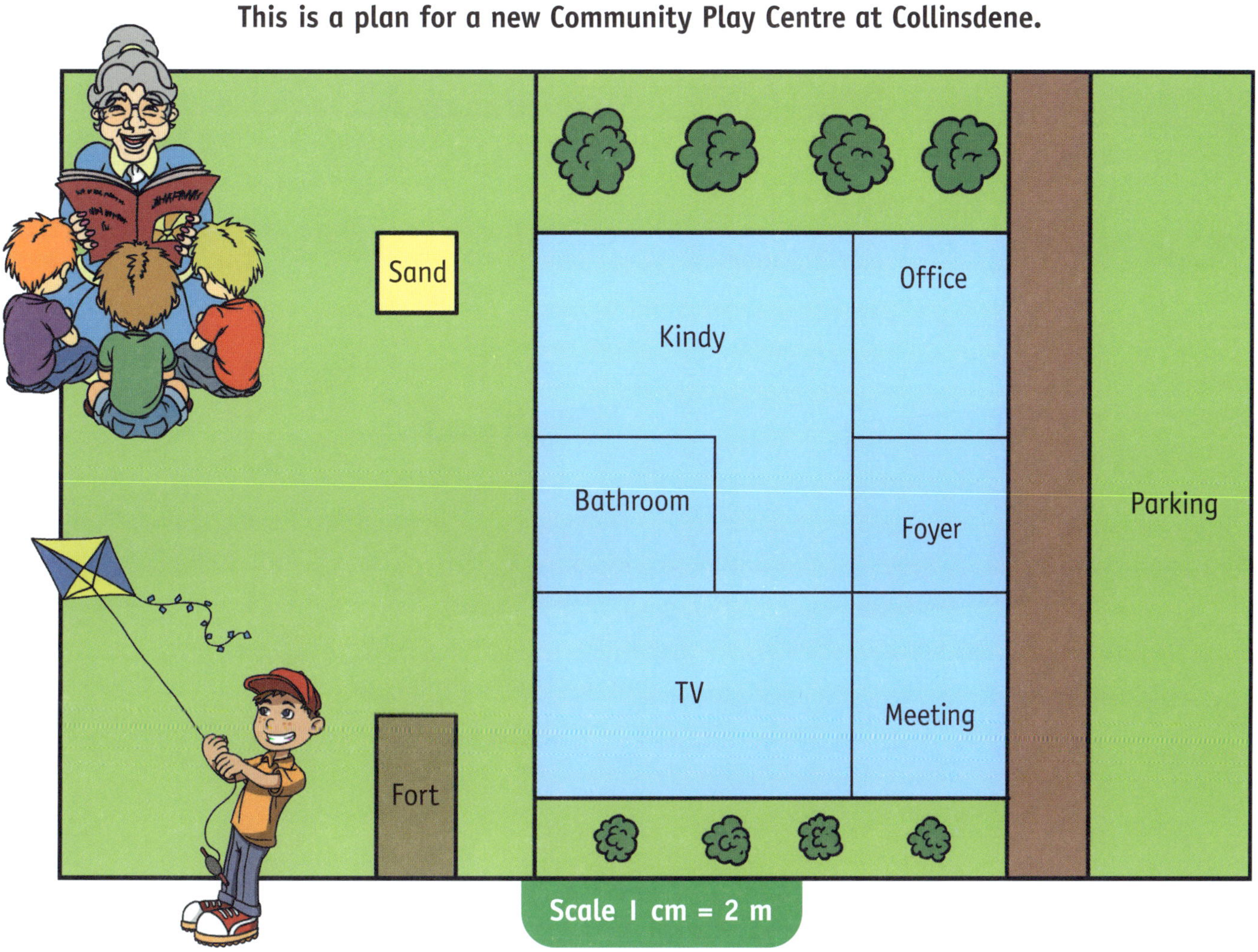

Sand

Kindy

Office

Bathroom

Foyer

Parking

TV

Meeting

Fort

Scale 1 cm = 2 m

1 Measure all sides to the nearest centimetre and convert to metres using the scale. Write measurements on the plan.

2 Fill in the builder's measurement chart in metres and square metres.

Area of irregular shapes

Divide the area into two small areas and add together.

Area of C = A + B

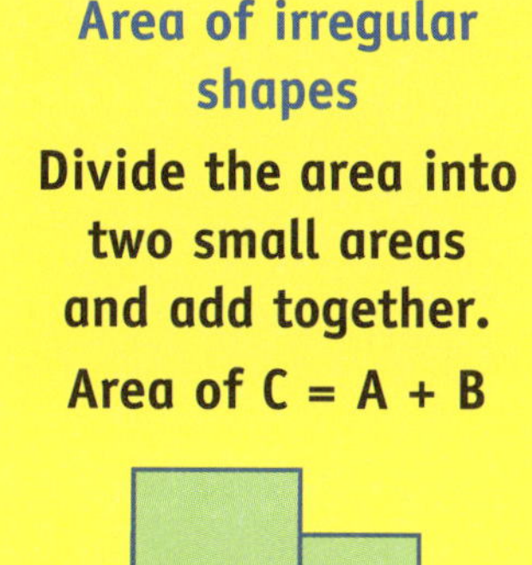

Room	Length	Width	Area	Perimeter
Foyer				
Office				
Kindy A				
B				
TV				
Meeting				
Bathroom				

Unit 37 Working with area and perimeter

1 Refer to the plan on page 171. Special carpet is ordered for the TV room, Meeting room and Kindy. How many square metres of carpet need to be ordered?

a TV room ____________ b Meeting room ____________ c Kindy ____________ d Total ____________

2 How much will the carpet cost at $45 per square metre?

a TV room ____________ b Meeting room ____________ c Kindy ____________ d Total ____________

3 Tiles to choose for the Bathroom floor. Write the total price for each. Circle your choice.

a $58 per m^2 ______

b $85 per m^2 ______

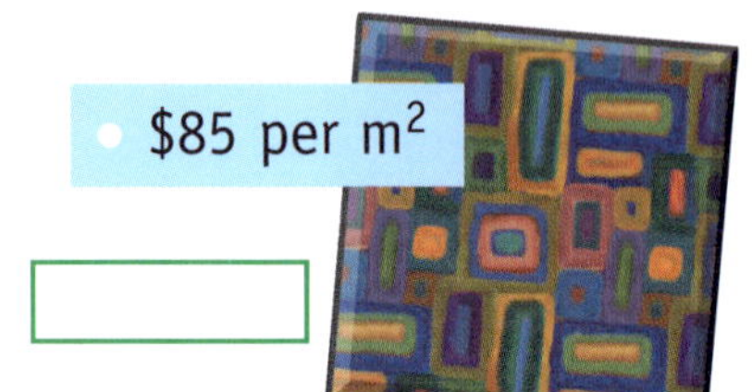

c $68 per m^2 ______

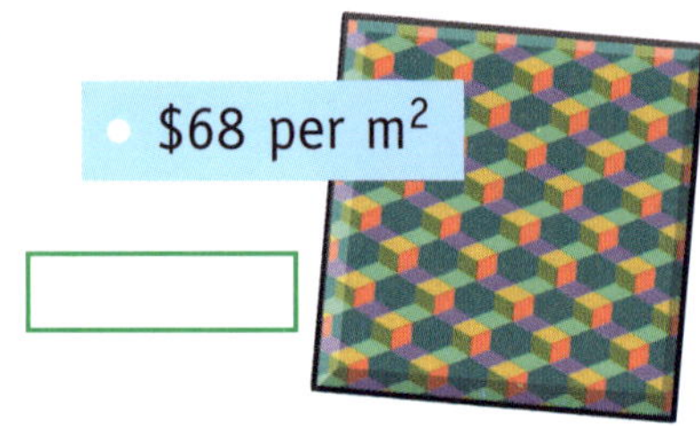

4 a Draw the TV room using the scale 1 cm = 1 m.

b Put an **X** for the TV screen. Draw a cushion area, an exercise area and a bookshelf in the room. Label each area.

c Add a wet area for painting away from the bookshelf. If you tiled the wet area with 50 cm tiles, how many would it take?

____

Four 50 cm square tiles will fit in one m^2.

Draw a diagram

Bill is building a fence around the sandpit and the fort.
Posts are 1 metre apart. How many posts are needed for each? ______

 AC9M6M02 Measurement **MA3-GM-02** Geometric measure A • Length: Use metres and kilometres for length and distances • **MA3-2DS-02** Two-dimensional spatial structure B • Area: Find the area of composite figures

Unit 37 Very large areas

1 hectare = 10 000 m²
ha stands for hectare.
Different shapes can be one hectare.

1 Each of the following areas is one hectare.
What are the missing measurements?

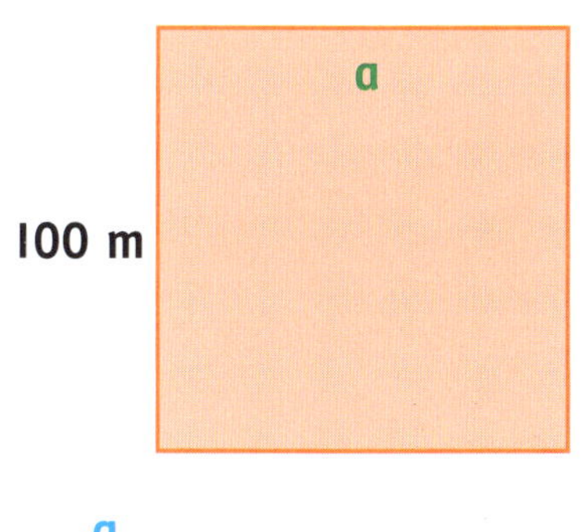

b

200 m

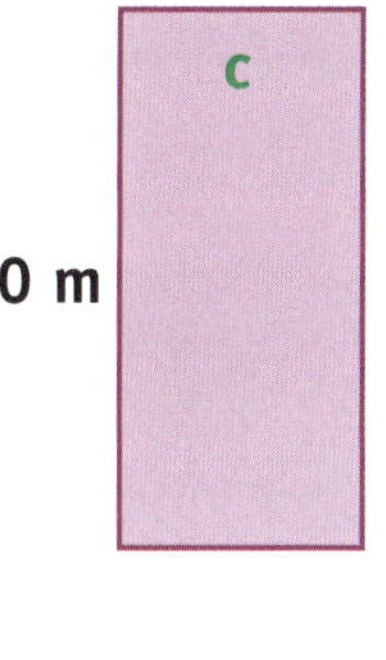

a ____________ b ____________ c ____________

2 True or false?

a A hectare can only be 100 m long and 100 m wide. ____________

b My patio has an area of 1 ha. ____________

c Uncle John's orchard covers 2·7 ha. ____________

d The perimeter of a hectare is 1000 m.

3 This is a scale drawing of a practice netball court.

a What scale is used? [ ]

b What is the area of the centre section? [ ]

c **A** passed the ball to **B**. What was the length of the pass? [ ]

d All straight lines are painted green. What is the total length of the green lines? [ ]

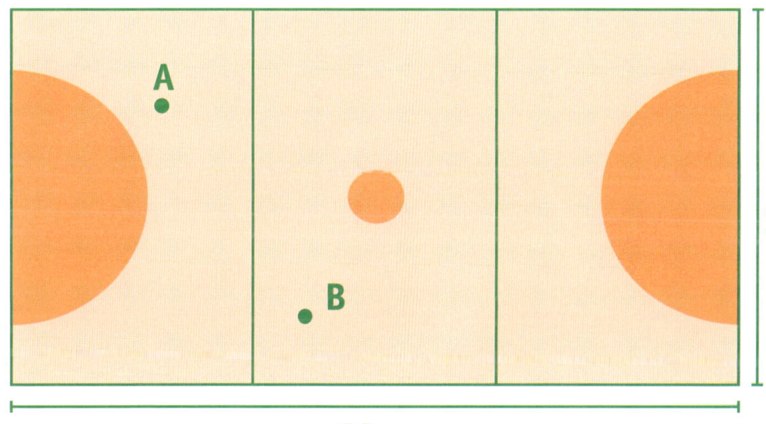

4 Australia's states and territories have the following areas. Match each with its area.

a 68 401 km² Tas.

b 800 642 km² ____________

c 227 416 km² ____________

d 1 349 129 km² ____________

e 983 482 km² ____________

f 2 529 875 km² ____________

g 2358 km² ____________

h 1 730 648 km² ____________

Mastery Checklist

I can:
- ☐ measure lengths
- ☐ convert metric units of length
- ☐ calculate perimeter
- ☐ calculate area
- ☐ draw a room to scale
- ☐ calculate large areas in hectares and km².

Unit 38 Timetable

Study the rail timetables for the Sydney to Melbourne 'ZZM'. Times are given in 24-hr time.

1 What time elapses between the departure of:

  a Train A and Train B? ______________

  b Train B and Train C? ______________

2 Complete the missing sections of the timetables.

3 The trains cross into Victoria at Albury.

  a How long is the NSW section of the trip?

  ____

  b How long is the Victorian section?

  ____

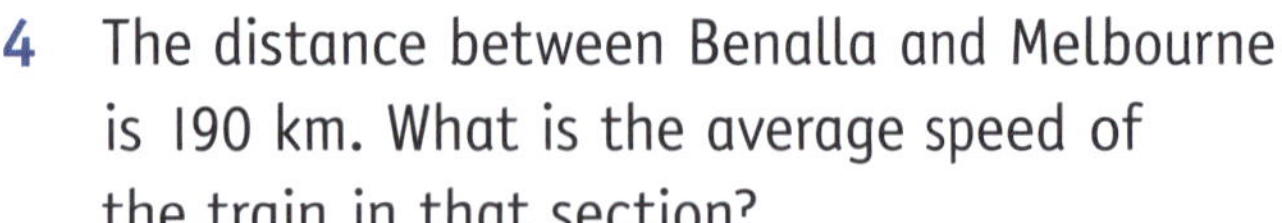

4 The distance between Benalla and Melbourne is 190 km. What is the average speed of the train in that section?

____

5 If the train leaves Melbourne at 08:15, when will it arrive in Sydney if it travels at the same rate as for Sydney to Melbourne?

____

6 If I arrive at Central Station in Sydney at 8:30 pm, how long do I have to wait before Train A leaves?

____

7 Which train will I catch to arrive in Wagga Wagga for a 1:30 pm workshop at the University?

____

8 On which train would you expect to have:

  a lunch? ______________

  b breakfast? ______________

  c dinner? ______________

Departure			City
A	B	C	
20:43	06:58	12:53	Sydney
20:54	07:09	13:04	Strathfield
21:26	07:41	13:36	Campbelltown
22:31	08:46	14:41	Moss Vale
23:19	09:34	15:29	Goulburn
00:24	10:39	-	Yass Junction
01:11	11:26	-	Harden
01:42	11:57	-	Cootamundra
02:18	12:33	-	Junee
02:43	12:58	-	Wagga Wagga
03:01	13:16	-	The Rock
03:17	13:32	-	Henty
03:28	13:43	19:38	Culcairn
03:55	-	20:05	Albury
04:36	-	20:46	Wangaratta
05:00	-	21:10	Benalla
07:00	-	23:10	Melbourne

Challenge! At midday, two trains depart their stations 200 km apart and travel towards each other. Puffing Billy travels at 20 km/h and Roddy Rocket travels at 80 km/h.

At what time will they meet? ______

AC9M6M03 Measurement **MA3-NSM-02** Non-spatial measure A • Time: Compare 12- and 24-hour time systems and convert between them • Non-spatial measure B • Time: Solve problems involving duration, using 12- and 24-hour time

Unit 38 Itineraries

1 Ruby is going on a cruise. She is planning her itinerary. Using the timetable, write the times Ruby can do her chosen activities.

Ruby's To Do List

Bingo: __________

Art auction: __________

Lunch buffet: __________

Ice cream: __________

Trivia: __________

Dinner at Oh la la: __________

Captain's Welcome: __________

Glamour Theme Night: __________

2 Archie is going on the same cruise. What time can he do his preferred activities?

a Breakfast: __________

b Ice cream: __________

c Basketball: __________

d Teen meet-up: __________

e Gym class – pump: __________

f Art class: __________

3 Are there any activities Archie may not be able to do due to timetable clashes with another activity? Explain.

____

____

____

WELCOME ABOARD PRINCESS M CRUISES

TIMETABLE: ACTIVITIES 29TH JULY

9:00	Stretch class
9:00	Morning walk
9:30	Breakfast: La Viva Cafe
9:30	Trivia session 1
9:30	Gym class – cardio
10:00	Bingo session 1
10:00	Library
10:15	Art auction
10:30	Splash competition
11:15	Trivia session 2
12:00	Lunch buffet
12:30	Ice cream open
13:00	Basketball
13:00	Name that song
14:00	Gym class – step
14:30	Ice cream open
14:00	Cafe Blue open
15:30	Teen meet-up
16:00	Kids dance party
17:00	Bingo Session 2
18:00	Oh La La dinner session 1
18:00	Gym class – stretch
18:30	Ice cream open
19:00	Captain's welcome
19:00	Art class
19:30	Gym class – Pump
20:00	Oh La La dinner session 2
20:30	Disco nights
21:00	Glamour theme night
* All activies 1 hour duration	
* All dinner sessions 2 hours	

Unit 38 Duration

1 Convert the times from 12-hour format to 24-hour format.

a 3:45 pm 15:45 b 9:40 am ________

c 7:15 pm ________ d 8:14 am ________

e 6:51 pm ________ f 12:01 am ________

2 Convert the times from 24-hour format to 12-hour format.

a 14:25 2:25 pm b 08:47 ________

c 21:39 ________ d 05:42 ________

e 23:19 ________ f 10:11 ________

3 Calculate the time difference. Answer in hours and minutes.

a 09:20 to 14:50 5 hours 30 minutes

b 10:00 to 10:47 ________

c 12:15 to 21:40 ________

d 16:43 to 17:01 ________

e 18:10 to 22:20 ________

f 06:35 to 09:48 ________

g 08:47 to 13:14 ________

h 18:15 to 18:59 ________

4 Solve these time word problems.

a A movie starts at 19:45 and goes for 2 hours and 16 minutes. What time will it end? Answer in 24-hour time format.

____

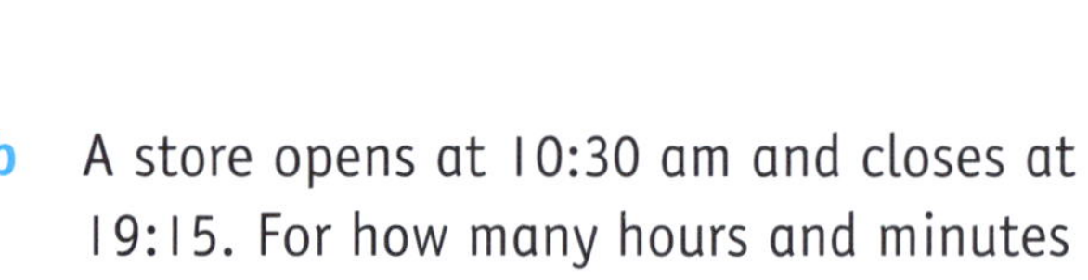

b A store opens at 10:30 am and closes at 19:15. For how many hours and minutes is it open?

____

c Juma starts baking biscuits at 09:40. They need to bake for 35 minutes. At what time will his biscuits be ready to eat? Answer in 12-hour time format.

____

d Your favourite TV show starts at 18:00 but you have basketball practice for $1\frac{1}{2}$ hours starting at 16:30. You live 20 minutes from basketball practice. Will you be able to watch your show?

____

AC9M6M03 Measurement **MA3-NSM-01** Non-spatial measure A • Time: Compare 12- and 24-hour time systems and convert between them • Non-spatial measure B • Time: Solve problems involving duration, using 12- and 24-hour time

Unit 38 More duration

1 Imagine you are planning a trip. Here is the flight schedule:

- Flight A departs at 09:35 and arrives at 14:20.
- Flight B departs at 17:15 and arrives at 21:50.
- Flight C departs at 22:10 and arrives at 02:35 the next day.

a How long in hours and minutes is Flight A? ______

b What time will you arrive at your destination if you take Flight B? ______

c Flight C crosses midnight. Calculate the duration of the flight in hours and minutes. ______

2 Imagine a typical school day for Kirra. Here is her schedule:

- School starts at 9:00 am.
- Lunch break is 12:15–13:00.
- Last class ends at 15:30.

a How many hours and minutes are there between the start of school and the lunch break? ______

b Calculate the duration of the last session if it begins after lunch and runs until the end of the day. ______

c How long does Kirra spend at school on this day? ______

3 Aydan is at the train station planning his journey. Here are the train departure times:

- Train A departs at 6:15 am.
- Train B departs at 14:55.
- Train C departs at 19:35.

a What time does Train A depart in 24-hour format? ______

b Calculate how many hours and minutes you have to wait for Train B to leave if you arrive at 1:30 pm. ______

c If train C is due to arrive at its destination after a journey of 5 hours and 45 minutes, what time is that? Answer in 12-hour format. ______

4 Hallie is going on an adventure with her friends. Here is their schedule:

- Start the journey at 10:00.
- Travel 45 minutes to the adventure destination.
- Have a picnic which will take $1\frac{1}{2}$ hours.
- After the picnic, go on a nature hike for $2\frac{1}{4}$ hours.

Hallie plans to finish the adventure by 16:45.

a What time will the picnic end if they have the picnic as soon as they arrive at their adventure destination? ______

b How long in minutes will the nature hike take? ______

c Hallie has to be home by 17:30. How much time do they have for extra adventure activities? ______

Mastery Checklist I can:

- ☐ read a timetable
- ☐ use an itinerary
- ☐ calculate how much time has passed
- ☐ use 12-hour and 24-hour time.

AC9M6M03 Measurement **MA3-NSM-01** Non-spatial measure A • Time: Compare 12- and 24-hour time systems and convert between them • Non-spatial measure B • Time: Solve problems involving duration, using 12- and 24-hour time

Unit 39 Equivalent number sentences

Equivalent number sentences have the same total.

Here, both sides equal 18:

3 × 6 = 9 × 2

18 18

Here, both sides equal 10:

60 ÷ 6 = 5 × 2

10 10

1 Write the missing value in these equivalent number sentences.

a 100 ÷ 4 = 5 × □

b 9 × 6 = 6 × □

c 55 ÷ □ = 1 × 5

d 90 ÷ □ = 20 ÷ 2

e 2 × 9 = 36 ÷ □

f 72 ÷ 8 = 9 × □

g 144 ÷ 12 = 24 ÷ □

h 6 × □ = 54 ÷ 6

i 36 ÷ 12 = 3 × □

j 9 × 8 = 1 × □

k 120 ÷ □ = 6 × 2

l 7 × 8 = 56 ÷ □

m 9 × 10 = 45 × □

n 6 × 3 = 9 × □

o 8 × 2 = □ × 1

p 4 × 3 = 144 ÷ □

q 7 × 5 = 70 ÷ □

r 3 × 8 = 24 ÷ □

s □ × 7 = 21 × 2

t 110 ÷ 10 = 11 × □

2 Make these into equivalent number sentences.

a  = 12 ÷ 3

b 60 ÷ 10 = ________________

c ________________ = 36 ÷ 3

d ________________ = 15 × 2

e 121 ÷ 11 = ________________

f 3 × 25 = ________________

Unit 39 Area model for multiplication

Strategies

To use the area model, partition the numbers to help you multiply.

23 × 5

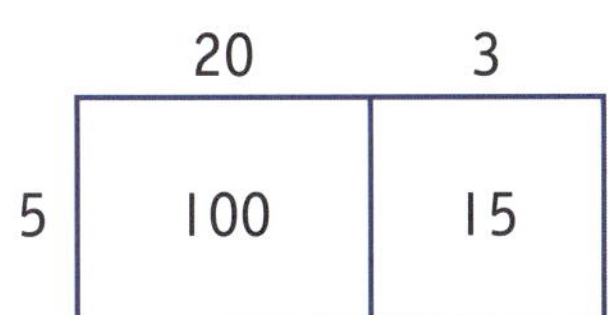

100 + 15 = 115

4593 × 7

	4000	500	90	3
7	28 000	3500	630	21

28 000 + 3500 + 630 + 21 = 32 151

1 Fill in the area models to help you multiply.

a 48 × 7

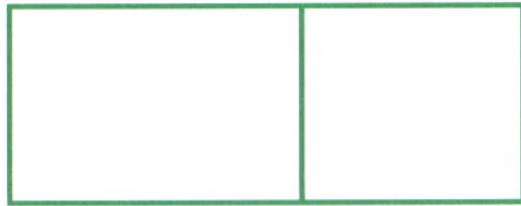

______ + ______ = ______

b 29 × 8

______ + ______ = ______

c 605 × 8

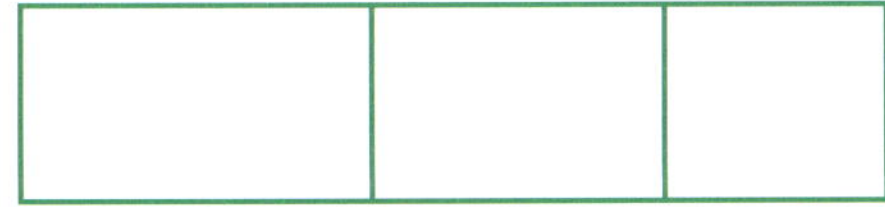

______ + ______ + ______ = ______

d 790 × 4

______ + ______ + ______ = ______

e 6492 × 4

______ + ______ + ______ + ______ = ______

f 8763 × 8

______ + ______ + ______ + ______ = ______

g 9234 × 6

______ + ______ + ______ + ______ = ______

h 4058 × 9

______ + ______ + ______ + ______ = ______

Unit 39 Multiply 2-digit × 2-digit numbers

2-digit × 2-digit

Area model

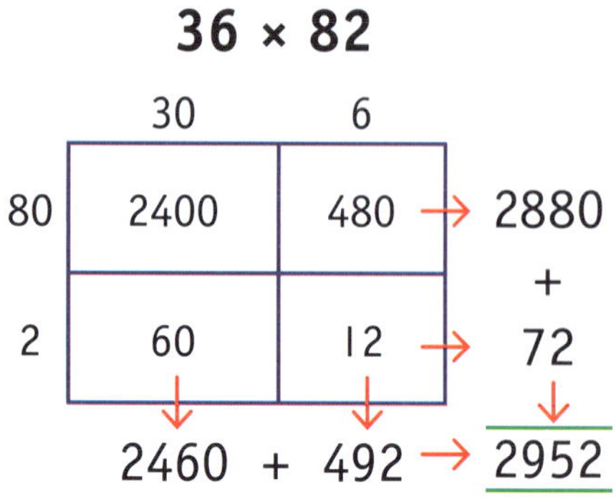

Algorithm method

```
  ⁴ ¹3 6
×     8 2
---------
    ¹ 7 2
+ 2 8 8 0
---------
  2 9 5 2
```

1 Solve the area models.

a 29 × 47

______ + ______ = ______

b 64 × 33

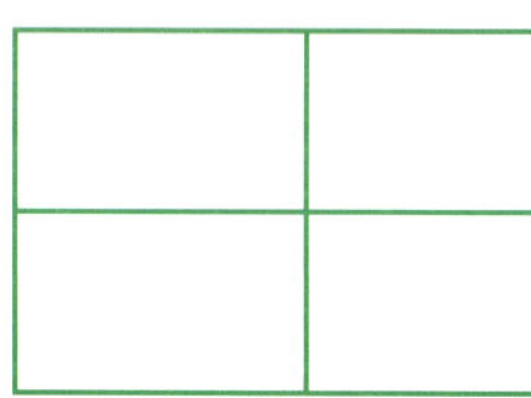

______ + ______ = ______

c 99 × 44

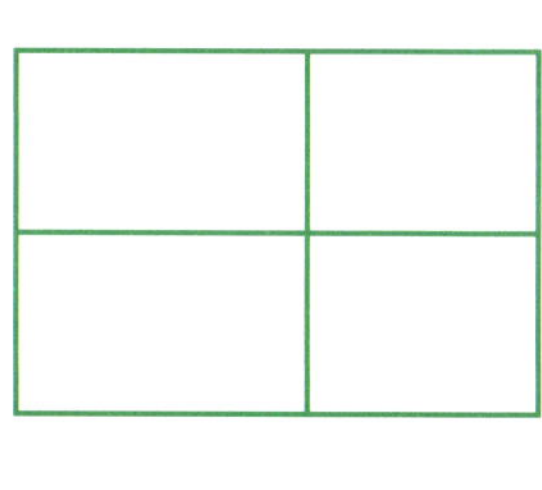

______ + ______ = ______

2 Solve the algorithms.

a 86 × 34

b 63 × 39

c 97 × 10

d 84 × 68

e 48 × 36

f 52 × 33

Unit 39 Multiply 3-digit × 2-digit numbers

1 Complete the multiplications using the area model.

eg 342 × 36

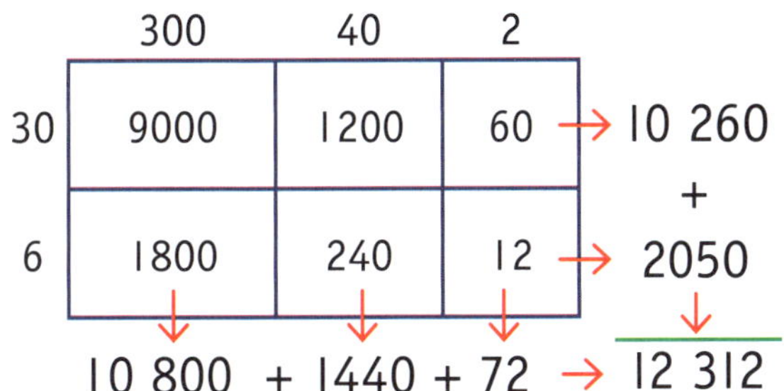

a 645 × 12

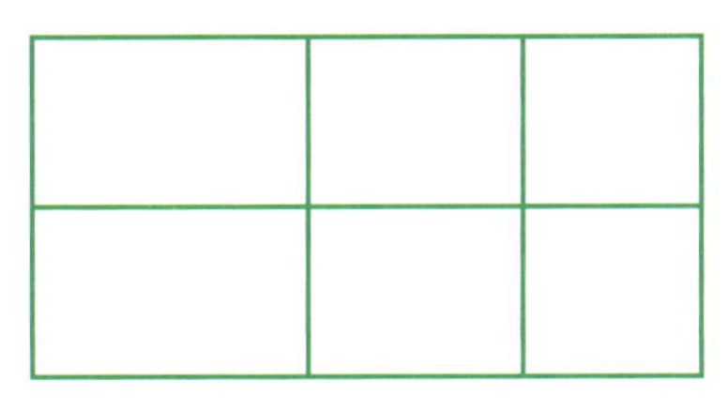

______ + ______ + ______ = ______

b 410 × 35

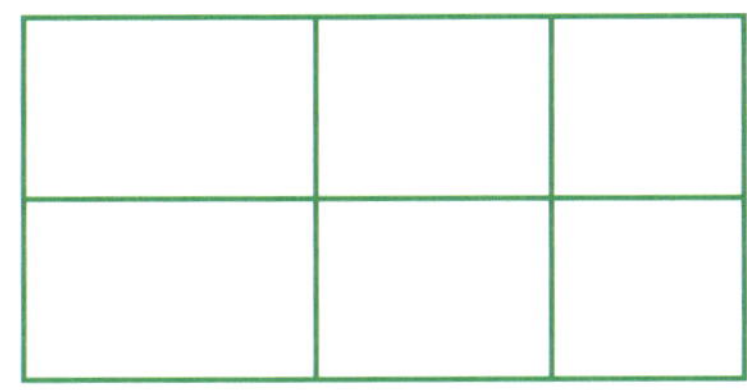

______ + ______ + ______ = ______

c 826 × 43

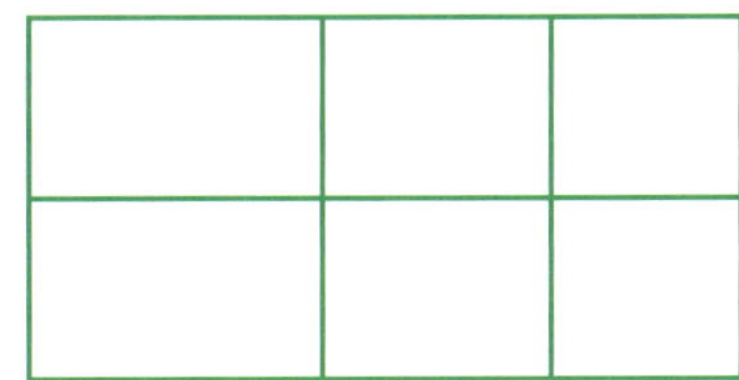

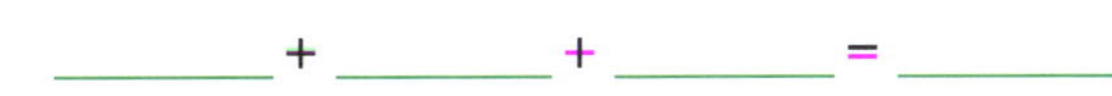

______ + ______ + ______ = ______

d 375 × 29

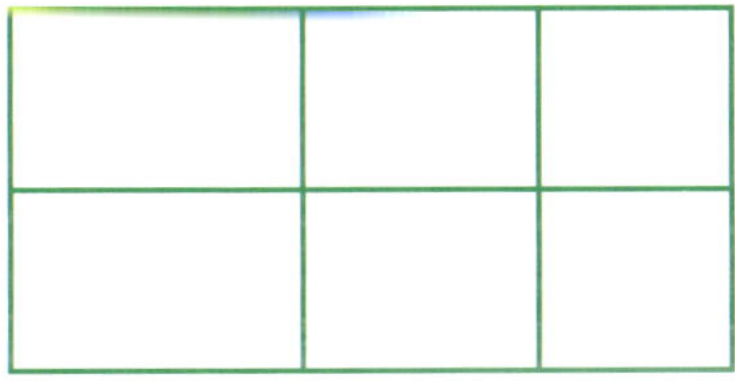

______ + ______ + ______ = ______

e 594 × 36

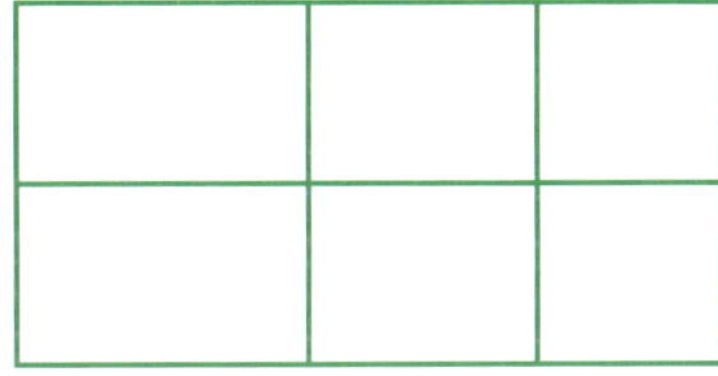

______ + ______ + ______ = ______

2 Complete the multiplications using algorithms.

eg

```
   1 1 2 3
     3 4 8
  ×    3 4
   1 3 9 2
+ 1 0 4 4 0
  1 1 8 3 2
```

a

```
   2 4 9
×    2 4
```

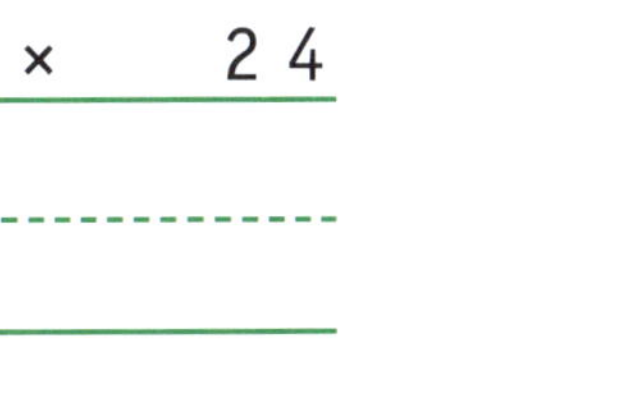

b

```
   6 0 9
×    4 8
```

c

```
   7 1 9
×    3 6
```

Mastery Checklist I can:

- ☐ use equivalence to find missing values
- ☐ use the area model to multiply
- ☐ use algorithms to multiply.

Furniture move

Investigation 4

Your task is to arrange the furniture in your classroom differently but still suit the needs of the teachers and the students.

Firstly, measure the classroom's length and width.

Draw a draft plan of your classroom to scale on this page.

Mark where doors and windows are located.

AC9M6M01 Measurement **MAO-WM-01** Working mathematically • choosing and applying mathematical techniques to solve problems • communicating thinking and reasoning coherently and clearly • **MA3-2DS-02** Two-dimensional spatial structure A • Area: Calculate the areas of rectangles using familiar metric units

Furniture move

Investigation 4

1 Make a good copy of your classroom plan, using drawing tools on the computer.

2 Find the best arrangement for the furniture that goes in the classroom by moving shapes for tables, desks, cupboards and shelves into place. Move them around until you are satisfied with the placement. You'll need to consider the following points.

- Leave enough room between furniture for people to move around.
- Make sure people can see what they need to see in the classroom when they are seated.
- Use the space to its best advantage.

3 Label any special features.

4 Write an exposition to argue for your plan being adopted as the best classroom plan.

5 Present your argument to the class using digital technology, eg PowerPoint.

To complete this task, I needed to:

- ☐ use technology to draw a plan of a room to scale
- ☐ use technology to place furniture in a room
- ☐ consider use of a room
- ☐ present a strong argument for the plan, using technology.

I enjoyed this task! ☆☆☆☆☆

Revision

1 Find two prime numbers that add to make 30.

Write your answer in the boxes.

2 How many minutes would there be in 46 years?

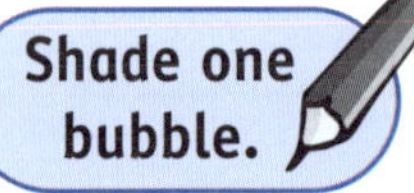

24 177 000 ○ 24 711 000 ○ 24 177 600 ○ 25 187 630 ○

3

5 equilateral triangles with 5 cm sides are joined.

What is the perimeter of the final shape?

55 cm ○ 30 cm ○ 75 cm ○ 35 cm ○

4

$$\frac{1}{2} + \frac{7}{12} = ?$$

$\frac{10}{12}$ ○ $\frac{11}{12}$ ○ $\frac{12}{12}$ ○ $\frac{13}{12}$ ○

5 One bus can carry 50 students.

How many buses will be needed to take the whole school of 361 students to the Carnival?

☐ buses

Write your answer in the box.

Revision

6 I boarded the train at 08:37.

The trip took $12\frac{1}{2}$ hours.

Which clock shows when my trip ended?

12:30 ◯ 21:07 ◯ 20:37 ◯ 21:17 ◯

7  Which diagram shows an equivalent fraction?

 ◯

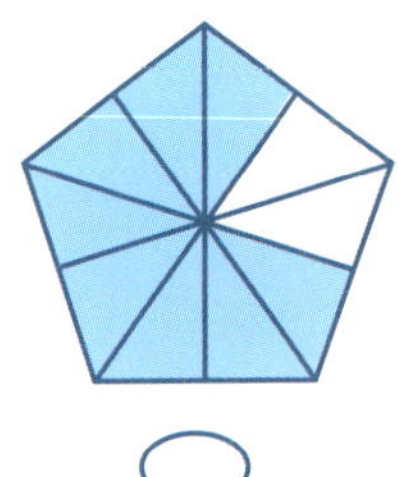 ◯

 ◯

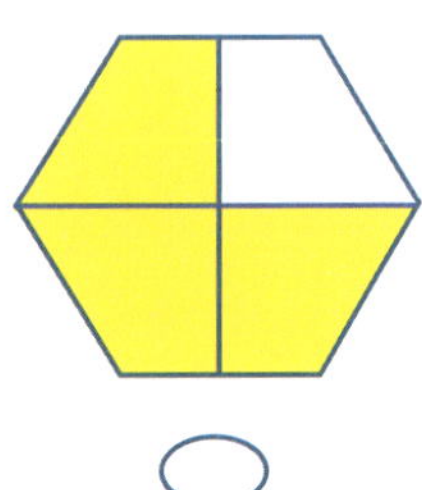 ◯

8 Round to 1 decimal place.

57·943

57·9 ◯ 58·0 ◯ 57·94 ◯ 57·90 ◯

9 Add 3·7 to 9·08.

12·7 ◯ 12·78 ◯ 12·8 ◯ 12·87 ◯

10 Solve.

$$60 - M = 5 \times 9$$

M = 13 ◯ M = 14 ◯ M = 15 ◯ M = 16 ◯

Unit 40 Views

build a model

1 Match the models to their front and top views.

Front views

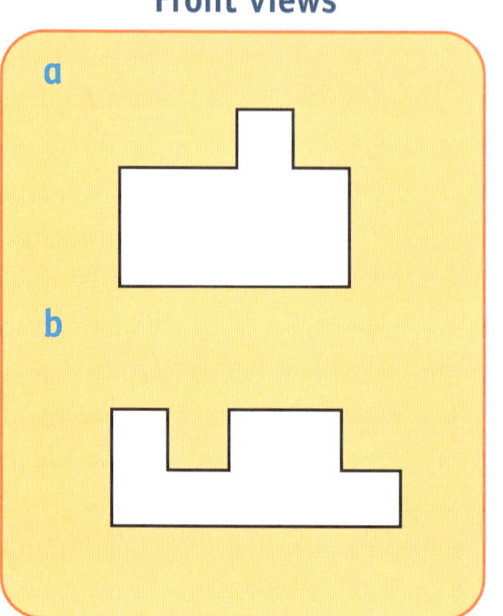

Models

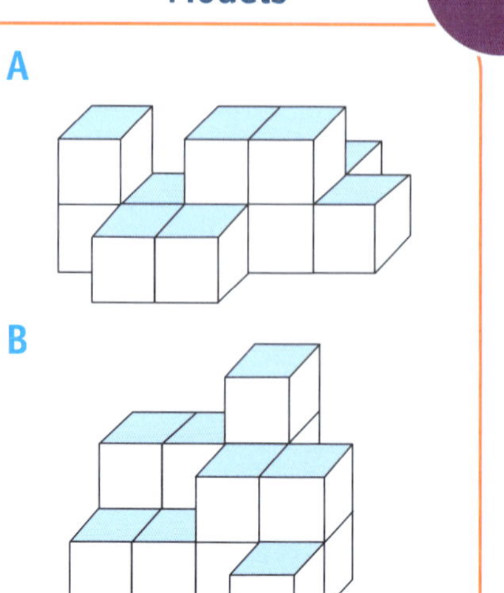

Top views

2 Build this model and draw the side and top views.

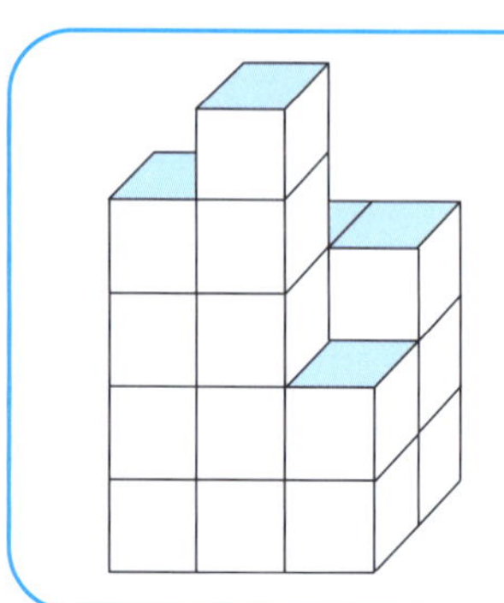

3 Build a model for which these are top, side and front views. Draw the model.

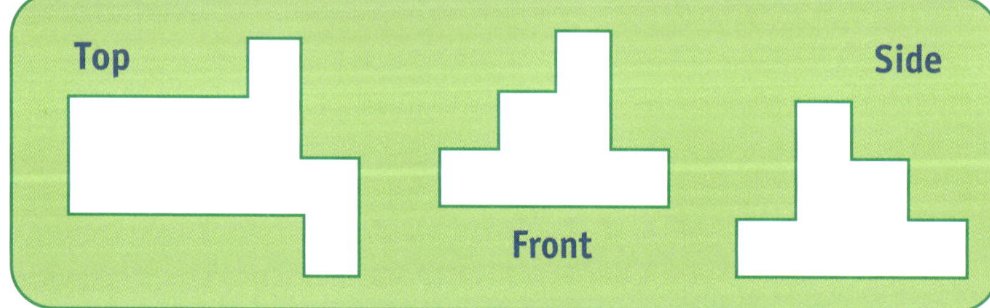

4 Match each model with its cross-section at the green line.

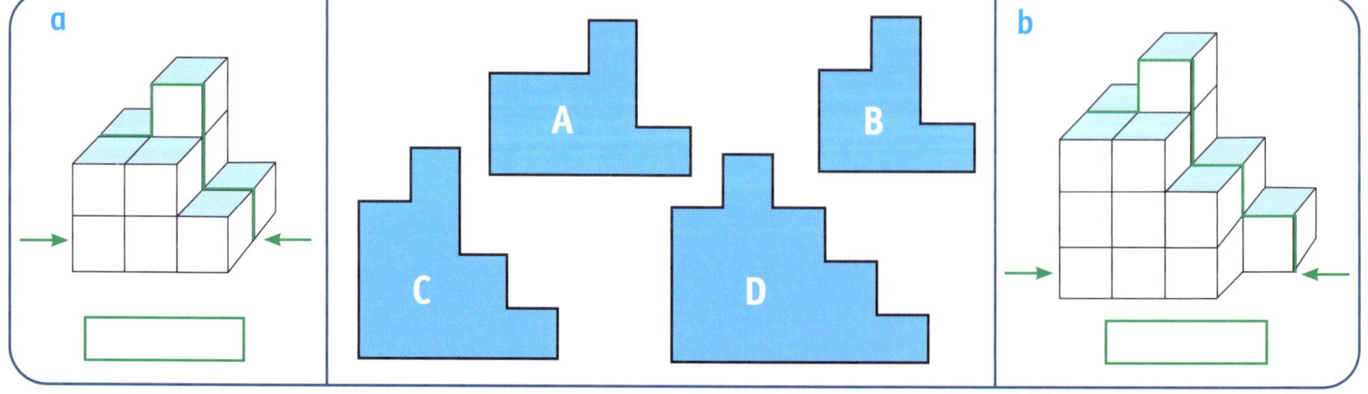

Unit 40 Drawing 3D objects

build models with cubes

1 Use these isometric drawings to build the model. How many cubes did you use?

a

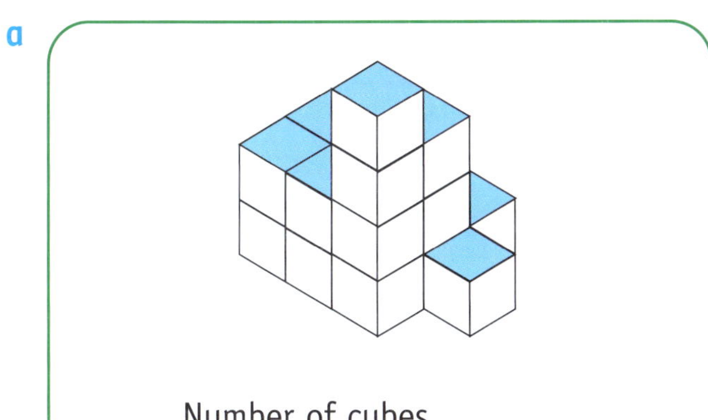

Number of cubes ________

b

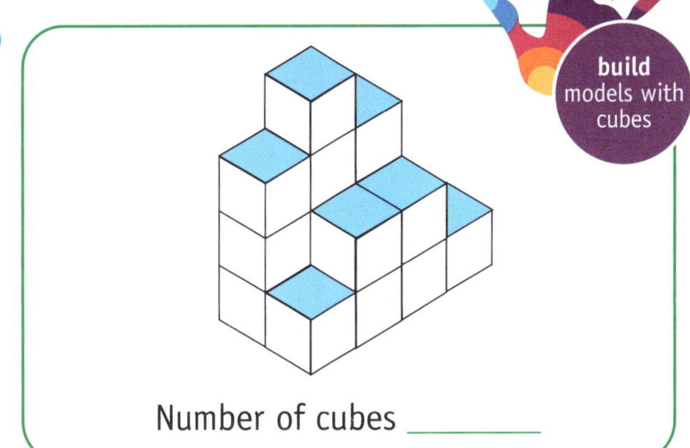

Number of cubes ________

2 Use these top and front views to build models and make isometric drawings.

a

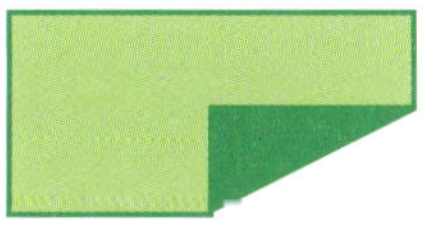

Top

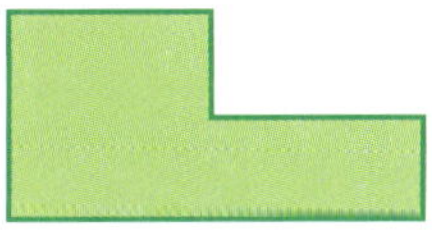

Front

b

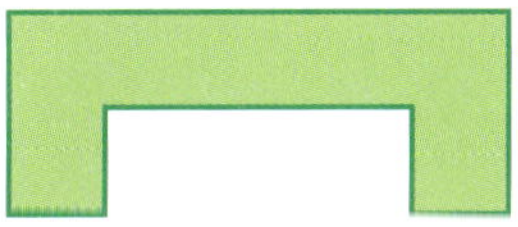

Top

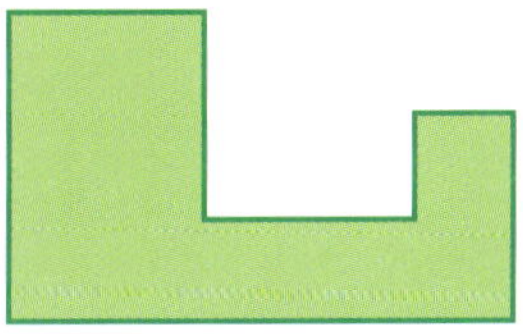

Front

Unit 40 Cross-sections

1 Circle the shape of the cross-section you would see.

a

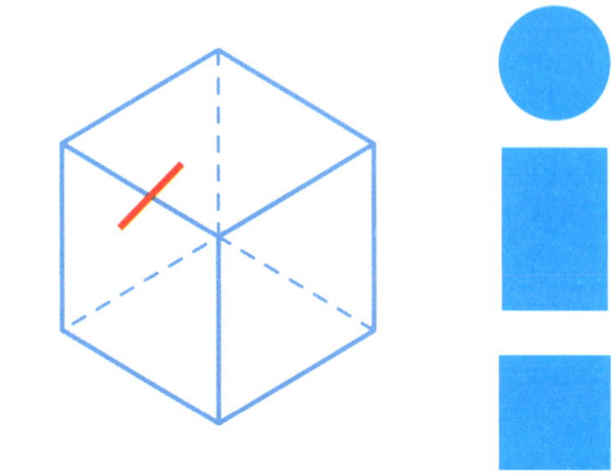

b

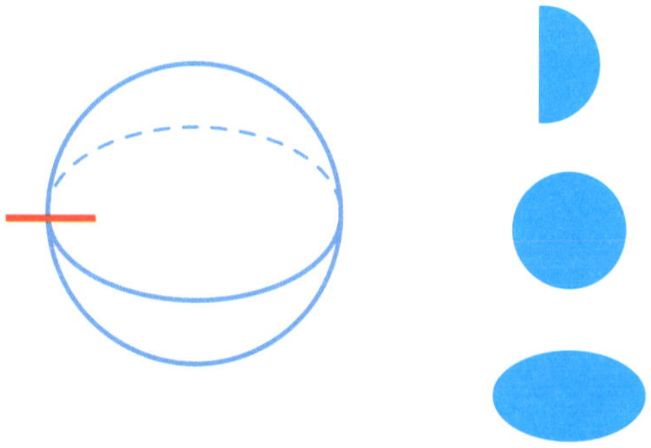

c

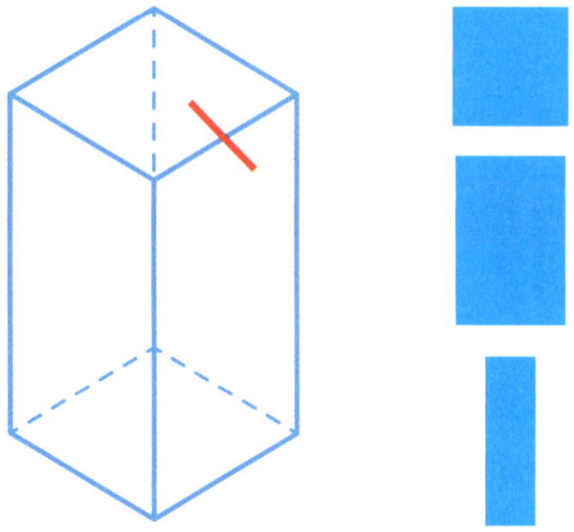

d

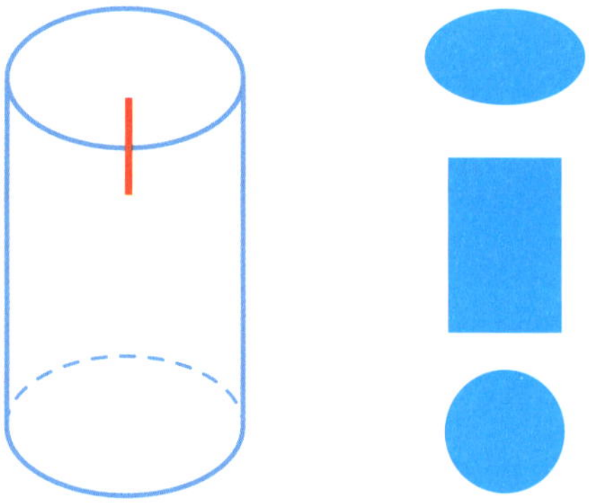

e

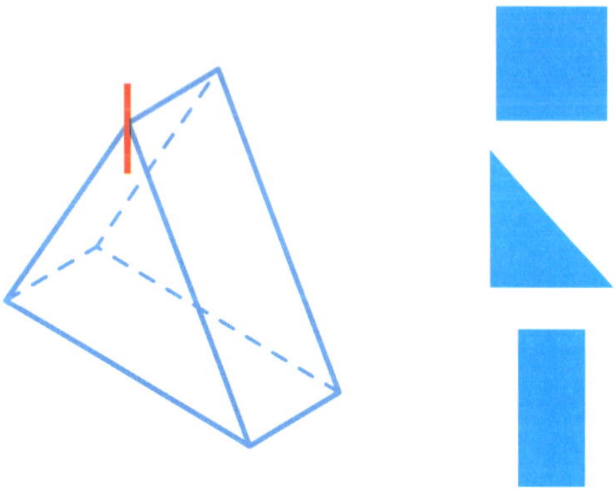

f

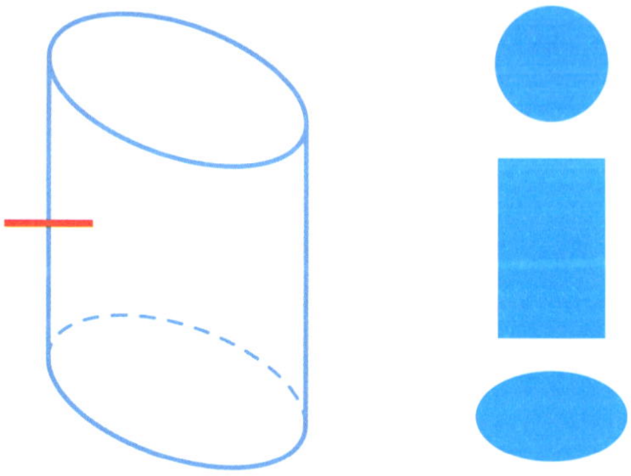

g

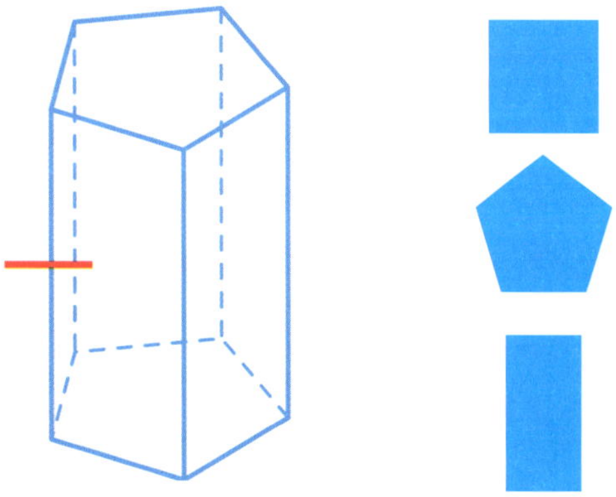

h

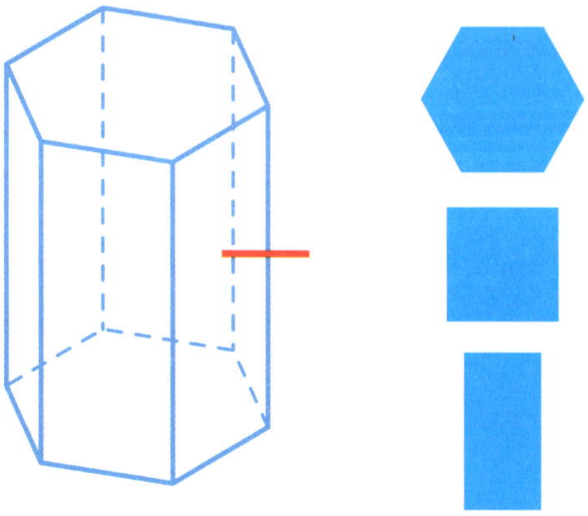

Unit 40 Cross-sections of prisms

A cross-section is the shape you see when you cut through a 3D object.

1 Draw the cross-section you would see for each prism.

a

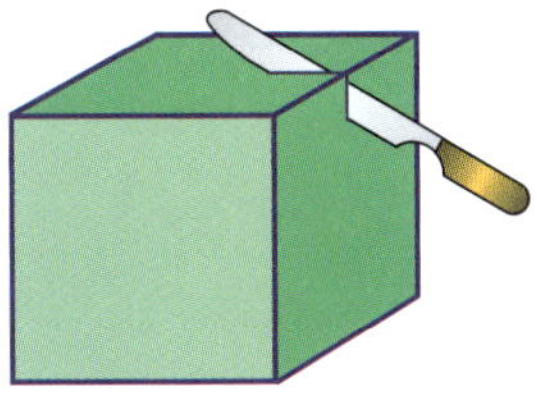

b

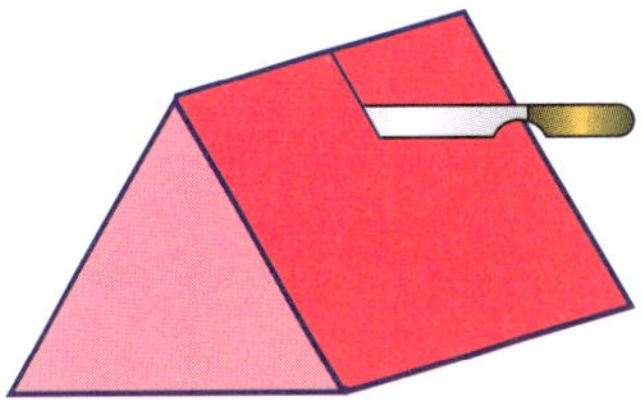

c

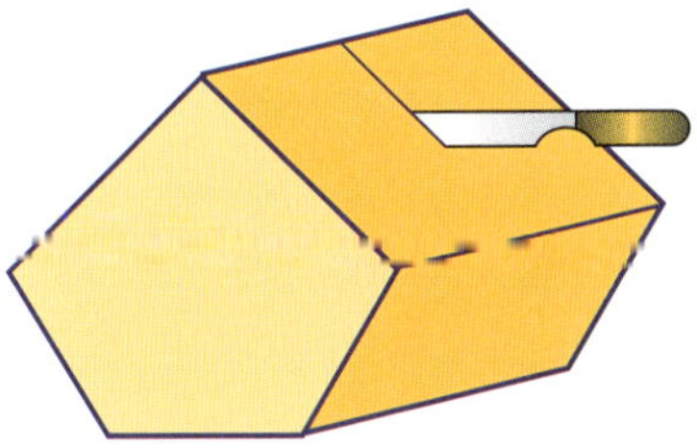

d

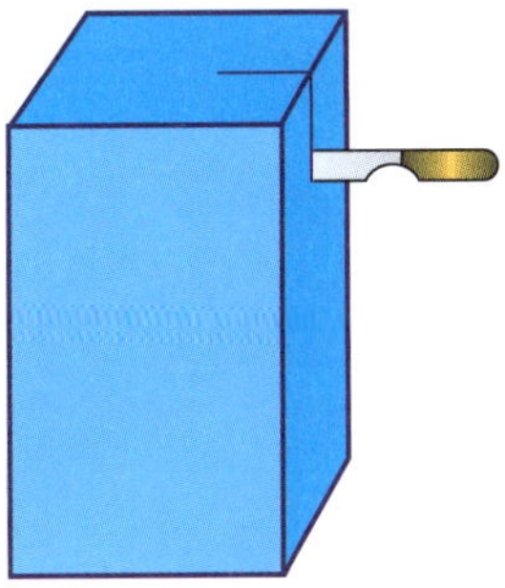

e

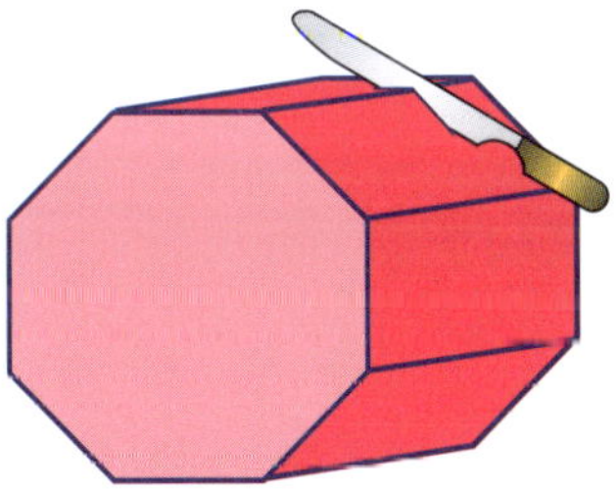

f

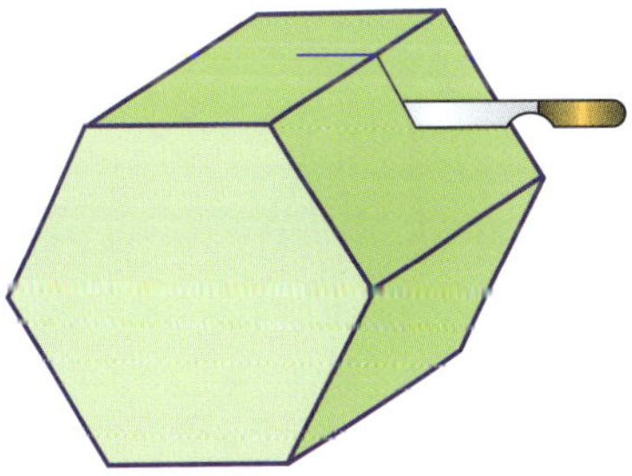

g

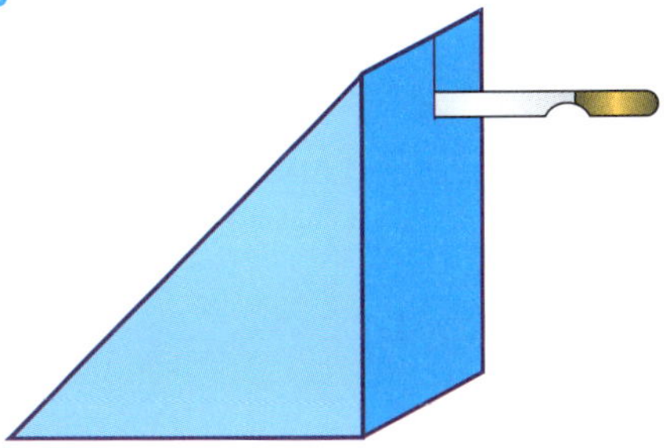

h

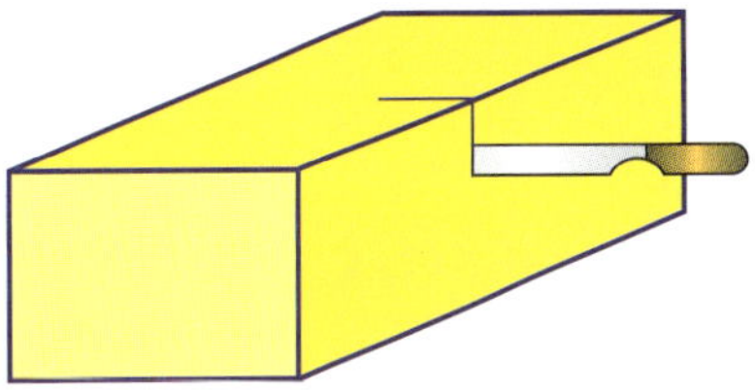

Unit 40 Cross-sections of pyramids

A cross-section is the shape you see when you cut through a 3D object.

1 Colour each pyramid and its matching cross-section the same colour.

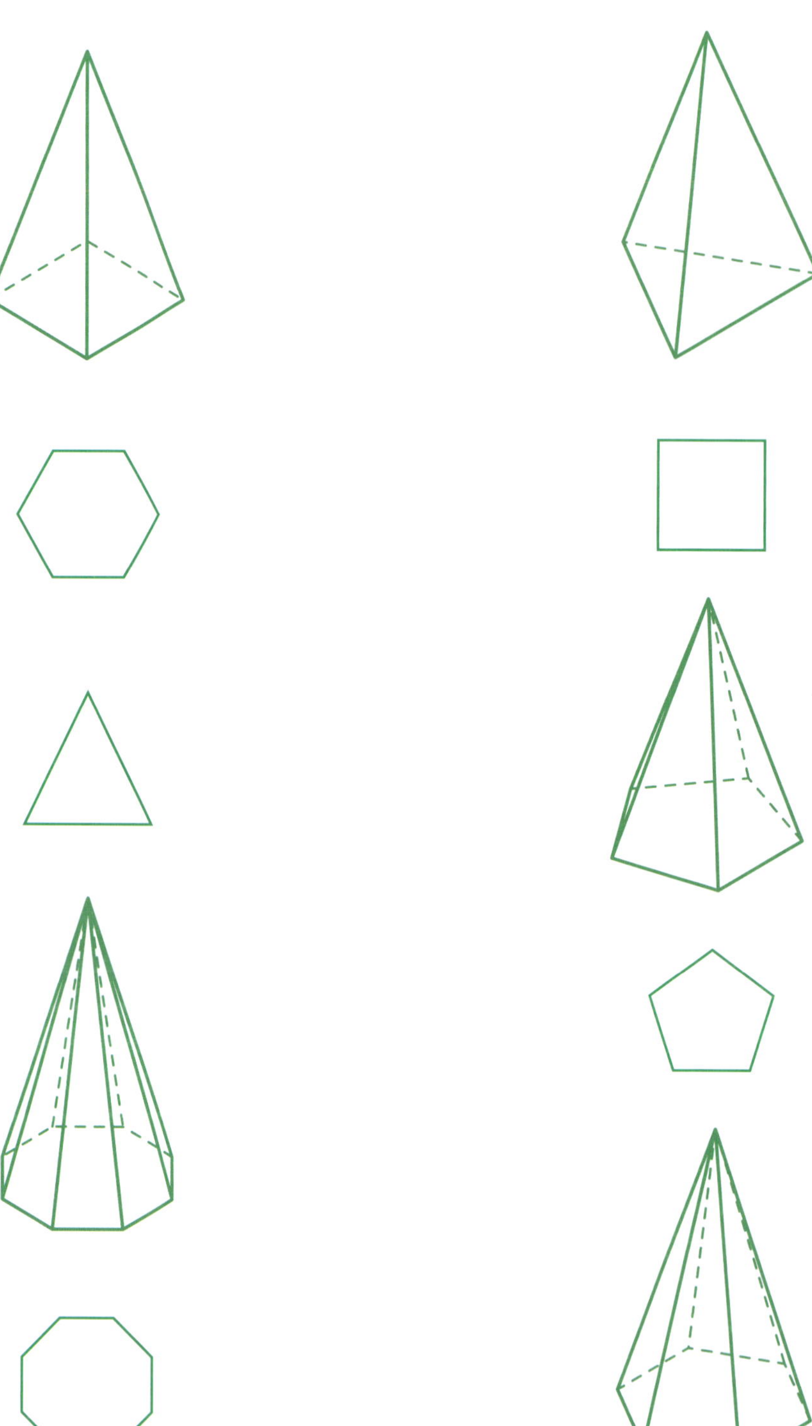

Mastery Checklist I can:

- ☐ draw top views, side views and front views
- ☐ identify cross-sections of 3D objects
- ☐ draw cross-sections of prisms
- ☐ match pyramids to the correct cross-sections.

Unit 41 Review of graphs

Match the graph to the report.

1

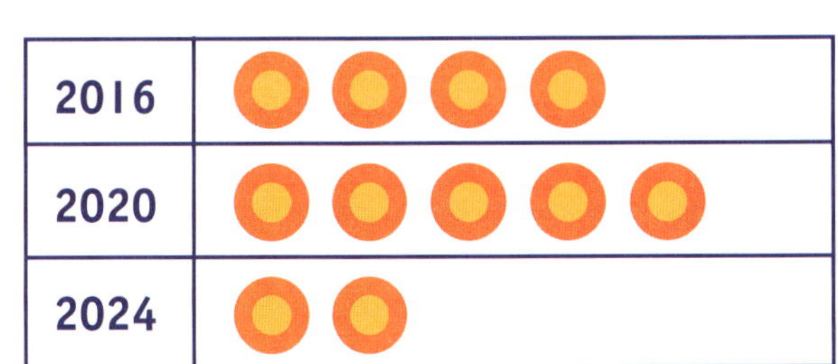

2

3

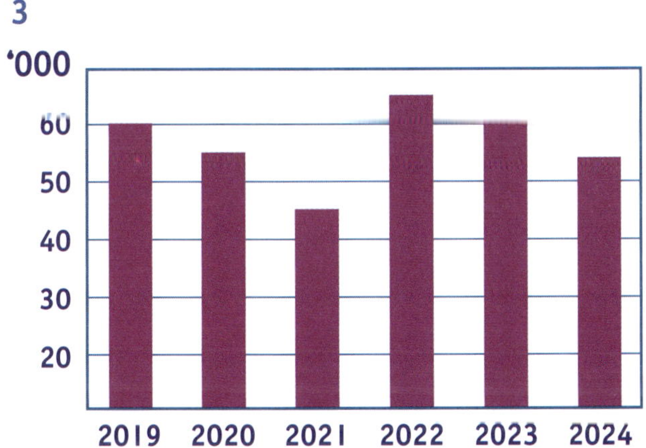

4

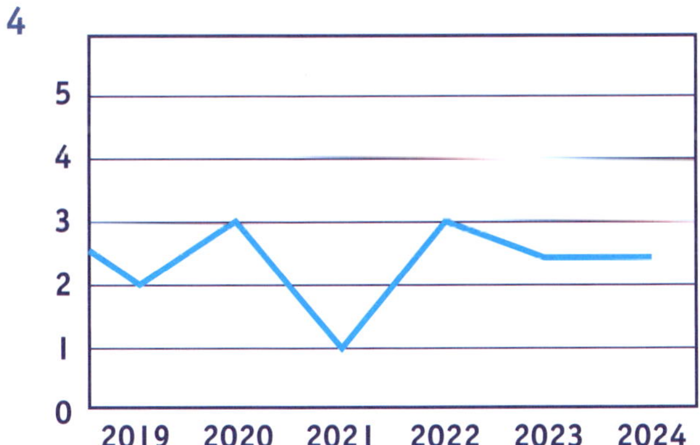

5

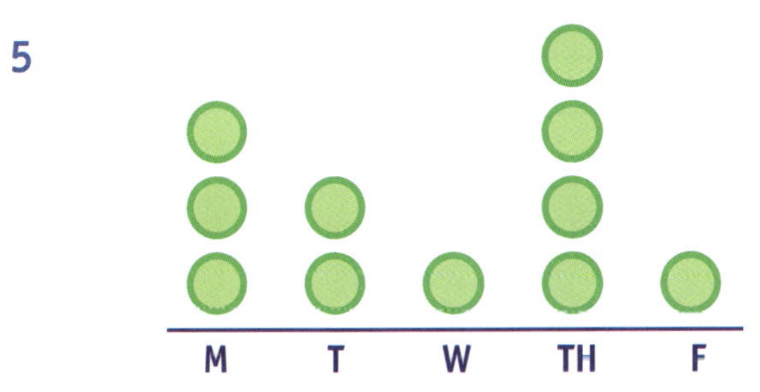

A More people own mobile phones
Fifteen to nineteen-year-olds own more mobile phones than the age group twenty to twenty-five-year-olds. Although the 20 to 25-year-olds have their own money to spend on mobile phones and plans ...

B Production down
Production of Spondas has dropped by more than 10% this year. Sponda CEO, Ms Ada Rayce puts the lower production down to ...

C Vegetables wilt
In spite of increased trade opportunities, green vegetable production in 2024 has fallen by 30 000 tonnes from previous years. The Greeneleafe Farm is being geared up to ...

D Savings go on appliances
Sales of the new IXL tablet at Joy Fulnez have fluctuated this week due to different reports about its functions. Only one IXL was sold on two days of the week.

E Interest rates
Average interest rates for this year have steadied and look set to increase slightly on past years, after two years of unpredictable rises and falls.

Unit 41 Interpreting graphs

Graphs 1 & 2

Refer to the graphs on page 191.

1 If production of vegetables is lower by 30 000 tonnes in 2024, how much was produced each year?

2016 ______________________, 2020 ______________________, 2024 ______________________

2 a About 14 million phones are owned by 15 to 25-year-olds in 2023.

How many are owned by 15 to 19-year-olds? ______________________

b Can you tell if 15 to 25-year-olds account for 50% of all mobile phones in the country in 2024? ______________________

c What may be some reasons people give for not owning a mobile phone?

____

3 a Roughly how many Spondas have been recorded on this graph? ______________________

b Between 2021 and 2022, production increased by ______________________.

c What factors might Ms Rayce mention as reasons for decreased production in any year?

____

____

d Years 2022–2024 account for more than 50% of total production shown. True or false?

____

4 a We pay interest to a bank for ____.

b In which year were average interest rates at their lowest? ______________________

c How would the average interest rate for twelve months be found? ______________________

5 Graph this data using a side-by-side column graph, as in graph 2, page 191.

	Girls	Boys
Year 6	32	36
Year 7	38	42
Year 8	40	38

Mobile Phones Owned By Students

Years

Number of phones

Unit 41 Gathering data

Graphs are drawn after data has been collected. Data can be collected by surveying people. Surveys ask special questions for people like marketers, developers, councils, governments, salespeople and educators.

1 Write three survey topics that local councils might use for their residents.

____

____

2 Write three survey topics that a movie theatre developer might use.

____

____

3 Write three survey topics that you might use in your class.

____

4 Tick the best questions to ask in a survey.

a What do you like for breakfast?

b Cereal, toast, fruit – which foods do you eat for breakfast?

c What schools do your brothers attend?

d Do you have brothers?

e Cricket, Softball, Soccer – which team sport do you play?

f What team sports do you play?

g Do you play a sport not listed here?

h Do you access the Internet regularly?

i What do you do with spare time?

j What sort of house do you own?

5 Why did you choose these questions? ______________________________

____

6 Many surveys ask you to put your choices in order.
Select six foods for survey respondents to place in order.

a ______________ b ______________

c ______________ d ______________

e ______________ f ______________

7 Select ten classmates to survey about their food choices from your list. Use tally marks to count responses. Number your food list from most popular to least popular.

a ______________ ____ b ______________ ____ c ______________ ____

d ______________ ____ e ______________ ____ f ______________ ____

8 A survey is done on how time is spent out of school.
Write six activities for respondents to place in order.

a ______________ b ______________

c ______________ d ______________

e ______________ f ______________

Challenge!

Ask 20 students to respond to question 8. From the results, place the activities on a number line from 0 (least likley) to 10 (most likely).

Unit 41 Data collection

survey

1 Tick a topic and a population to survey from the following lists. You will make two graphs of the results.

Population
20 students in your class
20 students in your school
20 teachers
20 neighbours or community members

Topic
Federal political party favoured for the next election
Choice of places for the ideal holiday
Favourite subjects to study throughout school
Use of Internet shopping sites

2 Make up six choices for your survey topic.

______________________ ______________________

______________________ ______________________

______________________ ______________________

3 Draw the two graphs of the same information. Label the axes.

4 a Which graph represented your results more accurately? ______________________

b Which graph is easiest to read? ______________________

5 Ask class mates to give an opinion of these questions as well.

Mastery Checklist I can:
- ☐ match graphs to reports
- ☐ analyse the data in different types of graphs
- ☐ explore why people conduct surveys
- ☐ conduct a survey and graph the results.

AC9M6ST01 • **AC9M6ST03** Statistics **MA3-DATA-02** Data A • Collect categorical and discrete numerical data by observation or survey • Choose and use appropriate tables and graphs • Describe and interpret different datasets in context

Unit 42 Chance experiment

Work with a partner.

1 You have two dice. You are going to throw them 20 times and total their numbers each time.

a Which total would you predict to have the:

greatest frequency? ________ least frequency? ________

Why? ____

____

b Take turns to throw the dice. Fill in Table 1 after each throw.

Table 1

Total	Die 1	Die 2
2		
3		
4		
5		
6		
7		
8		
9		
10		
11		
12		

Table 2

Total	Die 1	Die 2
2		
3		
4		
5		
6		
7		
8		
9		
10		
11		
12		

c Were your predictions accurate? ________

2 a Repeat the experiment. Use Table 2.

b What do you think is the probability of a similar result? ________________

c Why would you expect the probability of scores 2 and 12 occurring to be less frequent than that of 7?

____

____

d When would you use this method in everyday life? ________________

____

____

Unit 42 Test a sample

Chance

Aim: To carry out an experiment and estimate the proportion of counters of each colour in a bag.

Method: Place 40 coloured counters of three different colours in a bag.

Each pair of students is given a bag of counters made by someone else. They carry out this experiment to estimate the proportion of each colour in their bag, eg 40% blue, 50% green, 10% yellow.

After each set of pulls, do not replace the colours but keep pulling more.

1 a Take 10 pulls and record the colours pulled in the table below. Estimate what proportion of the total is each colour.

______ ______ ______

b Take another 10 pulls and make another estimate.

______ ______ ______

c Take another 10 pulls and make your final estimate.

______ ______ ______

Colour	Tally (10)	Tally (10)	Tally (10)	Total (30)

2 a Did your predictions change as you pulled out more counters? ______

b What could you learn from this? ______

3 When can this method of making estimates be used in real life? ______

______

4 **Complete:** To estimate the results from a population, we can test a ______.

5 Here is one question that could be asked of a population of people in a city.

Would you use a new bicycle path through your suburb (or town)?

Write two questions to ask of people in a city or town.

______

______

6 How many people need to be asked to have a good sample of a suburb or town? Circle one.

10 100 1000 5000 10 000

Discuss.

AC9M6P01 • AC9M6P02 Probability MA3-CHAN-01 Chance B • Compare observed frequencies of outcomes with expected results • Conduct chance experiments with both small and large numbers of trials

Unit 42 Probability puzzles

Solve the probability puzzles.

Write each answer as a fraction, a decimal and a percentage.

1 Coin toss

You toss a coin. What is the probability of getting heads?

Write your answer as a fraction, a decimal and a percentage.

Fraction:

Decimal:

Percentage:

2 Spinner probability

A spinner has 6 equal sections numbered 1 to 6. What is the probability of landing on an even number?

Fraction:

Decimal:

Percentage:

3 Rolling a dice

You roll a six-sided die. What is the probability of rolling a prime number?

Fraction:

Decimal:

Percentage:

4 Colour probability

In a bag there are 5 red marbles, 3 blue marbles and 2 yellow marbles. You pick out one marble without looking. What is the probability of getting a blue marble?

Fraction:

Decimal:

Percentage:

5 Deck of cards

You draw one card from a standard deck of 52 cards. What is the probability of drawing a diamond or a club?

Fraction:

Decimal:

Percentage:

6 Weather probability

The weather forecast says there is a 25% chance of rain tomorrow. What is the probability that it won't rain?

Fraction:

Decimal:

Percentage:

Mastery Checklist

I can:

- ☐ conduct a chance experiment
- ☐ compare predictions with actual results
- ☐ test a sample to make predictions
- ☐ express probability as a fraction, decimal and percentage.

Revision Term 4

1 **a**

$$\begin{array}{r} 508 \\ -\ 37 \\ \hline \end{array}$$

b

$$\begin{array}{r} 385 \\ 94 \\ 610 \\ +\ 336 \\ \hline \end{array}$$

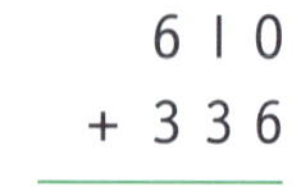

p 155

2 **a**

$$\begin{array}{r} 708 \\ \times\ 29 \\ \hline \end{array}$$

b

$$\begin{array}{r} 860 \\ \times\ 72 \\ \hline \end{array}$$

p 155

3 **a** $18 + 9 \times 37 =$ ______

b $68 \times 0 + 5 =$ ______

p 155

4 $P = 72 \div 2^3$

$P =$ ______

p 157

5 Write a number sentence for each story and work out the answer.

p 158

a Toby calls friends in Perth for 4 mins at 39c per minute and cousins in Darwin for 5 minutes at 52c per minute.

What is his phone bill? ______________

b What is the price for 6 adult tickets at $15 each and 3 children's tickets at half price?

____

6 What is the remainder?

p 160

a 8) 305 Remainder = ______

b 5) 3682 Remainder = ______

c 8) 5823 Remainder = ______

d 7) 9235 Remainder = ______

7 **a** Bought for $2350

Sold for $2785

Profit = ______

b Bought for $10 000

Sold for $8650

Loss = ______

p 161

8

p 161

	428
−9	
−50	
−13	
−25	
−66	

9 **Cooking Lesson**

p 165

Ingredients for 1 person:

$\frac{1}{2}$ cup choc-chips $\frac{1}{3}$ cup peanuts

$\frac{1}{4}$ cup butter $\frac{1}{5}$ cup condensed milk

Ingredients for 10 people:

____

10 Write in descending order.

p 166

a $\frac{2}{3}$, $\frac{3}{4}$, $\frac{4}{5}$, 0·82

b 0·25, $\frac{2}{9}$, $\frac{1}{12}$, $\frac{3}{5}$

c 0·45, 0·405, 0·004, 0·045

d $\frac{9}{10}$, $\frac{3}{4}$, $\frac{5}{8}$, $\frac{1}{1}$

Revision Term 4

11 Add. p 166

a $\frac{1}{4} + \frac{5}{12} =$ ______

b $\frac{3}{12} + \frac{1}{3} =$ ______

12 a $\frac{2}{3} \times 8$ b $\frac{4}{5} \times 6$ p 167

= ______ = ______

13 What is the perimeter of a rectangular room with an area of 30 m² and a length of 6 m? p 171

______

14 p 171

24 m

6·5 m

14 m

3 m

a Area of [orange] ______

b Area of [pink] ______

p 171

15 a What other dimensions of the orange shape would result in the same area?

______

b What would be the new perimeter?

______

16 p 173

400 m

100 m

Write the area in hectares. ______

17 Complete the dimensions for these areas which measure one hectare. p 173

a 100 m × ______

b 200 m × ______

c 250 m × ______

d 500 m × ______

18 Study the bus timetable. p 174

Stop	pm	pm	pm
Jinga Mall	3:25	3:55	4:10
Little St	3:28	3:58	4:13
Pryor St	3:33	–	4:18
Wallend St	3:39	–	4:24
Freear	3:44	4:08	4:29
Jolly St	3:49	–	4:34
Dreem Wharf	4:02	4:22	4:47

a If you miss the 3:25 at Jinga Mall by a minute, how long do you wait for the next bus? ______

b Arriving at the Jolly St stop at 4:10, how long must I wait for the next bus? ______

c What is the best bus to catch from Pryor St to catch a 4:30 ferry from the wharf? ______

d How long is the shortest bus trip from the Mall to the Ferry? ______

19 Calculate the time difference. Answer in hours and minutes. p 176

a 10:00 and 13:45 ______

b 11:30 and 16:00 ______

c 05:13 and 09:21 ______

d 22:00 and 01:15 ______

e 06:00 and 01:00 ______

20 Complete the equivalent number sentences. p 178

a 8 × 9 = ______ ÷ 4

b 12 + 15 + 9 + 3 = ______ × 13

c 9 × 5 = 15 × ______

d 125 ÷ 5 = 5 × ______

e (4 + 9) × (21 − 17) = ______ × 26

Revision Term 4

21 Use the area model to multiply. p 181

a 517 × 78

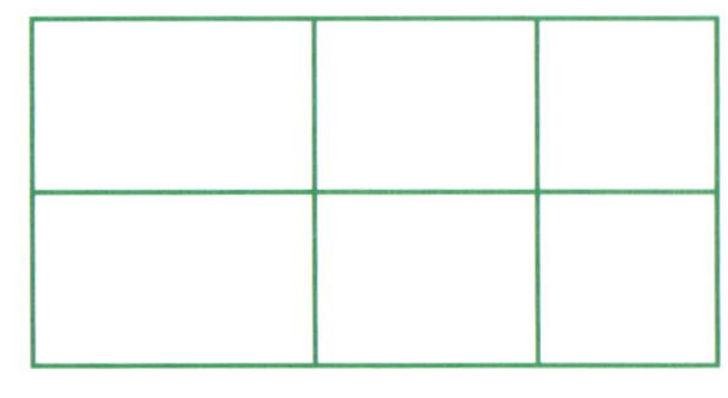

_____ + _____ + _____ = _____

b 487 × 42

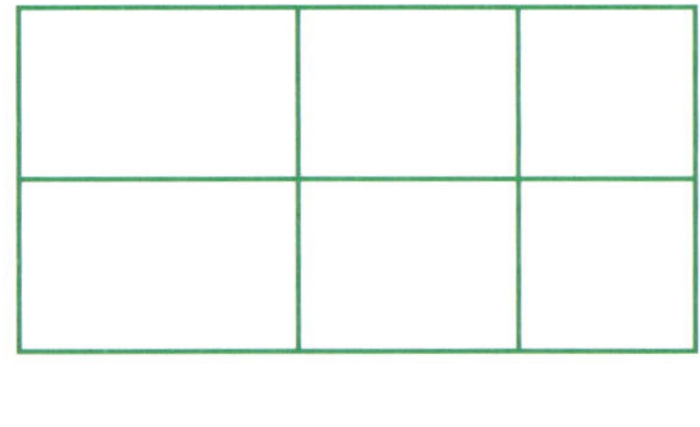

_____ + _____ + _____ = _____

22 Draw the top view of this model. p 187

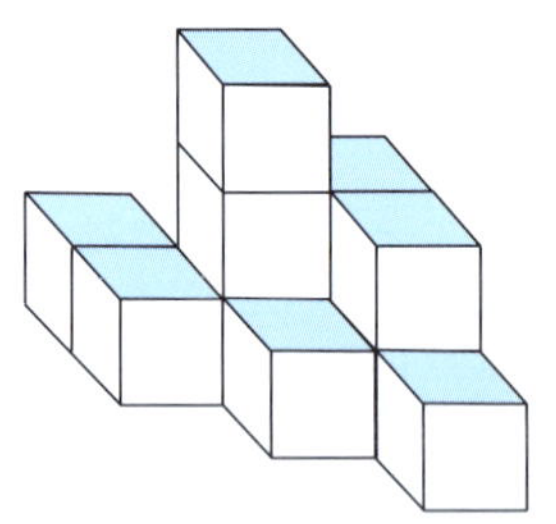

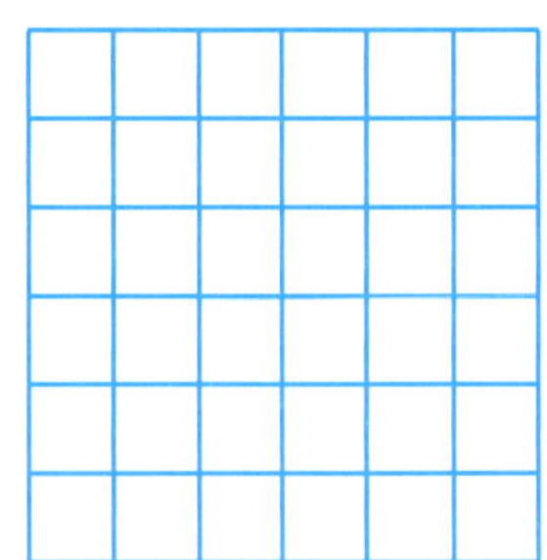

23 Draw the cross-section you would see when you cut through each 3D object. p 190

a

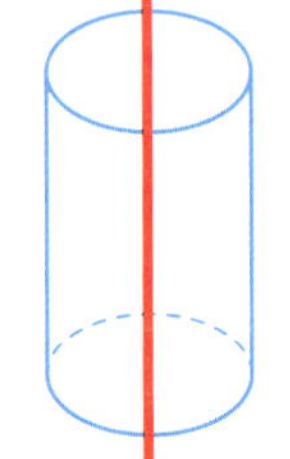

Cross-section:

b

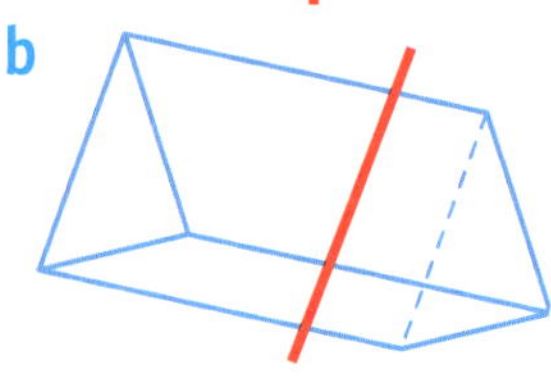

Cross-section:

c

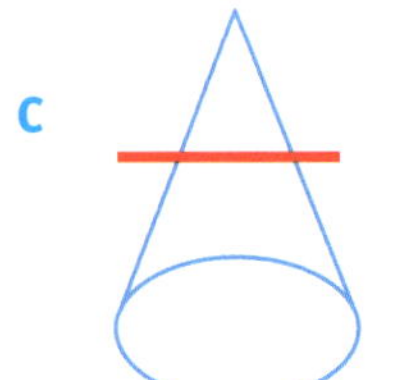

Cross-section:

24 Draw a line graph from this column graph. p 194

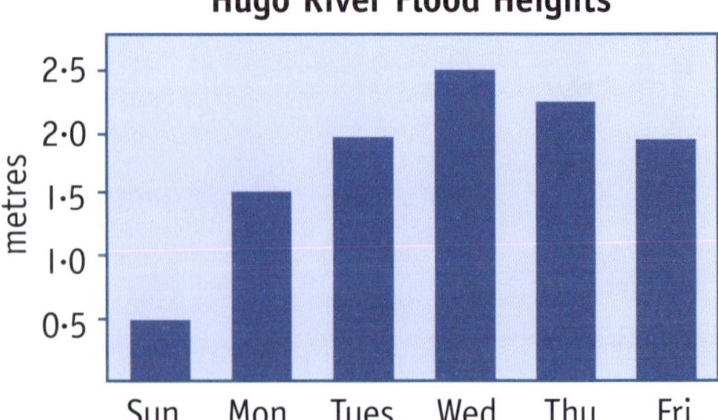

25 You pick 30 red marbles and no other colours out of a bag of 40 different coloured marbles. You could think that: p 195

____

____

26 True or false? p 195

When you throw a regular die, the probability of scoring:

a 1, 2, or 3 is 50% _____

b an even number is 100% _____

c an odd number is $\frac{1}{3}$ _____

d a 6 is $\frac{1}{6}$ _____

e a 1 is 0% _____

f a 4 is 1 in 6 _____

g a 7 is 0. _____